TOM WOOD
Anna's Boy

AN AMERICAN STORY

The autobiography of the grandson of a slave,
A modern-day pioneer and trail blazer's journey through
the winds, the rain, and the sunshine of change.

Print ISBN: 978-1-09832-087-4

eBook ISBN: 978-1-09832-088-1

AUTHOR CONTACT: taaaw26@gmail.com

TO

My parents Anna and Thomas Wood, whose genes, guidance, and sacrifices made my life the wonderful journey that it has been.
My late daughter, Vicki, whose gravitational warmth kept our family together.
Alice Gloster Burnette, who significantly helped to soften my transition into my "sunset years".
Muriel McCoy, who provided the support and environment for me to write my story.

CONTENTS

"I am still learning"

Michelangelo

ACKNOWLEDGMENTS

Put simply, Anna's Boy is a record of my cliffhanger journey through this mystery-cloaked existence called life. Hopefully, the documentation of some of the obstacles I encountered during my careers in the computer industry and corporate America, as well as my personal life, might help future travelers of color negotiate similar roads less traveled. Though much has changed, much more can be done.

In 2017, the Atlantic magazine reported that the Fortune 500 companies added eight new black CEOs between 2005 and 2011, a number that represented fewer than 2 percent of all Fortune 500 companies.

I also was motivated to leave a record of my business life for my children, Kay, Erik, Vicki, and Brian, who saw very little of me during their formative years. I want them, and their children to have a better understanding of what I did and why I spent many weeks and months away from home.

Many people helped produce this work and I'm grateful to them all. Alan Dynner, my longtime attorney and good friend, shared his writings and recollections of our Africa-related business relationship and adventures.

I offer a special thanks to Doug Smith, Doug and I met through Alice Burnette, who was my companion for almost twenty years before she passed of cancer in 2006. Doug encouraged me to write my life story, and offered to help. Doug provided the spark for me to do what I had thought about for a number of years, and not acted upon.

A shout out to Collin Woods for his cover image, it makes me look better than I did at a similar age.

I thank Wikipedia for much of the biographical material in my story.

"There is no FREE LUNCH"

MILTON FREIDMAN

A MESSAGE FROM THE AUTHOR

Anna's Boy is not a story of victimization. In spite of the struggles that we, blacks, have endured as a people, I've never considered myself to be a victim. Throughout the history of civilization life has been unfair to many and generous to many others. None of us chose our parents, our race, gender, the color of our eyes, or the country that became our first home. Had I been born in any other country than the United States, I doubt if I would have acquired the education and experiences needed to become the man I became. Despite tribulations, life has been good. Yet I know that there are many people with far less education and far fewer life experiences than I who are just as pleased with their lives.

I draw this conclusion from my own observations, which were supported in a recent study on happiness. The study determined that some of the happiest people in the world are in the Tonga tribe in southern Zambia and northern Zimbabwe, where they have next to nothing. They live in thatched huts, have no electricity, no running water, and no hospital system. Yet they're happy.

In Nature Boy, a song written by Brooklyn native Eden Ahbez and first recorded by Nat King Cole, one line reads: "The greatest thing you will ever learn, is just to love and be loved in return." If that's your perception of happiness, then there are many people in the world who are happy, despite not having any of the advantages that we in the Western world hold dear. I was born and raised in New York City and I know that the attitude of some New Yorkers is, "What good is happiness, can it buy money?" Is that the objective—to accumulate all the toys in the world?

I'm a product of the love and sacrifices of my parents and of so many others throughout who have made life safer, healthier, and more comfortable through advances in science, medicine, transportation, and housing. My bonus for having lived more than ninety years? I saw changes that I never dreamed possible in my younger years. I saw the U.S. Supreme Court end racial segregation in the United States, Nelson Mandela freed from South African prison, the end of apartheid in South Africa, and Mandela become president of the country that had imprisoned him for twenty-six years.

I attended the opening of the Smithsonian American Indian museum in Washington D.C.in 2005.The American Indian, had a much different struggle than we black Americans, such as dealing with the loss of their land due to "guns and germs"..They call Christopher Columbus's visit the "encounter" not the "discovery".The Indians won some battles, however the Indians lost the war.In the museum, the emphasis is not on all of the "struggles". Instead, the Indians have chosen to make the museum a celebration of Indian culture and values. In that spirit, that is the choice that I have made, to remember the past accurately, and I mean just that, accurately, and to focus on the present, and the future.

I was fortunate and grateful, too, that my life was briefly linked with three of the iconic figures of the 20th century: Martin Luther King Jr., David Rockefeller, and Jackie Robinson. By their words and through example, they helped shape the man I became. Although I never shook his hand or had a chance to chat with our nation's forty-fourth president, one of the most satisfying experiences of my life occurred when I traveled to Washington, D.C., in 2009 to see Barack Obama, a fellow Columbia University Alumnus, become the first black president of the United States.

I've enjoyed my life; I've enjoyed the daily contest, and I've enjoyed overcoming many, but not all, of the obstacles that blocked my way.

Tom Wood

"I don't believe in failure. Its not failure if you enjoyed the process".

OPRAH WINFREY

CHAPTER 1

"The arc of the moral universe
May bend towards justice, but it
Does not bend on its own"

BARACK OBAMA

"Yes, m'Lord".

These three words out of my mouth ricocheted off the walls of a London courtroom, their vibrations slapping me sharply across the face, as if to remind me that the theatre-type drama that was about to begin was not a dream. After years of delays, my time on the witness stand was here.

I sat in what the British called the dock, a witness stand that positioned me at eye-level with the three distinguished arbitrators: Lord Patrick Devlin, Sir David Cairns, and Sir Henry Fisher. They seemed relaxed, comfortable at home in their work in one of the four courts of historic Gray's Inn, where British law clerks and apprentices have been trained since the 14th century.

Mine was the only American accent heard during the courtroom proceedings, and with a wry smile I silently offered kudos to George Bernard Shaw for his profound description of America and Great Britain as two nations separated by a common language. Despite the precariousness of the moment, another breeze of humor blew through my mind, as I realized that the fate of my business career and–indeed–the course of my life would be determined by three English arbitrators who were more suitably adorned in white wigs and black robes than in business suits. More sobering thoughts chased my smiles away, as I pondered my situation, as I watched the three arbitrators huddled in animated discussion before I began my first of twelve days of intense interrogation.

I studied the three men and, for a moment, felt hopeful, knowing that the arbitration was in the hands of three of England's most respected legal minds. Lord Devlin, who was the youngest High Court judge to be appointed in the 20th century, was the chief/independent arbitrator. Known for his compassion, one of Devlin's most famous quotes is: "Trial by jury is the lamp that shows that freedom lives." Another former High Court judge said, "Patrick Devlin could have been the greatest among us," an opinion which was widely shared in the British legal profession.

Cairns, a English judge selected by Zambia, (the nation that I had taken to this English Court) was knighted in 1955. A Liberal Party politician, Cairns served as Chairman of the Monopolies and Restrictive Practices Commission and was Lord Justice of Appeal (1970-77). He presided over several notable cases, including the Exxon Corp v Exxon Insurance Consultants International Ltd.

Fisher, lauded for his quick apprehension and ability to analyze and organize voluminous material in the shortest possible time, was the arbitrator selected by my firm, TAW, which are my initials. He was a president of Wolfson College, and the eldest son of Geoffrey Fisher, the former Archbishop of Canterbury. Fisher became TAW's arbitrator, after Arthur Goldberg, a former U.S. Supreme Court Justice, stepped aside, at TAW's request.

The arbitrators' off-the-record platform chat heightened my anxiety and sent my mind whirling toward the hypothetical. Would this be the end of the line for me career-wise? What forces, I wondered, had guided this Harlem-bred black man to a higher level of the international business world in the 1970s and then sent him on a perilous spiral that now had him orbiting precariously above an abyss? I, the president and founder of TAW, an international leasing company that operated in fourteen African countries, wondered what it was all about. How had I become the central character in a U.S. $25 plus million lawsuit against the government of Zambia, a copper-rich landlocked country in southern Africa? How could I win this David vs. Goliath battle that pitted my seven-man legal team against Zambia's team, which was two dozen-strong?

I reflected on the many close calls and cliff-hanger entanglements that I had survived in my business life over the years. None, however, was as scary as this scenario, which developed when TAW's $80 million deal to transport tons of copper from Zambia to export in Dar es Salaam, Tanzania, fell apart. I wondered if years from now I would forever remember this sparsely decorated London courtroom as the site of my Waterloo. I wondered, too, might I have another odds-defying escape tucked deep within me?

Then I surveyed the room, focusing first on barrister Conrad Dehn, the leader of Government of Zambia's team of lawyers. Dehn was a member of one of Great Britain's preeminent law firms. A 1952 Holt Scholar of Gray's Inn, he was widely regarded as one of the leading advocates of his generation. People called him "a well-dressed bloodhound with manners." Dehn moved about the room deliberately and with an air of confidence attained, no doubt, from the reputation he built while breaking down witnesses on the stand with withering cross-examinations.

Lawyers in the British court system have different names and different functions than those in the American system. TAW was represented by lawyers from three countries, including three British lawyers (one barrister and two solicitors). In Great Britain, the barrister is the only lawyer allowed to function as an attorney in this courtroom. Barristers, most of whom are self-employed, are the advocates. They represent clients in criminal and civil cases, draft legal pleas, give expert legal opinions, and are usually hired by solicitors directly.

Solicitors, hired by firms or organizations, have direct contact with clients and may do transactional-type legal work. In the British court system, foreign lawyers can't participate in court procedures. Once the arbitration court convened, Alan Dynner, TAW's U.S. attorney, and I weren't allowed to discuss the case with each other because Alan, too, was to be called as a witness.

When I ended my scrutiny of Dehn from afar, I moved across the aisle and sought eye contact with members of my seven-man legal team, beginning with Alan, my attorney, who became a longtime friend and confidante. Alan came to TAW as an assistant to Norman Vander Clute, a partner in the company's first outside attorney. Their firm almost exclusively handled international projects. Intrigued by Africa, Alan urged Vander Clute to replace him as TAW's attorney. Vander Clute gave Alan the job, and he quickly proved to be an effective legal representative. The longer we worked together the more I realized that Alan, a Yale law graduate, not only was a brilliant lawyer, but he possessed the instincts of a seasoned businessman. We were often on the same wavelength, compatible from the start. We were so in tune with each other's thoughts that at times, we finished each other's sentences. When their law firm split, Vander Clute stayed with the founding firm; Alan went with the new firm. I chose to keep Alan as TAW's attorney.

During my business career I've always believed that the person doing the job was usually more important than the name on the door. Besides, Alan was genuinely interested in Africa and its people. Because of our fifteen-year age difference, Alan often called me his "big brother." In many of TAW's previous legal fights and negotiations, Alan's legal skills, managerial sensitivity, and tenacity helped us obtain the results we sought. His presence on TAW's team gave me a high level of confidence, as I prepared for a courtroom battle that could end with TAW in bankruptcy and my life in shambles.

Then I targeted Frank Presnell, my assistant solicitor. I was saddened when I discovered that he was a turncoat at heart, if not in deed. Presnell's admiration for Dehn's courtroom skills prompted him to commit what I considered to be a serious ethical faux pas. Though he was paid to represent TAW and me, he bet Alan that Dehn would break me down on the witness stand and we would lose the case. Frank Presnell never knew that I had learned of the Presnell/Dynner wager weeks earlier. From that moment, I watched Presnell, my assistant solicitor, with suspect eyes.

Then I locked on to Bruce Brodie, my chief solicitor and a South African native. Alan recommended Brodie for the job, with some reservations, only because he thought Brodie's South African roots might give me pause. Actually, Brodie and I became good friends, not only professionally, but socially.During the Arbitration, we broke bread together regularly. Once during lunch, he casually mentioned that his firm, Frere Cholmeley, was older than my country. The British firm was founded in 1750.

Brodie, described as cool, confident, and calm under pressure, came to us with high praise for his work in prior arbitrations, particularly international commercial arbitration. He was the recipient of a Blue, an award earned by British sportsmen and women attending universities and other schools for competing in athletic events at the university level. Of course, that earned him high marks from this hardworking former student/athlete. He was also John Lennon's solicitor. But Brodie wasn't without flaw. He had, after all, hired Presnell as his assistant solicitor.

A smile returned to my face as I gazed at David Hirst, my fearless, conscientious, and ebullient barrister. Some considered David, who had served as a Lord Justice on the Court of Appeal, somewhat of a showman. He spoke rapidly but always clearly, waved his arms dramatically during cross-examinations and waddled about the courtroom with penguin-like motions. He was a stickler for enforcing rules and decorum and once became emotionally agitated when someone, who worked for him, addressed him by his Christian name. He was subsequently knighted by the Queen, an honor which dubbed him "Sir David Hirst."

Sebastian Zulu's eyes were fixed on me before I looked his way. I returned his smile and was glad to have someone of his intellect, insight, and integrity on my side in a legal hassle involving Zambia, his home country. I met him when he was Zambia's solicitor general. He impressed me then when he openly opposed an order by Zambia's president to jail seventeen people.

The president relented, recognizing the wisdom in Sebastian's opposition. I leaned on Zulu heavily for legal advice for many years in the various African countries in which TAW did business.

After my legal team, my eyes turned to Frank Savage, an Equitable Life bank manager when I met him, still dressed the part. Clean-cut and stylishly outfitted, Frank came to mind when we landed the Zambia project. During our conversation, I told him that someone with his banking, financial, and organizing skills, combined with his love for Africa, should work with TAW. He agreed to join us as director of the Zambia project.I remembered vividly one of our early discussions after Frank joined TAW. I greatly respected Frank's rapid rise in the corporate world and his insight in evaluating people, as well as his abilities as a manager of people. My primary experience was in the technical world, one where the set of facts on which one made decisions were usually agreed upon. I was now operating in a world where the underlying facts were not always agreed upon. I learned early in my managerial career that"engineers are people who control things", "managers are people who control people", and therefore people who control people are more effective, powerful(however you may phrase it) than people who control things. Frank's ability to operate and succeed in this world was invaluable to me.The discussion involved a lengthy report Frank produced after making a trip on behalf of TAW. I said to Frank "I have read the report, now I want you to tell me what occurred "Frank replied "It is in the report", I answered "I want you to tell me what I should know about your trip" This really surprised Frank. I continued "Not that the report is not needed for the record, you may admit that you spent a great deal of time in making sure that history will be kind to what you have said in the report, I want to know what your instincts and experience tell you. Frank agreed. Later, Frank formed Savage Holdings LLC in 2001 and has served on several major boards, including Bloomberg LP, the New York Academy of Medicine, Lockheed Martin, and the New York Philharmonic.

Herb Cummings was neither a lawyer nor banker, but I considered him a valued member of my team. A multimillionaire and a gadfly, Herb often made me and the TAW team quite nervous, especially during court-room breaks, when he engaged in small-talk with the arbitrators. He had that must-talk-to-everyone personality. He could go into a bar and within ten minutes he'd know nearly everyone. My lawyers were concerned because they thought Herb might give away our plans while chatting socially with the arbitrators or opposing lawyers, but he never did. Herb had the air of a distinguished judge or physician. He was fashionably dressed and fashionably thin. I don't know how this came up, but later, one of the arbitrators told Alan that the arbitrators assumed that Herb was the banker and that Frank, the only other black American on my team, was one of my Hollywood buddies, just tagging along for moral support. They assumed Herb was the team member who was associated with those corporate boards.

Herb and I were about the same age and though we came from different worlds, we became close friends; the chemistry just worked between us. He was like a brother and had proven to me in so many ways that he didn't have a bigoted bone in his body. He accompanied me on many trips to Africa and on fund-raising trips, as well. He demonstrated his friendship most clearly when he made a last-minute financial gesture that helped my firm in a significant way. I knew Herb couldn't rescue me this time; my fate was in the hands of the three arbitrators still chatting among themselves. It was comforting, however, having Herb in my corner and a part of the fight.

After surveying the TAW team, I realized that some one who was instrumental in TAW's early success, was missing. That some one was Sam Howard. Sam joined TAW after a stint as a White House Fellow under U.N. Ambassador Arthur Goldberg. Sam left TAW to pursue "A Nobel Cause", he wanted to buy radio stations. I believe his desire resulted from his negotiations with the Prudential Insurance Co., on TAW's behalf. Sam basically headed the TAW team over the one year it required to complete the six million dollar loan from Prudential as one of the components necessary to start the leasing operation. Near the end of the negotiation, the Prudential Team Leader, who had recently negotiated a deal with NBC's Huntley – Brinkley to finance the purchase of the maximum, under the law, number of TV stations, told Sam, "we are impressed with Tom and your management skills, you should submit a proposal to acquire a series of radio stations". I told Sam I did not think I could manage that, a start up leasing company and a start up radio station operation, at the same time.My opinion at the time, and still is that no start up of any appreciable size is easy, there are always unforeseen problems, which would require full, and complete effort.

The reality of my sitting here in this London Courtroom attest to the requirement of full and complete effort, particularly a start up with six zero's before the decimal point.

My response was prophetic, for TAW had difficulty in raising the remaining equity for the leasing operation.

When Sam had the opportunity to pursue his "Nobel Cause" acquiring a radio stations, he decided to leave TAW.In addition to acquiring several radio stations, Sam went on to become the Treasurer of the Hospital Corporation of America (which at the time had one of the largest cash flows in the U.S.).Then Sam then went on to to found a groundbreaking Health Care company working with Tennessee's uninsured. After Sam left, there were several times that I missed his wise financial advice. Sam Howard and I remain close friends today.

A negative ruling would shut the doors at TAW and probably would damage my reputation beyond repair. Such an outcome undoubtedly would brighten the day for Marshall Mays, past chairman of the U.S. Overseas Private Investment Corporation (OPIC), who personally labored mightily to shove TAW into bankruptcy before the arbitration hearings began. I'm convinced that Mays, a staunch South Carolina conservative, had trouble concealing his disdain for any black man who dealt with him as an equal, as I did. Though Mays wasn't in the courtroom, I felt his presence, lingering over the proceeding like the proverbial 800-pound gorilla.

So much was at stake and not just money. Would corporate America take a pass on any future foreign deals that might be pitched by a black entrepreneur because the arbitrators ruled against TAW? More than anything, I knew I would accept a negative ruling as a badge of failure and would feel that I had let down the black business pioneers who had made it possible for me to pursue my goals.

As I waited to give testimony in this potentially life-altering arbitration, I drifted back in time, way beyond my early years in my hometown, New York, which was nearly four thousand miles away. In the few moments left before Lord Devlin banged his gavel, I asked myself, "How did this Harlem-born grandson of a slave manage to become the focal point of this London arbitration? I then began to consider the life and times of blacks in the America, that my grandparents knew as slaves.

"We may have all come on different ships,
But we are in the same boat now".

MARTIN LUTHER KING

CHAPTER 2

"We were proclaiming ourselves
Political hypocrites before the
World, by thus fostering human
Slavery and proclaiming ourselves
At the same time, the sole friends
Of human freedom"

ABRAHAM LINCOLN

My grandparents on my father's side were born into slavery in Virginia, during the Civil War. My father told me that about Grandpa and Grandma Wood, and little else. That was all he knew, or maybe that was all he wanted to tell. Did my great-grandmother when my grandmother was born into slavery in 1861, face a similar dilemma as Tony Morrison's heroine in the powerful novel "Beloved".

Here are a few, not widely remembered facts and dates covering slavery in the America's.

• 1501 Spanish and Portuguese bring slaves from Africa to the America's

• 1619 First slave ship arrives at what is known today as Hampton Roads Virginia.As was the usual case in such slave ship Atlantic crossings, about half the slaves carried aboard died in the Atlantic crossing.

- For we black's living in what is now the United States, black slavery lasted longer than freedom for blacks has existed.

- Slavery 1619 to 1865

- Freedom 1865 to 2020

- Aproximately 250 years under slavery.

- Aproximately 150 years under legal freedom.

- Black slavery in the U.S. lasted approximately 100 years longer than black freedom.

- Massachusetts was the first state to legalize slavery, Mississippi became the last state to abolish slavery. (delayed ratification of the 13 th Admendment)

- 1819 The Attoney General of Canada declared, by residing in Canada black resident's were set free.An estimated upper limit of the number of U.S. slaves that fled to Canada is 100 thousand.

- 1829 President Guerrero of Mexico abolished slavery in Mexico, which then included what is now Texas. This triggered a series of events leading to Texas becoming part of slave holding United States in 1845.

- 1859 The last slave ship with slaves destined for the U.S. lands in Mobile Bay Alabama.

- Crispus Attucks (1723-1770) who was of African and Native American descent was the first person killed in the Boston Massacre and thus the first American killed in the American Revolution.

- John Baptiste Point du Sable (1750-1818) was of African descent and is regarded by historians as the first permanent non-indigenous settler of what later became Chicago, and is recognized by historians as the "Founder of Chicago".

- The slave trade displaced more than 12 million Africans,
  some 5 million to Brazil, 3 million to the Caribbean,
  and less than ½ million to North America.

- It should be noted, that at the time of my grandparents birth,
  the population of the United States was approximately 30 million, with 4 million slaves (13% of the population) as of
  this writing, the United States population is well over 300
  million, and blacks make up approximately 13%).

According to Dr. Drew Gilpin Faust, the 28th and first woman President of Harvard University, who grew up in Clark County Virginia ; "Our nation's experience with slavery began in Virginia, when some 20 captive Africans arrived on a warship in Jamestown in 1619.Black bondage existed in Virginia for close to two and a half centuries, very much longer than black freedom has.Slavery made colonial Virginia prosperous, creating a plantation society founded on toabacco production, social and economic stratification, and unfree labor.It also produced a class of white owners whose daily witness to the degradations of bondage instilled in them a fierce devotion to their own freedom.They were determined to be the masters not just of their house-holds, their estates, and their laborers, but also of their society, their polity, and their destiny. George Washington, Thomas Jefferson, James Madison, James Monroe, George Mason were– slaveholders all. That so many of the Founding Fathers, including the leaders of the Revolution and the aurthors of the Declaration of Independence, the Constitution, and the Bill of Rights, were slaveholders is both an irony and a paradox.The Nation conceived in liberty was also the Nation conceived in slavery. Commitment to a repub-lican form of government was incompatible with the absolute power that defined the system of slavery.Thomas Jefferson's attraction to Sally Hemings (Jefferson's slave), with whom he fathered five children, embodied the tragedy present at the very creation of "American freedom". Many white Virginians (and white Americans — my comment —)created a narrative of an invented past and a distorted portrait of their own time to reassure themselves of the justice of their social order and of their own benevolence. The cult of the Lost Cause embraced an apocryphal history suffused with nostalgia for a world of valorous Confederates, kindly masters, and contented slaves. And it mischaracterized the present, extolling the "Virginia Way", a distinctive form of Jim Crow in which blacks and whites lived peaceably together in lives of "separation by consent". The Founders embraced both slavery and freedom. We have inherited the legacy, and the cost, of both".

I believe that, as a nation, we have not yet lived up to the Declaration of Independence "All men are created equal" statement. However, as individuals, many Americans have lived up to these ideals. America throught its history has moved towards these ideals, despite pertubations and wavering. We as a nation, particulary today, are continually tested as to our resolve to make these ideals an every day reality. We should not waver.

I don't remember my father ever telling me Grandpa Wood's first name, nor did he ever talk about the things Grandpa liked or disliked. My father rarely shared with me any of the father-son experiences he may have had with his father, and he never spoke of the things that brought Grandpa joy or made him cry. There must have been more sadness than happiness in Grandpa Wood's early years as a freed young slave, and I suspect that he focused on just making it through each day rather than dreaming of a brighter future.

Muriel McCoy, one of the persons mentioned in the book's dedication, can trace one of her male ancestors to the 18th century. Nero Hawley (1742-1817). This trace can be made because Nero became a "free man", after his Army service during the American Revolutionary War. Many American black families can not make this trace(including my family) unless the subject's slaveholder(s) kept records of their "human property".Muriel's relative, became a brick maker. Born into slavery in Stratford, CT, Nero earned his freedom after enlisting in George Washington's Continental Army. He survived the famous 'Winter at Valley Forge.' His historic life is featured in historian E. Merrill Beach's book, From Valley Forge to Freedom. Nero's grandsons, Grant and Peter Hawley were named trustees of the Colored Methodist Episcopal

Church in June 1835, now known as Walter's Memorial African Methodist Episcopal Zion Church, the oldest black church in Bridgeport, CT. The church celebrated its 175th anniversary in 2010.

Throughout history, stories I've read about a person's life in slavery have been more disturbing than uplifting. The African slaves, who were first brought to the New World in chains several centuries ago, endured horrific conditions during their ocean journey and after their arrival in 1619. A glimmer of hope of freedom crept into the psyche of American slaves in 1847 when Dred Scott, a former slave, began a ten-year judicial fight to gain his freedom. Scott's slave master brought him out of the South to Missouri and then Illinois, a state that had banned slavery. The United States Supreme Court dashed the dreams of black folk in an 1857 ruling that today's scholars and historians call "the worst decision" ever made by the U.S. highest court.

With Chief Justice Roger B. Taney presiding, the court ruled 7-2 that blacks–whether free or enslaved–were considered inferior when the U.S. Constitution was drafted, and they could not be considered citizens of America. Which meant, of course, that when then slave owner Thomas Jefferson penned this enduring line–"We hold these truths to be self-evident that all men are created equal"–it didn't apply to the nation's sixty thousand slave population.

In the Court's majority opinion, Taney wrote, "It is difficult at this day to realize the state of public opinion in regard to that unfortunate race which prevailed in the civilized and enlightened portions of the world at the time of the Declaration of Independence, and when the Constitution of the United States was framed and adopted; but the public history of every European nation displays it in a manner too plain to be mistaken. They had for more than a century before been regarded as beings of an inferior order, and altogether unfit to associate with the white race, either in social or political relations, and so far unfit that they had no rights which the white man was bound to respect."

I wonder how my grandparents reacted when they learned of that ruling, which was announced just four years before the start of the Civil War. Taney's Court also declared the Missouri Compromise unconstitutional, thus permitting slavery in all the nation's territories. Taney had hoped that the Court's decision, declaring federal restrictions on slavery unconstitutional, would put the issue to rest. Instead, it galvanized Northern opposition to slavery and stoked the flames that ignited the Civil War.

In the book Black Manhattan, author James Weldon Johnson wrote, "The Dred Scott decision proved to be the beginning of the end of slavery. History changing events followed in portentous succession. In 1859 John Brown was at Harper's Ferry. In 1860 Abraham Lincoln was nominated by the newly organized Republican Party. In 1861 Ft. Sumter was fired upon and the 'irrepressible conflict' . . . became a reality."

Regardless of the hardships and racial barriers I had to circumvent, I've never considered myself a victim because my ancestors were slaves. And I've tried to nullify the defense that many whites—and some blacks—have used to rationalize slavery in America, which goes, "You were initially enslaved by other Africans, your own people, so it isn't the white man's fault." The notion that people of the same race or ethnicity enslaved their own isn't unique. Throughout history, people, if they could, enslaved their own people.

The Vikings, plunderers of the 9th and 10th centuries, were probably the most successful at it. Rather than kill their captors, they enslaved them. The Vikings enslaved their neighbors. They tried to enslave Ireland, Scotland, France, and Constantinople, too. The word "thrall" means slave in the Norse language. "Enthralled" meant you were enslaved. People of all races, religions, and ethnicities have been abused and oppressed at various times throughout history. Slavery in some ancient civilizations was better than others. In some systems, the duties of slaves included educating the children of their slave owners, and in others, slaves were set free after serving an agreed upon time.

Slavery in ancient Greece and Rome was not as oppressive. Blond, blue-eyed Anglo-Saxons worked side-by-side with blacks from Africa or brown-skinned folks from Asia. However, slavery in America, which lasted for more than two and a half centuries, was extremely oppressive and dehumanizing. According to Chief Justice Taney, Negroes were " . . . beings of an inferior order . . . unfit to associate with the white race, either in social or political relations . . . " The impact of that sordid chapter in America's history lingers still.

The American slaves' dream of a better life finally took shape during the Civil War when President Abraham Lincoln signed the Emancipation Proclamation that promised freedom for slaves in the Confederacy once the Union armies reached them. Expressing his thoughts to three prominent Kentucky figures, including newspaper editor Albert Hodges, Lincoln wrote, "I am naturally anti-slavery. If slavery is not wrong, nothing is wrong . . . And yet I have never understood that the Presidency conferred upon me an unrestricted right to act officially upon this judgment and feeling . . . I claim not to have controlled events but confess plainly that events have controlled me."

In his autobiography, Up from Slavery, Booker T. Washington, educator and founder of Tuskegee Institute, recalled celebrating the landmark moment as a nine-year-old boy. Washington wrote, "As the great day drew nearer, there was more singing in the slave quarters than usual. It was bolder, had more ring, and lasted later into the night. Most of the verses in the plantation songs had some reference to freedom. Some man who seemed to be a stranger made a little speech and then read a rather long paper - the Emancipation Proclamation, I think. After the reading, we were told that we were free and could go when and where we pleased. My mother, who was standing by my side, leaned over and kissed her children, while tears of joy ran down her cheeks. She explained what it all meant, that this was the day that she had been so long praying but fearing that she would never live to see."

Ten years before the Barack Obama presidency began, black America dubbed Bill Clinton "the first black president" because of his progressive policies that were sensitive to the black experience. But Clinton wasn't the "first black president"; Lincoln was. The newly freed slaves and whites called Lincoln the first "black Republican president" when he signed the Emancipation Proclamation, and, of course, it was a pejorative by the majority of white southerners. Lincoln was hated by southern whites for abolishing slavery, and for many years they did not celebrate his birthday in the South.

In 1866, all governments in the former Confederate states were dissolved (except Tennessee's) and Congress passed the Civil Rights Act and four Reconstruction Acts, which opened the door for freed slaves to hold public office. Four years later, Joseph Rainey of South Carolina became the first black member of Congress. During the Reconstruction Era, other ex-slaves–all Republicans–also held seats in the Senate and House of Representatives from southern states, including Mississippi, Alabama, Georgia, and Louisiana.

Southern Democrats moved quickly to regain control of southern legislatures and restore white supremacy. They stayed in power by restricting the rights of the majority of blacks to vote by imposing nuisance changes, such as poll taxes, literacy tests, and other residential requirements. To me, it is so ironic that today's Republican Party, which freed the slaves and gave them the vote, are using similar tactics to keep minorities particularly blacks from voting booths.

Actually, legislation designed to keep free blacks out of the mainstream of American society existed–in the North and South–as early as the 1800s. Before slavery was abolished, these laws were called "Slave Codes." In 1865 and 1866, the name was changed to the Black Codes. Mississippi was the first state to pass the Black Codes, which prevented blacks from bearing arms, learning to read and write, and testifying against whites in court, and denying blacks the right to own property and access to employment in skilled positions. Many blacks not working in the fields were the plantation handymen, busying themselves as carpenters, masons, bricklayers, plumbers, and so on, but weren't able to find work using those skills in the South or North.

Several border states also had the Black Codes. Illinois prohibited blacks from outside the state from staying in the state more than ten days.

Those who stayed beyond ten days were subject to arrest, detention, a fifty-dollar fine, or deportation. Maryland required blacks to obtain licenses from whites before doing business. All the former slave states banned the marriage between whites and blacks.

When I was a kid, I thought racism was the worst thing in the world, but it isn't. After my first trip to Africa, I thought poverty was the worst thing in the world, but it isn't. Ignorance is the worst thing in the world. It's the catalyst that produces racism and poverty; it's people being taken advantage of because they're ignorant.

Fortunately for me, my early years were relatively free of the hardships my ancestors suffered. I'm grateful that my life journey began in an environment well-suited for someone like me who possessed an adventurous heart and a curious mind. My turn to explore the tangible qualities, as well as the intangible mysteries of life, had arrived.

CHAPTER 3

"Harlem was home; where we belonged;where we knew and were known in return;where we felt most alive. Harlem defined us, claiming our consciousness, and I suspect, our unconsciousness."

RUBY DEE/OSSIE DAVIS

The Harlem that I knew during my formative years no longer exists, but vivid memories of that wondrous era must have been etched in my bones. Eighty years later, they linger still.

The Harlem that I knew does not exist because of the availability of "drugs".

The Harlem that I knew does not exist because of the availibility of "guns".

The Harlem that I knew does not exist because of relatively recent "upward mobility" for blacks.In the United States, upward mobility, in general has always been avialiable to whites, sometimes aided by name changes. Changing skin color is a bit more difficult than a name change. Note: most black families who have been in the United States for more than five generations, already have experienced a name change.

The Harlem that I knew was a place where almost no one had an air conditioned home.

The Harlem that I knew was one with "a thousand eyes" observing from open windows, what was happening below.

The Harlem that I knew was one where my mother, a woman alone because my father, traveled as a Pullman Porter with the railroad, could on occasion, in the summer heat, with two small children take my sister and I to sleep in a local park, without fear of harm to herself or her children. My mother would sit on a park bench and watch over my sister and I while we slept.

That, was the Harlem that I knew as a schoolboy, and now does not exsist.

Luckily, I came into this world smack in the middle of the Harlem Renaissance. W.E.B. Du Bois, Langston Hughes, Paul Lawrence Dunbar, Zora Neale Hurston, Joe Louis, George Gregory, and other prominent black authors and achievers strolled Harlem streets during the "New Negro Movement," which began in 1919 and extended into the 1930s.

Hurston, an American folklorist, anthropologist, and native of Eatonville, Florida, penned four novels and more than fifty short stories. Her biographer, Robert Hemenway, described her as "a brown skinned, big boned, with freckles and high cheekbones . . . a striking woman: her dark brown eyes were both impish and intelligent, her voice was rich and black – with the map of Florida on her tongue." Commenting on the racial barriers of that time, she once wrote, "Sometimes I feel discriminated against, but it does not make me angry. It merely astonishes me. How can any deny themselves the pleasure of my company? It's beyond me."

Even now, I walk in lockstep with Hurston on that point and look back on my life, grateful that my parents–Thomas and Anna Lamont Wood–left Virginia in the 1920s and made Harlem their hometown. Being black in New York City, residing in Harlem for much of my early life, I considered living to be a contest, involving rules and ethics. As a black person, you could bend the unjust man-made rules, but an inner voice wouldn't allow you to bend your own ethics. My search for the meaning of life began in a community that included many of the world's most accomplished and respected black achievers, and I acknowledge their sway in the educational and career paths I chose. Dubbed "Black Manhattan" by James Weldon Johnson in his book of the same name, Harlem became my intellectual and emotional incubator. But not mine alone. Beginning in the 1920s, more African American journalists, poets, intellectuals, composers, actors, and entertainers lived in "Black Manhattan" than in all other U.S. cities combined. It was an inspirational/motivational reservoir for young black achievers of the next generation and beyond.

Harlem, however, wasn't always the black oasis that I knew as a child. In his book, This Was Harlem (1981-82, Harper Collins), author Jervis Anderson describes its roots:

" . . . At times, it was easy to forget that Harlem was originally the Dutch name 'Haarlem'; that the community it described had been founded by people from Holland; and that for most of its three centuries – it was first settled in the 1600's – it had been occupied by white New Yorkers.

"Harlem became synonymous with black life and black style in Manhattan. Blacks living there used the word as if they had coined it themselves . . . . As the years passed, Harlem assumed an even larger meaning. In the words of Adam Clayton Powell, Sr., the pastor of the Abyssinian Baptist Church, Harlem 'became the symbol of liberty and the Promised Land to Negroes everywhere'.

My mother, was born in Milford, Virginia, which is about thirty miles north of Richmond, the state capital. After my grandparents died, my mother, then six, and her siblings, were parceled out to be raised by other relatives. I later learned that some of my mother's family Used "Mont" as their last name; others, including my mother's changed their last name to "LaMont." No explanation for the name change was ever offered, but many blacks altered their last names for various reasons during that time.

Anna Wood was big-boned and tall (5'10"); dressed conservatively, Victorian style, and nearly always wore her hair raised with a bun in the back.

She wore Emma J shoes, the kind with laces and slight heels. They were very popular back then. She was soft-spoken and rarely emotional. I would call her sedate. I found out later that as an adult, my mother was a beer drinker, but that was before my sister and I came along, after that, she didn't allowed alcohol in the house. Occasionally, one of my father's brothers used to come to the house intoxicated but my mother would stop him at the door and say, "You're not coming in here with profanity or alcohol!"

My mother rarely complained about anything. She was very strict, but less strict with me because of the convention of that time which said, "boys are allowed freedom, but girls are not." My sister, Frances, who was three years younger than me, virtually stayed in the house throughout her school years because my mother wouldn't allow her to go outside to play by herself. My parents called me "Junior," but Frances had difficulty pronouncing Junior, so she called me "Duna." That nickname stuck and I'm glad it did. Many years later, when I became the only uncle to her children, they called me Uncle Duna, which is much better than referring to me as "Uncle Tom."

My grandparents on my father's side was born into a world in which their soul was claimed by a white God and their bodies were claimed by a white man. To me, it's a miracle that they produced a man like my father, who was honest, loving, prudent, and hardworking. Thomas Wood, a soft-spoken man, was raised in South Boston, Virginia, which is 115 miles southwest of Richmond. Occasionally, we traveled to South Boston to visit my grandfather. My father had two brothers and a sister. He might have had other siblings as well, but those were the only ones he mentioned. Neither of my parents had more than a sixth-grade education. My father, a World War I veteran, served in France. After the war, he returned to Richmond, Va., where he met my mother.

My parents left Virginia and moved to New York's West Side in a section called San Juan Hill because of a heavy influx of black veterans, who fought in the Spanish- American War. My father was thirty-five and my mother was twenty-six when I was born at a lower Manhattan hospital in a white neighborhood. Actor/civil rights activist Harry Belafonte was born at the same hospital. On my birth certificate, my parents are listed as blacks: my mother, a housewife, my father, a porter. My father, a World War I veteran, worked for many years as a Pullman Porter.

I was named Thomas Alexander Wood, but was not listed as a junior on my birth certificate. Still, whenever I said or did something that displeased my mother, she'd yell, "Thomas Junior!" Her tone of voice signaled the degree of trouble I was in.

We resided at 232 W. 149th Street in Harlem, within an area noted for its broad streets and spacious apartment buildings. When Harlem expanded to include "sugar hill", several mansions were added to those already sprinkled throughout the neighborhood, including one owned by James A. Bailey, cofounder of the Barnum & Bailey Circus. Bailey built the house, which included numerous stained-glass windows and hand-carved wood throughout the interior. According to The Wall Street Journal, in 2008 the asking price for Bailey's former home was ten million dollars.

The black migration from the Caribbean, and the American South to San Juan Hill, and other sections of the mid-West Side to upper Manhattan began in the 1920s. Upper Manhattan soon became a black oasis, a "Promised Land" for blacks everywhere and the site of the internationally recognized Harlem Renaissance. Like many of the southern blacks of that era, my father was a fiscally conservative Republican. My mother was a FDR Democrat. My father would not recognize the Republican Party of 2020. I believe that if my father were alive today, he would comment; "like a virus, the parasitic * white suprematist members of the democratic party of his day, have simply changed its "hosts", and joined the conservative wing of the republican party of my son's day.(* as defined by the net flow of federal tax dollars to the states)

For most of its existence, "the white south felt it needed something akin to a diplomatic strategy with the rest of America". * The white south had been trying to balance its top priority "the enforcement of white supremacy" held in place by the dual weapons of law and violence with its forced membership in the broader United States. (* "Why we are Polarized" by Ezra Klein)

As I grew older, in my teens, I followed in my mother's political food-steps. When I became old enough to vote (then 21) and witnessing scandal's on both sides of the aisle, I considered my self an independent, while voting with the democrats on most issues and candidates. Barry Goldwater, Richard Nixon and Lee Atwater with their "southern strategy" caused me to retrace and continue in my mother's democrat footsteps.

The southern strategy is a republican party strategy to gain and maintain political support among white voters in the south by appealing to racism against blacks.

Richard Nixon's "southern strategy" to borrow a Barrack Obama phrase called for the republican party to "put lipstick on the pig"of southern racial bias, in order to allow the republican party and the racially biased south to enter into a lasting embrace. I believe that Lee Atwater who became Chairman of the Republican National Committee, was one of the major spear carriers for this strategy. Atwater became a political strategist for Nixon, after being an activist in the campaigns of South Carolina's Senator Strom Thurmond.

Richard Nixon's "southern strategy" became infamous in the black community as well other communities in the northern states when Lee Atwater in opposition to the Voting Rights Act, was caught saying "You start out in 1954 by saying nigger, nigger, nigger. By 1968 you can't say nigger – that hurts you. Backfires. So you say stuff like forced busing, states' rights and all that stuff. You are getting so abstract now, you are talking about cutting taxes—-the things you are talking about are totally economic things and a byproduct of them is blacks get hurt worse than whites.—I'm saying that if it is getting that abstract, and that coded, that we are doing away with the racial problem one way or another —because obviously sitting around saying we want to cut this is much more abstract than even the busing thing, and a hell of a lot more abstract than nigger, nigger.

Lee Atwater's duality on race is evident, if one examines his musical preferences, and assiociates. The American duality on race is diminishing with each generation.In my generation and community this American duality on multiple levels is caputured by the off repeated joke, "In the south blacks can get close to whites, but never equal;in the north blacks can get equal to whites, but never close."

Lee Atwater loved the "blues" and would often play in concerts with B.B.King and other black musucians in clubs and church basements.Atwater recorded a blues album with B.B.King, Issac Hayes, and other black musicians.Lee Atwater sought and became a member of the historically black Howard University Board of Trustees. When the Howard students rose up in protest, Atwater resigned.

In 1990 Atwater discovered he had brain cancer and announced that he had converted to Roman Catholicism, and on his death bed he recanted the racist views he espoused most of his life.

How I came to be born in a white hospital, what my father did in the war, how my father felt about life, and specifics about my ancestors are among the many mysteries of my family life. In my house, children didn't question their parents about anything at any time. We just sat and listened. Children were never included in family discussions. Over the years, friends have urged me to research my family genealogy to learn more about my ancestors. The few morsels of family history I received from my parents came in dribs and drabs.

My parents frequently talked about a person named Maggie Walker. When I became a young adult, I assumed they were referring to Madame C. J. Walker, the hairdresser. Instead, they were talking about Maggie L. Walker, a black teacher and businesswoman from Richmond, who was the first woman of any race to charter and become founder and president of a bank in the United States.

My father spoke with a slight, southern accent, but my mother spoke with perfect diction, grammar, and without a hint of a southern accent. My

Jewish and Italian schoolmates would come to my house and comment on my mother's English because their parents were recent immigrants and spoke with noticeable accents. My understanding is that my mother went to live with a relative who worked for a white northern physician in Richmond, who helped my mother become a facile student of the English language. Later in life, I met one of my mother's sisters. She didn't speak English as accent free as my mother did.

My sister, Frances, was born after we moved across the street into the Dunbar, an upscale apartment complex that was built by the Rockefellers. They built a similar high-rise in Midtown Manhattan. The Rockefellers hoped the Dunbar would improve the quality of life in the black community. It had a security force, but it was not a gated community. Bill "Bojangles" Robinson, the tap dancer and actor, lived in the Dunbar and sponsored an annual picnic. He used to distribute dimes to all the kids on the playground. Archie Parsons, a Michigan graduate and New York Herald Tribune reporter, grew up in the Dunbar. He was one of the first black journalists to work for a major newspaper.

I was told that after we moved there, John D. Rockefeller, the family patriarch, also came and distributed dimes to kids. Rockefeller, then the richest person in modern history, was an oil industry businessman and philanthropist. He and his brother William Rockefeller Jr., were cofounders of Standard Oil. John's wife, Laura Spelman Rockefeller, was an abolitionist, philanthropist, schoolteacher, and founder of Spelman College in 1884 to educate black women in Atlanta, Georgia. Mrs. Rockefeller's parents were longtime activists in the antislavery movement.

When my sister was in preschool, my mother allowed her to go with me to a big sandy area on the playground to play on the swings, seesaws and monkey bars. We'd go in the morning and get dirty playing in the sand. We'd go home for lunch, bathe and then mother would dress us in clean clothes. That was every day, and that was my mother.

I was my mother's favorite and Frances filled my father's face with joy. There was one chore that I never complained about doing because my mother and I did it as a team. We, then, lived in a six-floor walkup apartment, and washing the windows was a tricky task. I would sit on the windowsill, with my back outside. My mother would hold my legs while I washed the window. When I finished the lower panes, I would stand to wash the upper panes and she would hold me while I did that. One of the big events in my young life occurred when I was ten. That's when I graduated from knickers to long pants. Young boys today surely should be thankful that they never had to wear knickers.

My father smoked cigarettes; my mother didn't smoke, and she wouldn't allow him to smoke in the house. My sister and I weren't allowed to drink coffee or tea. As a young teen, I disobeyed her one Sunday during services at St. James Presbyterian Church. When tea was offered to everyone, I drank a cup and felt like I had committed a mortal sin. I didn't know how to tell my parents that I had succumbed. My parents didn't know about it because they attended services at a different church, Abyssinian Baptist Church.

My parents also never knew about my involvement, which for me, was one of Harlem's most dangerous after-school activities for boys: gang fights. On several occasions, I was among two groups of kids chucking rocks at each other on Edgecombe Avenue. I was under ten at the time, young and dumb, hoping that the teeth that might get knocked out wouldn't be mine. Once, as I was about to sling a missile at a rival combatant during a Halloween rock fight, Rev. Edler Hawkins, an assistant pastor at St. Presbyterian Church, yanked my shirt and spun me around. "Why are you out here wasting your time fighting on the streets?" he asked, not expecting an answer. "Don't you want to do something with your life besides throw rocks at people? Don't you ever want to be able to hold your head high?"

For singling me out, I put Rev. Hawkins' name at the top of my people-I-don't-like list, but it didn't stay there very long. His lecture stuck with me and shortly thereafter, I realized that he had changed the course of my life.

Soon after, I found a new group of friends that included Lester Florant, I then developed interest in safer and saner activities. I played sports, mainly basketball and stickball, attended St. James' Sunday services regularly, and became active in various other church functions. Occasionally, I was chosen to say the opening prayer at some church functions, with all my new friends sitting in the front row, giggling and making funny faces. Their antics were silly and distractive, but, they weren't throwing rocks! Obviously, Rev. Hawkins helped shape the new "me."

Ironically, a few years later, an incident involving Rev. Hawkins pushed me away from the Church and my pursuit of a spiritual connection. When I was a young teen member of St. James, Rev. Hawkins loomed as one of the Presbyterian church's rising stars. At a Presbyterian conference in Cleveland, Ohio, he was selected to become a bishop. The promotion was later withdrawn without explanation and a white pastor received the promotion. The rumor that spread through the black community—and indeed the Church—was that Rev. Hawkins was turned away because he was black. This incident occurred in the 1940s, so it shouldn't have come as a surprise. As a bishop, Rev. Hawkins would have had domain over white Presbyterian churches as well as black Presbyterian churches. Still, it shook my faith in the Presbyterian Church and in religion in general. My attitude was that if the Church truly believed in the teachings of Christ, how could it support such a blatantly racist decision?

Despite my concerns about organized religion often not living up to its own sacred values, when I became a father years later, I sent all my children to Sunday School because I felt it was a good place to learn civic values.

Discussions I had with friends, including Lester Florant, heightened my doubts about religion. Lester and I kind of gravitated toward each other mainly because we had similar interests besides playing stickball. Lester was a year older and two years ahead of me in school. We were the same height, about 6-1. People who saw us together often assumed we were brothers. We talked a lot, and frequently engaged in intellectual debates, or more accurately, abstract discussions, something that didn't happened in the Wood home. In my era, children were to be seen, not heard, at the family dinner table.

I always felt loved by my parents, especially my mother. I hear kids today say, "I hate my parents," and I know I could never have said that because that's so far from the experience I had while growing up. There were hardships, I got spanked and punished for doing this or that which I shouldn't have done, but my parents were loving providers.

I don't ever remember going hungry as a kid. We didn't have sumptuous, fancy meals, but we had good meals. We didn't get everything we wanted, but most of the major things were provided. During Easter week, I usually got a new suit and Frances got a new dress. At Christmas, we got a few presents, not like what kids get today. We got one toy-like present each year. I got a pair of skates, a hockey stick, baseball glove, or a bike. That was it.

My sister and I were not very close when we were teenagers, not because we didn't like each other, but because we lived in two different worlds. That was the culture of that day and probably more the culture of the black community, though I don't know that for sure. I had free range, I could go out and play with the kids on the block; my mother wouldn't let my sister do that. Basically, my mother wouldn't let my sister out of the house without her supervision, except to go to school. That limited my sister's range of activities. Boys could go outside and play; girls couldn't. That was the distinction.

My sister and I were competitive, but the competition involved activities within the home, not outdoors. I thought I could do anything she could do, and she thought she could do anything I could do. I had the advantage because I learned to knit and do all the things that girls did, and she tried to play ping-pong, but she couldn't play stick ball and other games I played outside the house. Girls went to school, came straight home and stayed there. They hardly had any social life.

My father's career as a Pullman porter got off to a shaky start. He spent the first few years waiting for established porters to miss their job (or run) due to illness or other emergencies. Sometimes, he'd wait twenty-four hours or longer for an opportunity to take a run. Porters with seniority had priority over newcomers or those with less experience. My father missed many runs because someone with greater seniority would be given the assignment. From time to time, many of those waiting left, and my father began to get runs because he simply outwaited the competition. He persevered.Later, with seniority, his job as a full-fledged Pullman porter placed him among a precious few steady bread-winners in the black community.

His job regularly kept him away from home for long stretches, but we were thankful that his extended absences were balanced equally by long stays at home. His routine schedule consisted of five-day trips to California, followed by five days off in California, and ended with a five-day return trip to New York. He then had fifteen days off before starting another cycle. The same home/away scheduling was applicable regardless of his days on the run. For example, for a three-day trip, he would have three days off upon arrival at his destination, and after his three-day return trip, he would have nine days off.

His long stays at home made the social time we had together that much more special. Occasionally, he'd take me fishing with him. I believe I was about seven years old when my father snagged himself with a fish hook. The hook was lodged in the skin between his thumb and forefinger. The tip of the hook went all the way through his flesh, which made it impossible for him to pull it back through without damaging that part of his hand. With help from others, the hook finally was removed without causing serious damage to his hand. I don't recall how they managed to remove it, but as I watched, I do remember thinking how brave my father was. They cut it out without applying any anesthesia. They just cut it out right there on the spot.

My father often worked during holidays, but one year, he was off Christmas Eve and I went with him to get a Christmas tree. I was about ten at the time. He had hoped to pay no more than twenty cents, maybe twenty-five cents. We walked miles all over Harlem in the snow looking for a tree. Finally, it got dark and we were freezing, so he gave up and paid seventy-five cents for a tree. That was one of the few times I spent an entire day with my father during the holidays.

It was during another Christmas season that my father taught me a lesson I never forgot. Just a few days after getting a new two wheel bike for Christmas, a big kid took it away from me. I ran home crying the blues to my father, but he had no interest in my sad song. "You go and get your bike back," he commanded. I did and got beat up again, but I got my bike back. My father was proud of me. My dad said, "If I had gone with you, we would have gotten your bike back, but someone else would have taken it again when I wasn't around. If you stand up to them, they'll leave you alone. They're not going to bother anyone who'll fight back." The older I get, the smarter my father gets.

Chicago industrialist George Pullman revolutionized travel in 1867 when he leased his first Pullman cars to the railroad. The cars came equipped with well-trained porters, many of whom were recently freed slaves. My understanding is that Pullman hired only black porters and paid them 20 percent less than he would have to pay white employees. The Pullman Rail Car Company quickly became one of the largest employer of blacks in the nation. Only whites were hired as Pullman train conductors.

Pullman porters were reputable workers in the black community because they traveled across America, weren't required to do heavy physical labor, and had steady incomes. Historian Timuel Black described them as " . . . good-looking, clean and immaculate in their dress and . . . had a sense of intelligence about them."

Pullman porters and U.S. Postal workers probablly had some of the best permanent, good-paying jobs in the black community. That's why the Wood family could afford to live at the Dunbar. My father's job kept him away from home half the time, but I never thought it was unnatural for him to be away, even for extended periods. I didn't think my dad was doing something out of the norm, because I knew many dads didn't have jobs and I understood what that meant for their families. I knew we were fortunate to have a father with a steady job. Besides, I don't believe I would have gotten to know him any better if he had come home every night. Raising the children was my mother's full-time job and I doubt if she would have shared that responsibility with my father.

Because of his job as a Pullman porter, my father worked during the entire Depression. If we had a financial crisis, he'd resolve it because he saved his money. His life as a young man was quite different in Virginia, where he wasn't allowed to open a bank account. At the time, my father worked as a driver for a man named Camp. "Old man" Camp, as he was known, was an influential guy. When he learned that my father was denied a bank account, he sent a letter to the bank manager. Camp wrote: "This "boy" is a hardworking guy, etc., etc. Open an account for him." They still wouldn't let him open an account.

Fiscally conservative by nature, my father, who spoke with a southern accent, was influenced greatly by the wealthy folk he met in his railroad job. John D. Rockefeller and his grand sons occasionally rode my father's train. My father shined John D. Rockefeller's shoes, but was told by Rockefeller, "Don't shine my grand sons' shoes, they shine their own shoes." Movie stars Jackie Gleason, Mae West, and Joan Crawford also were Pullman Porter favorites. In 2012, I saw a musical entitled Pullman Porter Blues, in Washington D.C.'s Arena Stage about the Pullman cars, described by some as "hotels on wheels". The play helped me remember the experience my father would talk about. My father ocasionally received hefty tips—one hundred dollars or more. He learned to invest in the stock market and save his money.

Before my father left Richmond Virginia, my father had over time deposited more than three hundred dollars in a Bank in Richmond. That was a lot of money in those days. Unfortunately, he lost that money when the bank manager stole the bank's deposits and skipped town. My father was among a small number of black people with a Deposit Account (DA) at Macy's Department store in New York. A DA was a credit card in reverse. You had to put the money in the store's credit account first and then you could use it to purchase items. Basically, you were using your own money. When my father died in 1960, he left more than ten thousand dollars in stocks and bonds, an unusual amount of money for a working-class black man at that time, without life insurance.During most of my father's life, almost all of the major life insurance companies, such as Metropolitian Life, would not insure blacks.

As the real head of our household, my mother decided where we lived, how we dressed, how we spoke, and where we went to school. I remember preparing to attend first grade in a school building just outside the Dunbar complex, but my mother nixed that idea. She didn't like the Harlem school system, so we moved to Westchester County because she believed the schools were better. My mother made the decision to move, though there must have been some discussion about moving because the move made my father's commute more difficult. We didn't have a car, so it was difficult for him to get to work. We left Westchester County after a year, but we didn't move back to Harlem.

We moved to the Bronx and later, we moved from the Bronx back to Harlem. We lived at 367 Edgecombe Ave., which was known as striver's row and/or Sugar Hill. The entire street was situated on a bluff, a beautiful vista that overlooked Yankee Stadium. If you traveled further up the road, you were on Coogan's Bluff and could see the Polo Grounds baseball stadium, where the New York Giants played. That area was home to America's black elite. Many of the nation's top political leaders, artists, and entertainers were among its residents, and it seemed to me to be infused with an air of importance, excitement, and creative energy.

Adam Clayton Powell, Thurgood Marshall, and W.E.B. Du Bois were among the notables who lived a few doors up the block from us in 409 Edgecombe, a red-bricked tower building. Walter White, who was head of the NAACP, also lived in there. Up the road further, at 555 Edgecombe, Duke Ellington, the great jazz pianist, songstress Lena Horne, singer Paul

Robeson, and Roy Wilkins, another former NAACP president, lived in an apartment house that was twelve stories high and had a uniformed doorman.

The Nicholas Brothers, who were tap dancing sensations during that era, and actress Dorothy Dandridge were neighbors; they lived south of 150th street on Edgecombe Ave. When boxing great Joe Louis came to fight in New York, he stayed a few doors up the street from me. My friends and I used to go to the backyard of the house where he lived and hang on the fence, hoping to catch a glimpse of him.

In January 2010, The New York Times published a feature article about the historical significance of Edgecombe Avenue under this banner headline: "In Sugar Hill, a Street Nurtured Black Talent when the World Wouldn't." The reporter described Sugar Hill as "the neighborhood of choice for elegant black musicians, dapper actors, successful professionals – and those who aspired to be like them."

But Harlem wasn't merely a haven for black entertainers and achievers; it was an oasis of irrepressible style, culture, and class. The Times also provided its readers with an occasional glimpse of the cruelty that many blacks endured throughout the country. It published stories about the lynching of blacks, mainly in the South, the daily injustices fostered by the South's "Separate but Equal" laws, and de facto segregation in various other parts of the nation. In some ways, white supremacy in the North kept blacks as segregated and servile as we were in the South. The success of a few top entertainers and celebrities didn't significantly alter reality for most blacks of my generation. Later, several black writers, Richard Wright, James Baldwin, Ralph Ellison, and others, provided the lens through which white America clearly could see the barriers and feel the anguish created in black America. In his bestselling novel Invisible Man, published in 1952, Ralph Ellison captured the inner-frustration and shame felt by blacks, particularly black men, during that era.

I was twelve when I first recognized and expressed rage toward those whites who looked upon me and those who looked like me, with disdain and disgust. This was greatly diminished and later eliminated in my university years with understanding. I don't remember my father sharing his inner-feelings with me or my sister, at times, but I sensed he felt a similar rage. His job provided the comfort and security every family covets, and he clearly was proud of his status as the family breadwinner. Years later, I learned of the role that A. Philip Randolph, an early leader of the civil rights movement, played in improving the working conditions and salaries for Pullman Porters. In 1925, the year before my parents moved to Harlem, Randolph was elected president of the Brotherhood of Sleeping Car Porters, which was the first predominantly black labor union.

Published reports regarding early union negotiations reveal that Pullman offered his five thousand porters relatively steady employment, but most porters faced poor working conditions and received skimpy paychecks. During Randolph's negotiations for changes, acts of violence and firings shrunk union membership to less than seven hundred. In 1932, the election of Franklin D. Roosevelt as president sparked positive changes for the union organizers. Amendments to the Railway Labor Act (1934) granted porters rights under federal law and union membership rose to seven thousand. A year later, the Pullman company negotiated with Randolph and agreed to a contract, which was signed in 1937. Employees gained two million dollars in pay increases, a shorter workweek, and overtime pay.

Randolph's success with the Pullman Porters prompted him to challenge other racial barriers. In 1941, he led a March on Washington Movement, which prompted President FDR to issue an Executive Order that ended discrimination in the defense industries during World War II. Later, he helped persuade President Harry S. Truman to issue an executive order that ended segregation in the armed services. Randolph solidified his status as one of the most influential civil activists of the 20th century by taking the lead role in the 1963 March on Washington, where Martin Luther King Jr. delivered his revolutionary "I have a dream" speech. I was there.

As leader of the Brotherhood of Sleeping Car Porters, Randolph had a significant impact on my father's career. I'm sure his name was bounced about quite often during the many private conversations my parents had when my sister and I were out of earshot.

CHAPTER 4

*"At the dawn of the twenty-first Century, when knowledge is
literally power, where it unlocks the gates of, opportunity, and
success, we all have responsibilities as parents, as librarians,
as educators, as politicians to instill in our children a love
of reading so that we can give them a chance to fulfill
their dreams"*

BARACK OBAMA

I love books now as much as I did when I was a kid in the 1930s.

There were no books in my house back then; well actually, there was
one, Little Caesar, which is the kind of book that today would fall under the
genre of pulp fiction. It was not a great book, though Edward G. Robinson
became a star, playing the title character in the 1931 movie. That was the only
book I remember seeing in our house. My father probably got it off the train.

I now believe that my interest in reading and education was fueled by
my interest in finding out "how things work".

I remember, at the age of five or six, taking apart the family's' "grandfather clock", to find out how the pendulum made the clock hands move, and
not being able to put the clock back together. I also remember being severely
punished for doing so. The "grandfather clock was given to my mother by
her parents, and as such became a prize possession of the Wood household."

My elementary schoolteachers showed me mystery-filled avenues I could travel and awesome vistas I could summon through reading. The library was within walking distance of my house. I got my library card when I was in grade school and visited it on a regular basis to check out books. Mrs. Falk, a heavyset Irish woman, was quite cerebral. We basically read The New York Times nearly every day in her third-grade class. She called the Daily News "trash" and never brought it to class for us to read. I didn't always understand what I was reading in The Times, but it was in her class where I developed the process of reading.

Like many blacks, who were a generation removed from slavery, my parents–above everything else–emphasized the importance of education, though neither dared help with my homework. Maybe they didn't want to compete with my teachers or maybe they couldn't because of their limited education. The latter, I believe, was closer to the truth. They did, however, encourage me to go to school every day and try to do my very best.

Determined to give us an edge, my mother moved us around like gypsies, searching for the best school system. Finally, she made Sugar Hill, the upscale, black concave that was immortalized by resident Duke Ellington in his" Take the A Train" 1942 theme song, our home. Sugar Hill was then geographically defined by 155th Street to the north, 145th Street to the south, Edgecombe Avenue to the east, and Amsterdam Avenue to the west. It acquired its name in the 1920s when blacks who learned of its existence longed to be a part of what they perceived to be "the sweet life."

I attended P.S. 146 (grades 1-6) in the Edgecombe Avenue school zone. The school was later destroyed by a fire. I started the second grade there, which really was the beginning of my distinct recollection of my life. Though we later moved back to the Dunbar, I never left P.S. 146. My daily walk to school from the Dunbar, which began with a climb up a high stairway that led up the hill, was a tough hike. I was among a large group of kids who took that daily trek. The good company definitely made it easier to bear.

During our family' stay at 367 Edgecombe Ave in a 3'rd floor walkup, I began to play "stick ball". A version of baseball for city kids. We used a broom stick without the broom(smile) for the bat and a rubber ball, the street waste water covers were our basses, home plate one cover the next cover, second base etc.One of my stick ball buddies was Connie Kirnon, later to become Connie Kay, the drummer for the Modern Jazz Quartet.I remember when I was a senior in engineering at the University of Michigan, walking by a record shop with a display of a new record cover with 4 black men with beards, one of them looked familiar—it was Connie, now Kay not Kirnon, the drummer with the Modern Jazz Quartet, Much later in our lives we would cross paths again in such places as Los Angeles, San Francisco, London, and Paris

Another school classmate from those days and Columbia University was Lt. Commander Earl L. Carter, who later became one of first three black U.S. Navy Fighter Pilots. The other two were Jessie Brown, and Alfred Floyd. (Jet Magazine Aug 21 1952)

We later moved to 450 west 152 st., a six floor walk up, where I spent most of my early formative years, grade 3 through my second year at Stuyvesant High School.There was a park at the end of the block, with a full basket ball court.This is where I began to play basketball. At the time the block that we lived in, was the edge of expanded Harlem.In the 1930's, to the west across Amsterdam Ave. began a "whites only"neighborhood.With the exception of several Pentecostal churches, the major black churches were at the black population center of gravity.The Abyssinian Baptist Church was quite a distance from our home. As most Harlemites, the Wood family did not own a car, the difficulty using public transportation, in getting to the Abyssinian Bapist Church, caused my mother to stop regular attendance at Abyssinian.My mother began to listen, each Sunday on the radio, to Dr. Harry Emerson Fosdick, of the River Side Church, which was in the Columbia University area.

Surprise! To this day, I vividly remember the opening hymn before Dr. Fosdick's sermon, which begins with;

"He walks with me, and He talks with me, and He tells me I am his own"— After the sermon by Dr.Fosdick, my mother would listen to the Charioteers.The Charioteers was organized at Wilberforce University in 1930.They would start the program with the Gospel rendition of "Swing Low, Sweet Chariot"

When my sister and I began to attend church alone, we attended St. James Presbyterian Church which was 11 blocks away from our home, it was the closest major black church.The 11 block distance was comparable to the 12 block distance to my Jr. High School.Each were withen walking distance.

A historical note: Alexander Hamilton's home is a few blocks from St James, on Sugar Hill and within the expanded Harlem.

My mother often reminded me that my classroom was my home-away-from-home and I should never allow anything or anyone to distract me from my assignments. My father drove home the same message later, when I was a young teen. When he contemplated buying a six thousand-dollar house in Long Island, I urged him to allow me to quit school, so I could get a job and help him pay for it. He nixed that idea without a moment's hesitation. My parents also nixed my plan to take a paper route, so I could earn spending money. In essence, they said jointly, "Spend your spare time perusing the books you so passionately love, not placing newspapers in doorways of neighbors' homes and apartment buildings." So, I did.

It was not until I attended Stuyvesant High School that I began to work at a job that I received an income. Because of the relative limited classroom space, Stuyvesant had two school sessions, one in the morning, and one in the afternoon. Upperclassmen attended the morning session. When the basketball season ended (in the spring semester), I began work after school. I had a variety of jobs, from silk screen printing to packing overcoats for shipment. Thus at the age of sixteen, I became relatively independent financially of my parents, except for meals and lodging. This continued until I left home to attend Columbia University at the age of eighteen, under a Naval

Officers Trainning Program at which time I became financially independent of my parents.

The New York school system used a tracking system, which allowed the smartest students to stay in the same home room and attend the same classes together each year throughout elementary school. The only thing I remember vividly about my Edward W. Stitt middle school is, that a kid that I believe was Alan Greenspan and I were booted out of the smart class after our first year. Greenspan, who is a bit more than a month older than I am, later became chairman of the Federal Reserve. I remember Alan because he was a very slight, small, academic-looking guy, who never spoke up in class. I took him with me to the principal's office and I told the principal, in the vernacular of Brooklyn Dodgers' fans, "We were robbed, just robbed!"

Our grades certainly were high enough for us to have remained in the fast-track class. Alan didn't say a word, but I guess it was my mother in me that caused me to raise my voice at school officials about being dumped from the smart class. I was the only black male in that class, which also included a couple of black females. School officials later relented and returned us to the fast track. I finished Stitt with my reputation as a bookworm intact.

I grew up with what I think were very limited ambitions only because of the limited career choices I and other blacks had before the Civil Rights era. Back then, if you were black you'd see interesting jobs in the newspapers, but you'd decide that it wouldn't be realistic to pursue them. You would say to yourself, "That's not for me. They won't let me do that." You knew there was a black world and there was a white world, and that blacks, no matter how talented, couldn't cross most economic and social lines.

My mother was the only one, in my young life, who kept telling me, "that I was able to do anything I wanted to, if I worked hard, did my best, lived a respectable life, and had a little luck. As I saw it then, financially successful blacks were in sports, the rackets, or doctors. Looking back, I now recognize, during this time, the dilemma of many well meaning teachers in trying to advise black youth.: "to encourage hope where there was little, or to suppress hope where there was some."

I do not remember any guidance counselors through my high school days. I had my first encounter with a University providing advice on my career path, when I reached Columbia University. The advice given was incorrect, for in the long run the world is not static, ; and that long arc of the moral universe had begun to bend towards justice, and equality for blacks a little faster, as a result of World War II.

The advice, very well meaning, that I received from the Asst. Dean of the Columbia Engineering School was "that I should switch to teaching for I would not be able to find employment in the engineering field". He was correct at the time the advice was given, however that long arc of the moral universe did not stop bending. I have been the beneficiary of that movement from time to time, in my adult life.

One of the most significant crossroads of my life, which I didn't think about much at the time, occurred in 1940 near the end of the first semester of my final year at Stitt, Middle School. Students in my homeroom class were invited to take an exam to determine if any of us were bright enough to handle the workload offered at the New York City's most selective public specialized high schools. By passing that exam, I earned a three-year stint at Stuyvesant, which then was one of New York's three original Specialized High Schools that offered tuition-free accelerated academics to city residents. Brooklyn Technical High School and the Bronx High School of Science were the other two specialized high schools.

Stuyvesant still ranks among the top high schools in the nation. Each November, more than 28, 000 eighth and ninth graders take the 2 ½ hour exam, but only eight hundred (less than 3 percent) are accepted. Stuyvesant was located at 345 East 15th Street when I attended but was moved to a waterfront building in Battery Park City in 1992. Enrollment supposedly was based solely on the entrance exam but during the 1940s, students who lived within a ten-block radius of the school district were allowed to attend without taking the exam. Stuyvesant High School has, over the years, produced four Nobel Prize winners, as well as over two hundred world wide or United States winners of major awards in the fields of physics, mathematics, chemistry, medicine, music, education, business, film, politics, etc..This list includes a Nobel Prize Winner in my Stuyvesant class of 1944, Robert Fogel, the 1993 Nobel Prize winner in Economic Sciences.

I knew for some time that Eric Holder, Attorney General of the United States under President Obama and President Obama were both undergrauates at Columbia (not at the same time). Barack Obama went on to Law School at Harvard, Eric Holder went on to Columbia Law School. What I have learned recently is that Eric Holder is also a graduate of Stuyvesant High School, and played freshman basketball at Columbia.

Stuyvesant was a boys' only school back then; girls were admitted beginning in 1969. By 2002 the female population had grown to 42%. I'm sure my sister, Frances, would have passed the test if girls had been allowed to take it. She was much smarter than I, and an excellent test taker. Her scores ranged in the 140s on the IQ tests that she took. My IQ test scores were in the 110 range. There were only about a dozen blacks out of a four thousand student-population when I attended Stuyvesant.

Besides having one of the nation's most rigorous scholastic curriculum, in the early '40s Stuyvesant's faculty had its share of quirky characters, including my English teacher, Mr. Lowenthal. I don't remember his first name. He was tall and very, very thin and had a lock of black hair that fell across his forehead. He might have been in theatrics. Back then, all students were required to pass the New York State Regents exam at each grade level. We were given a regent exam in every subject every term and it was an intense process. On the first day of class Mr. Lowenthal allayed our fears, with this preamble: "I can teach you enough English to get you past the regents, so don't worry about it. I want us to spend most of our time talking about life."

He began a series of conversations leading us in discussions about literature, morality, ethics, and life, some of which I still remember. On the first day of class, Mr. Lowenthal said, "If you want to make money, don't go to college. Consider the Sanitation Department. Workers there make more money than teachers!" At the time, that was true in New York and it was true when I moved to Teaneck, New Jersey, where owners of sanitation companies had some of the biggest houses. He then recited a list of people, Henry Ford and other famous dropouts, who made it big. Then he said, "But if you want to have a rewarding life and learn how to excel in a challenging and sometimes complicated world, then the Stuyvesant experience will prepare you to do that." Mr. Lowenthal was a great teacher, as was my physics teacher.

I can't recall his first or last name, but he couldn't remember my name or the names of any of the other students in our class. He called everyone Pancho or Pedro. He offered this explanation: "I know I'm not going to remember everybody's name, so it's easier for me to say Pancho or Pedro." That was an odd memory. I took six semesters of physics before I left high school and he was my physics teacher! Occasionally, he'd talk about flamenco dancers and other things. Like Mr. Lowenthal, my physics teacher was different but impressive. However, Dr. Samuel Ellner, a short, slender guy, easily was the most unforgettable teacher I had at Stuyvesant.

Dr. Ellner was a rarity, a basketball coach with a PhD in chemistry, and by example, he taught me to respect athletic achievers as much as I did academic achievers. In the early '40s, I idolized white athletes in general, only because there were very few black athletes at any level. I was a Brooklyn Dodger fan and admired them all. I felt lucky when Jackie Robinson joined the team a few years later. Still, I didn't really respect athletes because I saw them as being good at their sport but not much else.

Dr. Ellner encouraged me to strive to be more than a good student and pushed me to try out for the varsity basketball team. Norman Skinner and I became friends the first day of school. We both went out for the basketball team. He made it; I didn't. He was a much better athlete than I was. In fact, he later played semi-pro ball for a team in Scranton, Pennsylvania, while attending Harvard Business School. There were no black players in the National

Basketball Association (NBA) during that time. Chuck Cooper, picked by the Boston Celtics in the second round in 1950, became the first black to be drafted into the NBA. Cooper was an All-American at Duquesne University.

The next semester, I practiced every free hour I had and made the team. I didn't possess the gifts of a great athlete, but compared to most of my opponents, I was big(for those days), agile, and could grab a lot of rebounds for my team. I felt that I could out jump any one my own height, or even one to two inches taller. I was delighted to be recognized as a high school rarity: a student-athlete. More importantly, as a competitor, I tapped into some of the intangibles that, I believe, lead to success in many of life's other challenges. Take a shooter in basketball. He doesn't think about the ten consecutive shots he missed; he focuses on the next one that could win the game. Take a 400 hitter in base ball, a relative rarity, and, by definition, that person has failed to hit 6 out of 10 times at bat, that hitter usually is confident when the out come of the game is on the line, and they are at bat, they will succeed and get a hit. That has always been my outlook. I discovered that if I honed my skills, with a little bit of luck, I could persevere when the odds were against me. You have to have confidence in yourself.

I do not recall what Stuyvesant's basketball won-loss record was for the two years I was on the starting five. I do remember in my last year, our won-loss record was good enough for Stuyvesant to play in the Manhattan high school finals against Benjamin Franklin High School in Madison Square Garden. We lost. The reason I remember, is that this was the only time in my basketball career, Stuyvesant High School and Columbia University, that my mother and father saw me play.—and WE LOST.

In spite of this set back, which at the time, I thought was a major one, I felt that, if the opportunity were available, I could be a winner in most arena's of competitive life. To use the old Vince Lombardi phrase, I could "run to daylight." I was determined to keep probing and probing in the world and when I saw daylight, I was gone. I would find a way to get out of Harlem, metaphorically, not necessarily move away from home. I wanted to move away, beyond the notion that the color of my skin would prevent me from realizing any goals I chose to pursue. I venture to say that the upshot of what I tried to do in my life was to prove to white people that black people can do these things.

Paul Robeson, one of only a few black superstars of that era, was also one of my idols. Robeson, the son of an ex-slave, who escaped from a plantation, was born in Princeton New Jersey in 1898, and after graduation from high school was refused admission to Princeton University, in 1915 won an academic scholarship to Rutgers University where he was the third black student ever enrolled at Rutgers ; became an All-American football star later inducted into the college Football Hall of Fame; and graduated No. 1 in his class. While at Rutgers Robeson joined the debating team, he also sang with the Rutgers Glee Club unofficially, as membership in the Glee Club required attending all-white mixers. In 1922, he earned his LLB from Columbia Law School while playing in the National Football League (NFL), he studied at the School of Oriental and African Studies in London England in 1934 and later became an internationally-acclaimed singer and actor. When Robeson returned to the U.S., he supported black civil rights and pro -Soviet policies. When World War II ended Robeson was placed on the U.S. Attorney's List of Subversive Organizations. Robeson's passport was revoked and his income took a nose dive. Much later he regained his U.S. passport as a result of a 1958 U.S. Supreme Court decision. Paul Leroy Robeson lived his remaining years in Philadelphia Pa.

My "love" connection to Robeson materialized through his niece, Bennie Robeson. She was my first date. We were both sixteen. I met her at a party in New York City. Basil Paterson and his future wife, Portia, were among the guests. Basil became one of New York City's top political leaders.

I moved to the next level of my formal education during World War II, an uncertain and anxious time in our country—and, indeed, the world. As fate would have it, my ability to pass an exam again pushed me in the right direction. With the war still raging, the U.S. Army and Navy needed additional commissioned officers in their respective branches of service. Many high school graduates were drafted or volunteered for active duty service, so the war also caused a severe drop in enrollment at many top U.S. colleges and universities, forcing some to consider closing.

The U.S. government fixed its officer shortage problem by solving the colleges' enrollment problem. The Navy created a V-12 College Training Program which enrolled more than 125, 000 men in 131 U.S. colleges and universities. The Navy's V-12 program began in June 1942; The V-12 program was created to grant college degrees to future Navy and Marine Corps officers, and though the Armed Forces were legally racially segregated during World War II, the V-12 program did not bar blacks who passed the exam; but black cadets weren't allowed to share dorm rooms with white cadets. I didn't have a roommate during my stay at Columbia. President Harry Truman's executive order, signed July 26, 1948, desegregated the Armed Forces six years after the Navy's V-12 program accepted black cadets.

Uncle Sam paid tuition fees to participating colleges and universities for each qualified candidate. Once a degree was obtained, the future officer's next step was to attend a U.S. Naval Reserve Midshipman's School to complete a four-month course. Graduates then were commissioned as ensigns in the U.S. Naval Reserve before joining the U.S. fleet in combat. Samuel Gravely, the first black admiral, was in the Columbia Midshipmen's School Program while I was in the V-12 program at Columbia. He was commissioned an ensign on November 14, 1944, and later became the first black to command a Navy ship, the first fleet commander, and the first to command a ship in combat.

I was eighteen when I joined the Navy out of high school. Norman Skinner, my teammate on Stuyvesant's varsity basketball squad, and I took the V-12 exam at the same time. Norman didn't pass; I did. If I had my druthers, I would have gone to Cornell because that was Jerome (Brud) Holland and Samuel Pierce's alma mater. Brud was an All-American football player at Cornell and Sam earned bachelor and law degrees from Cornell and a

Masters of Law degree from New York University. I idolized both. Sam served two terms (1981-89) as Ronald Reagan's Secretary of Housing and Urban Development (HUD) and became one of my closest friends. He also became my legal advisor and confidant during the early years of my business career.

I also considered Harvard and Stanford. The Navy told me that if I picked a school close to home, I most likely would get my first choice, and if I didn't, I probably would not. I didn't discuss this with my parents, mainly because I didn't believe they could help. I picked Columbia because it was right in the neighborhood. Even though I'd spent just about all my life in New York, I had never been to Columbia. I strolled proudly onto that Ivy League campus, hoping that good decisions were sometimes made out of ignorance.

CHAPTER 5

"When education is viewed as a private investment yielding private returns, there is no reason why anyone other than the "investor" should pay for it. But when understood as a public good underlying our democracy, all of us have a responsibility to ensure that it is of high quality, and available to all"

ROBERT REICH

In 1944, the typical freshman at an Ivy League college arrived on campus dressed stylishly, brimming with confidence. The atypical Ivy League freshmen, such as yours truly, attended classes in attire more associated with swabbing decks and burdened with doubt generated by a heavy course-load.

I attended Columbia University courtesy of a legally segregated U.S. Navy. The United States Armed Forces in the summer of 1944, were legally segregated in "our fight against Hitler's theory of Aryan (smile) superiority". It was amusing to me that any paper trail that I made during my stay in the Navy brought out a huge rubber stamp marked "COLORED" in an attempt to prevent any mistakes. I walked the hallowed grounds of that upper Manhattan-based university grateful to my Uncle Sam for footing the bill. The Navy had established basic training regimens and curricula at several "elite" college level institutions that were dubbed "Equivalent of Annapolis" schools. Columbia was one of them. We attended undergraduate classes with the regular students, but because of mandatory military courses, we carried nearly twice the load. We averaged twenty-two to twenty four hours per semester; the regular undergraduates usually took twelve hours.

The Navy's V-12 recruits had a structured and more demanding curriculum. We wore uniforms to all classes and adhered to Navy protocol at all times; that is, we kept our dorm rooms spotless, saluted the officers at the appropriate time and place, and saluted the flag whenever we left the dorm. At bugle call each Monday morning, we rushed downstairs and stood on the field at parade rest. We began each week day with the same routine. Our weekend leaves began at noon each Saturday, but those who didn't pass a white glove inspection of their rooms couldn't leave campus.

In those days, Columbia wasn't what today's computer savvy teens would call "user friendly" to blacks. No "colored only" or "whites only" signs were displayed, but we knew that many of the segregationist rules of the South were in effect. The dorms generally housed two students per room, but blacks were never assigned rooms with white cadets. I had a room to myself. There were no black fraternities on campus. I traveled a few blocks to Harlem for my haircuts.

I never feared walking the streets of Harlem day or night. Quite often in black neighborhoods, its people put cocoons around their young star athletes, entertainers, or high achievers. I think that's why Norman Skinner and I were never robbed, hassled, or mistreated in Harlem. We were never pressured to smoke or drink when socializing with friends who did. The people of Harlem understood how tough it was for us to excel at Stuyvesant and Columbia and they respected us, were proud of us, and wanted us to succeed. While Harlem had its share of unsavory characters during that time, they never bothered us.

I had two separate sets of friends throughout my high school and collegiate years. One group consisted of the intellectually gifted students; the other consisted of gifted athletes. I tried to fit in with both. My closest friend, Lester Florant, was among the smart group. We were like brothers. Lester was a better student than I, but I was the better athlete. Norman Skinner was my best friend among the athletes. Academically, we were about the same, except my inclination was toward engineering and science and he preferred literature and the arts. Norman was very bright. I'd put him in both groups.

Lester and his family lived around the corner from me at 848 St. Nicholas Avenue. We were raised in families guided by both parents, who stressed discipline and academics. Our fathers had steady incomes and were good providers; the mothers' job was to manage the households. We played stickball in the streets, attended the same church, and focused on our classroom work. Generally, we socialized with like-minded students. While Lester attended Howard University, I was at Columbia. We kept up with each other through letters and postcards.

Lester's father, who was born on a small island in the Caribbean, Dominica, worked as a house painter. He had eight children, he taught all the boys to house paint. I learned much later that Lester's father owned a six-story apartment building in the neighborhood. He acquired the building during the 1929 Depression from his landlord in a peculiar way. Lester's father completed numerous painting jobs throughout the neighborhood for his landlord, but the landlord couldn't pay him. He settled his debt with (Lester's dad) through a transaction called a mortgage overture, which allowed the landlord to transfer the deed to Lester's father. That was unusual in those days. All eight Florant children–five boys and three girls– were exceptionally bright. Six of them graduated from Howard; Stanley, the oldest, was the first black to graduate from Columbia University with a degree in architecture. Lester's brother, Lionel, taught at Howard and later worked for black historian E. Franklin Frazier.

Norman was raised in a single-parent household. His mother didn't speak English very well and had health problems. She worked as a maid. Norman's father left the family when Norman was very young. He was never a part of Norman's life.

Basketball brought Norman and I together. We were teammates on Stuyvesant's varsity basketball team and as freshmen on Columbia's team.

Norman made Stuyvesant's varsity as a ninth grader; I was selected as a tenth grader. Norman was 6-2, more muscular, and an inch taller than I was. We were both starters on Stuyvesant's basketball team during my junior and senior years. I felt that we were equals in scholastics, but he was more talkative and had better social skills than I did.

I was surprised when he didn't pass the Navy's V-12 test because we took the same courses and roughly had the same grades. Academically, the only difference between us was that I favored engineering and science and he, like the typical Columbia student, was more interested in reading books, but not the technical fields. Had Norman passed that test, he would have qualified for an all-expenses paid college education. The V-12 package was better than the scholarship that Norman had.

He instead attended Columbia on a general scholarship, which was awarded to many star athletes, but it was not an athletic scholarship. It was given to deserving students who were unable to pay tuition and board but theoretically not linked to their performance as athletes. I remember one outstanding football player couldn't get along with the head coach, so he quit the team, but was permitted to complete his studies on his scholarship, and graduate with his class.

Norman received a scholarship to attend Columbia, but his college days were interrupted for two years when he was drafted into the Army. He served at an Army post in the South, but he was a different man when he returned to Columbia during my third year. Prior to his Army service in the American south, Norman almost always had a smile on his face. When Norman returned after his Army service, that smile was rarely seen. He never wanted to discuss his time in the Army with me. After finishing Columbia, Norman earned a graduate degree from Harvard's business school.

I met most of my other athletic friends playing basketball in the park near my house, including Sonny Lewis, one of the legendary players in the Harlem parks. I lost track of Sonny after I left Stuyvesant, many years later, I saw a window washer while riding the subway who resembled Sonny. It was Sonny! His arm was extended through the handle of the pail, which was bumping against his backside, so he didn't have to carry it. Sonny was five or six years older than I was, but he looked like he was fifty. He was about 6-4, tall in my day, and was an outstanding park player. I idolized this guy, and I was shocked to see him looking grizzly and disheveled. I said to myself, "There for the grace of God . . . "

Incidentally, another friend named Sonny Lewis lived across the street from me during my elementary school years. He wasn't a basketball player. His cousin was Colin Powell, the four-star general, who later served as U.S. Secretary of State during President George W. Bush's second administration. I learned of his connection to Powell while reading Powell's autobiography. In it Powell mentions an uncle named Shirley Lewis. That had to be Sonny's father.

On what turned out to be a glad-I-was-in Harlem-black-history-making moment, I attended a political meeting held by the Rev. Adam Clayton Powell Jr., who, in 1945, became the fourth black since the Reconstruction Era to be elected to Congress. Powell was a mesmerizing orator in the pulpit, and not too shabby at a political podium. Once Powell took his seat in Congress, he rarely hesitated to display his contempt for the racial bigotry that blacks endured daily. To the chagrin of his southern white congressmen, Powell did something that was not able to be accomplished by the few black Congessmen elected before Powell.

At the Harlem meeting I attended, he told us of the instructions he gave to his staff upon his arrival. He said, "One of the first things I did was demand that everyone on my staff use the congressional facilities, dining room, bathroom, etc. I told them if you don't use the cafeteria, if you don't use the barbershops, if you don't use the bathrooms, if you don't use the swimming pools, I'm going to fire you." Those southern congressmen hated him for that, but that was the way he was. He single-handedly ended racial segregation of Congressional facilities in Congress.

My mother was a longtime member of the Abyssinian Baptist Church, where Adam Clayton Powell Jr. succeeded his father as pastor in 1937. I can still see the excitement in her eyes whenever she retold a Powell story about a black man who joined a church in the north with a mixed congregation.

Continuing the story, my mother said, "Years later, the man moved back to the South and tried to join a church of the same denomination, but he was turned away. When he left the church after being turned away, God stopped him on the steps and said, 'Don't worry about it. I can't get in there either.'"

My mother loved telling that story. Powell also had a reputation for using questionable tactics to get what he wanted. Years later, when I needed political help in New York, I asked my longtime friend Samuel Pierce, then a prominent Republican, if I should talk to Powell. Sam said, "Don't go near him because if he puts his hand in your pocket and you take it out, you'll be his enemy for life. Don't go near him."

Though located so close to the heart of Harlem, Columbia felt and seemed so far removed, so distant and void of the hometown vibes I had grown to love as a kid. During most of my elementary and high school days in Manhattan and the Bronx, I was often the only black in the class, but I never felt lonely. In my world away from school back then, I found the love and happiness I needed to have an enjoyable social life at home with my family and friends.

In the Ivy League, if you sought a professional degree, as I did, you usually had to complete six years of college-level work. The Ivy League wanted its students to absorb the "Ivy League Culture," so all students were required to take the core humanities courses (literature, music, art, and so forth). The Navy had its own core courses related to the military, I attended Columbia for four years, then moved on to the University of Michigan. It took me six years to earn an AB in mathematics from Columbia and a Bachelor of Science degree in Electrical Engineering (BSEE) from Michigan.

The V-12 was a special program to me for another reason: it integrated Princeton University. John Howard, one of my friends, was the first black person to earn a degree from Princeton (1947). Several others had tried. In 1935, Bruce M. Wright became the first known black admitted to Princeton in the 20th century, but once Wright arrived on campus and his race became obvious, he was sent packing. Wright, who became a New York judge, was dubbed "Turn 'em Loose, Bruce," by the New York Transit Union for releasing blacks on their own recognizance when defendants had no previous record and strong family and community ties. During a 1979 lecture at Columbia University Law School, Judge Wright said a more appropriate nickname would have been "Civil" Wright. Princeton was the last male Ivy League college to accept U.S. blacks.

John and Melvin Murchison Jr. already were enrolled as V-12 trainees at Columbia when I arrived. They were roommates. John was a premed student and son of a prominent New York doctor, who had offices in Harlem. Actually, John was enrolled at Columbia before he joined V-12. Mel transferred to Columbia from regular naval duty. Previously Mel attended Virginia Union University, where he played football. As a V-12 student, he also played football for Columbia, and after the transfer, Mel played football for Princeton. The Navy decided to transfer all premed students to other colleges, perhaps because it felt there were too many applicants for Columbia.

John, Mel, James Ward and Arthur "Pete" Wilson Jr. became the first blacks accepted by Princeton, and that historic breakthrough occurred only because the Navy sent them there. Princeton must have believed that it would have stirred a great deal of controversy if the black naval recruits had been rejected.

Of the four, Mel was the only one to leave Princeton without a degree. He left without explanation. I was told that Mel wanted to continue to play football for Princeton, but several Princeton alumni paid him ten thousand dollars not to return because they didn't want a black man on the team. I don't know the truth of that, but when I saw him some time after that, he just said that he didn't go back. I haven't seen or spoken to him since. Mel and Pete Wilson, to my knowledge, were the first black's to play varsity sports at Princeton, Mel in football and Pete in basketball. We were all pioneers in the struggle for racial justice and acceptance during that pre-Civil Rights era, but I don't believe any of us drew satisfaction from that at the time. As the only black in the Columbia V-12 program, when they left for Princeton, I felt somewhat abandoned after John and Mel left. They had provided that comfortable, social link that naturally develops among most dormitory-bound college students.

According to the Harvard Gazette, "Little known facts about Albert Einstein, who resided in Princeton are, that he invited Marian Anderson to stay at his home in Princeton, when the singer was refused a room at the Nassau Inn at Princeton, and that in 1946 Einstein visited HBCU Lincoln University, where he gave a speech in which he called racism "a disease of white people".(which was ignored by the mainstream press) Some members of Princeton's black community, at the turn of the last century, remembered the white-haired, disheveled figure of Einstein walking through their streets, stopping to chat, and handing out candy to children.

I considered myself to be a pretty good student-athlete at Stuyvesant High School, but at Columbia my grades slipped a bit, as did my athletic ability against tougher competition. Still, I was good enough to be on the starting five on Columbia's varsity basketball team as a freshman, and as a sophomore, an achievement that probably helped me land another high-profile date. My childhood friend, Lester, took a group of his friends from Howard University to a Columbia vs. Navy game in Annapolis, Maryland, to see me play. My date for that evening was Jean Drew, the niece of Dr. Charles Drew, the black physician who developed techniques in the storage of blood plasma during World War II. His work led to the development of the American Red Cross Blood Bank.

I got them tickets near the team bench, but naval administrators wouldn't let them stay there even though they had regular grandstand seats.

My friends were forced to sit in the balcony. Once again, it was clear to me that racial segregation wasn't just a practice peculiar to the deep South.

Lou Rossini was my teammate in my second year as a starter with a 20 won, 11 loss record, under coach Paul Mooney's return to Columbia after World War 11. Lou was the outstanding mature player on the team. Shortly after graduating Lou became the head coach at Columbia.In his first year as coach, Lou guided the basket ball team to a 21 won 1 loss season with a NCAA Tournament appearance. Lou coached Chet Forte, who won a national basket ball title, and earned more fame as director of "Monday Night Football".

With me, coming into the game from the bench, Columbia's varsity team was quite successful during my final two years. Norm Skinner, who had returned to Columbia after a two-year Army stint, was a starter.

Elmer Ripley was my basketball coach as a freshman. He was one of the great college coaches. Elmer attended Brown and left at the age of 19 to play professionally. Elmer Ripley was inducted in 1973 into the Basketball Hall Of Fame. I had three different coaches during the four years I played for Columbia, preparing me for the real world I would face later in life. We won the Ivy League Championship in 1947-48 season and beat Holy Cross when former Boston Celtic great Bob Cousy was an All-American. Many pundits of the game have commented that, good high school and college athletic programs teaches one "how to win with grace, and how to lose with diginity"

In those days, basketball was in its Neanderthal phase compared to today's game. A two-handed set shot was the form for shooting from beyond the free throw line. One-handed shots were used mainly for layups; one handed jump shots were a no-no. Indeed, most players taking one handed jump shots spent the rest of the game on the bench. The dunk shot was still a few years away.I frequently tell people that, I played basketball in the "ice age".The basketball player of today is bigger, stronger, and definitely more skilled than those of my day.I would go out on a limb, and say "that today's championship high school basketball team, would defeat the average professional basketball team of my day. Examples are, Lebron James, Magic Johnson, Larry Bird Kobie Bryant;, naturally one would want to include Michael Jordan in this list, .However Michael did not mature in high school, in fact, as I recall Michael had trouble making his freshman high school team. Michael Jordan was not a "man child" like Lebron James.Michael matured later, in my opinion in terms of skill and will Michael Jordan is the greatest to play the game.

My sentimental choice is Bill Russell,Russell's Boston Celtics won 11 of 13 Professional Basketball Championships in the years Russell played for the Celtics. ----- and I suppose I can add the fact, that When leaving the basketball court at half-time,in one of those classic Russell/Chamberlin ChampionshipPlay-off match ups, Bill Russell rubbed my son Erik's head.

In the 1940s, I believe there were fewer than a dozen blacks in the country playing basketball with major colleges and relatively few competing in the nation's, (with the exception of track and field), other major sports arenas throughout the first half of the 20th century.

Among the most notable were:

* Joe Louis. Best heavyweight boxer of all time. Heavyweight Champion from 1937 to 1949. The Joe Louis cultural impact was world wide. He was the first black American to become a nationwide hero within the United States. Louis integrated golf, appearing as a sponsor's exemption in a PGA event. Joe Louis grew up in rural Alabama, ; his family threatened by the Klu Klux Klan moved to Detroit Michigan in 1926. Louis had 69 professional fights with only 3 losses, held the heavyweight championship longer than any heavyweight from 1937 to1949. When Louis defeated Braddock, it was a special moment for black Americans. Langston Hughes described the Louis effect. "Each time Joe Louis won a fight in those depression years, even before he became champion, thousands of black Americans on relief or W.P.A., and poor, would throng out into the streets all across the land to march and cheer and yell and cry because of Joe's one-man triumphs. No one

else in the United States has ever had such an effect on Negro emotions-or on mine. I marched and cheered and yelled and cried too".

The June 1936 defeat of Louis by Max Schmeling, of Germany, set up one of the most famous boxing matches of all time. Schmeling's victory over a black American was hailed by the Nazi's as proof of Aryan superiority. The rematch was held in Yankee Stadium with a crowd of over 70, 000, and broadcast world wide.Joe Louis won, decisively, Schmeling was knocked down 3 times and only managed to throw 2 punches. The fight lasted 2 minutes and 4 seconds.Prior to the fight, Louis visited the White House, where president Roosevelt told Joe Louis "Joe, we need muscles like yours to beat Germany". Joe Louis' popularity across all walks of American life, resulted in some unexpected difficulties, which I did not find out about until I became an electrical engineering student at the University of Michigan.To my knowledge, the magnitude of this problem did not exist before the Joe Louis era, and became moot since. The difficulty, the technical problem, was caused by the very high percentage nationwide of the American population, who listened to the fight on the radio.(No TV in the Joe Louis era) No one knew in advance when the fight would end.When the fight was over, the house lights, and the radio were turned off.The unpredicted removal of the "load" on the electrical generators tended to cause the generators to run faster and faster and by doing so cause costly damage.For normal activity statistical data can make the problem manageable.The Electrical Power Engineers were grateful when the Joe Louis Era was over.

* Jack Johnson. In 1908, Johnson, nicknamed the "Galveston (Texas) Giant," became the first black to capture the heavyweight boxing title. During his seven-year reign, the flamboyant and controversial Johnson dated white women and reigned with undisguised arrogance. He claimed the title, defeating Tommy Burns, and kept it by defeating a series of "Great White Hopes," including former heavyweight champion Jim Jeffries. That victory sparked race riots in twenty-five states and fifty cities and led to the deaths of twenty people and injuries to more than one hundred others.

* Paul Robeson. He was mentioned in a previous chapter. He was the most gifted black student-athlete of that era . . . and one of my role models. Robeson was an All-American football player for Rutgers and valedictorian of his 1919 graduating class. He also earned a law degree from Columbia in 1923. He later became an outstanding singer and actor. His son and I became friends during our college years.

* Jesse Owens. He became a national hero after breaking three world records on his way to capturing four gold medals in the 100 meters, 200 meters, long jump, and 4x 100 meters relay at the 1936 Olympic Games in Berlin, Germany. With Adolph Hitler among the spectators, Owens shattered the German führer's myth of Aryan superiority in about forty-five minutes.

* Jackie Robinson. In 1939, Robinson became the first athlete at UCLA to earn varsity letters in four sports: baseball, basketball, football, and track. Robinson made his most significant contribution to his country in 1947, the start of my final year at Columbia, by signing with the Brooklyn Dodgers to become the first black to play for a major league baseball team. I was a Dodger fan before Jackie joined "Dem Bums," so it was quite a thrill for me to see him run around the bases at Ebbets Field. Years later, I had the privilege of spending a week end with the sports icon after he joined me in the business world.

* George Gregory. The first black All American basketball player. He was the captain and star center of the Columbia University basketball team in the 1930-31 season, when Columbia won its first League Championship. George was born in New York City in 1906. After graduation from Columbia, he earned a law degree at night from St John University and would serve on the New York City Civil Service Commission.

Gregory became involved with the Harlem Center of the Children's Aid Society while an undergraduate. From 1931 to 1953, he headed youth programs in Harlem and the Forest House in the Bronx, where I worked for him as a youth councilor for two summers.

Memories of my four-year stint at Columbia are bittersweet. Some of the good and not-so good moments grew out of my connection to the Navy's V-12 program. During my second year as a V-12 student, I was the only black in the V12 program at Columbia University. Just being selected as a candidate and getting the opportunity to become a graduate of an Ivy League school was quite special, despite the rigorous workload.

The daily Navy regimen, combined with the study demands imposed routinely by Ivy League colleges, led to a very high dropout/flunkout rate. A couple of my friends, who were Columbia undergraduates before they joined the program, flunked out because they couldn't adjust. A lot of trainees dropped out because they couldn't cope with the discipline. There were about two hundred students enrolled in my freshmen class. When the program ended twenty-eight months later, about twenty trainees were left, and I wasn't among them.

I didn't drop out or flunk out. I intentionally got kicked out of the program because I missed curfew three consecutive days. My military instructors knew my grades overall were strong, and they suspected I was trying to get kicked out of the program. Each time they asked me why I broke the rules, I didn't respond. By breaking the rules, I thought that I increased my odds of returning to Columbia for my final years under congressional legislation, the G.I. Bill which provided greater opportunities and benefits to veterans of war. Sounds strange, I know, but true.

The GI Bill, passed in 1944, provided a range of benefits for World War II veterans, including payment of tuition and living expenses to attend a college/university, high school, or vocational school. I believed that my status as a Navy seaman guaranteed my eligibility for GI Bill benefits, but my status as a trainee in the V-12 program did not. Rumors had it as probable. World War II ended in 1945, during my second year at Columbia. Strong rumors floated throughout the Navy that funding for the V-12 program would be dropped and that trainees wouldn't be eligible for GI Bill benefits. I took the gamble only because a few other trainees had done it earlier for the same reason and they were discharged without punishment. I also was discharged without punishment.

The V-12 program was shut down in June 1946, a year after the war ended, the rumors were untrue. Trainees were allowed to continue their education, if they chose to do so. I went back to Columbia on the GI Bill.

Subsequently, I frequently joked that the reward for my mistaken, ill-informed analysis by a nineteen year old, based on rumor, and a few isolated cases, was to be assigned to the "spud locker" at the naval base in Long Beach, Long Island, from which I was honorably discharged from the navy, as World War II had ended.

I was lucky, as in golf, where your objective is to land the ball on the preferred side of the hole, even when you do not hit the golf ball correctly. Fourtunately my mistake or misjudgement did not put me at a permanent disadvantage

This was another life lesson, I have always remembered, "do not make potential life changing decisions based on rumor".

When I returned to Columbia in 1946, I was uncertain of my long term goals. I was uncertain about my academic, athletic, and career prospects.

The very well meaning Asst. Dean of the Columbia School of Enginneering had advised me "that I should switch from engineering to another field, as I would not be able to work as an engineer in industry because of my race.

The Columbia basket ball team suddenly became ten times better, with the arrival of Walter Budko, a six foot six inch center, and several other players returning from the war. My direct competition was Bruce Gerke, a tight end from the football team at six foot three and 210 pounds. I weighed in soaking wet at 170 pounds and six foot even. My basket ball skills had improved only slightly compared to the skill level of the team.

The fact that the National Basketball League at that time, did not allow blacks to play in the League, was a turn off, however it really did not effect me directly — for I knew that my basket ball skills were not at a level that I could remotely play in the NBA.

President Dwight David Eisenhower's name is on my AB Degree from Columbia. He left the Columbia Presidency to become the President of the United States. During his term as President of Columbia, he would on occasion walk around the campus, greeting the students. Out of uniform, his appearance was that of a "middle age" gentleman who lived in the surrounding reasonably affluent community. Often as not, a Columbia student, acclimated to the "New York City" general environment would not return his greeting. When he had the rare opportunity to speak to students in small informal groups, I would hear him say "something to the effect—"when I greet you on campus, please return my greeting, where I come from, that is the normal response".

Note: Columbia is in the middle of a city of 7 plus million people, and is not blocked off from non university traffic, both pedestrian and motor vehicles.

I met Yolanda Marquez at a party. I soon began taking regular trips to Smith College in Northampton Massachusetts, where she was a student. Smith College is one of the Seven Sisters, a consortium of women's colleges, the counterpart to the predominantly male Ivy League. I was twentyone; she was eighteen, and very pretty. I thought of myself as more of an athlete than a student, but she challenged me intellectually, culturally, and showed me a different Harlem, a Harlem known only to the black elite. I like to say that her impact on my life is best summarized in one line: "She introduced civilization to the unwashed."

She took me to the opera, the ballet, classical music concerts, and steered me toward books that in the past I had never considered reading, and I quickly came to understand their value. She took me by the hand and opened my eyes to a different level of black society. Through her, I met Harlem's brightest and wealthiest residents, beginning with her father, Cecil Marquez, who was one of Harlem's richest physicians. Marquez finished medical school when he was twenty. He married Yolanda's mother, Gloria, when she was sixteen. Gloria could easily have passed for white. She had a brother who did pass.

Through Yolanda, I met Dr. Ralph Bunche and his family. Dr. Bunche received the 1950 Nobel Peace Prize for his negotiations in the Arab-Israeli conflict in the 1940s. I met E. Simms Campbell, a very talented black cartoonist for Esquire during the 1930s, who once took me to his upstate New York home, where he had a three-car garage with his own gas pumps, and a Japanese butler. I couldn't really call these people friends. I just met them through Yolanda.

I also met Hazel and Ralph Sharper, who were then the Kennedys of Harlem society. Hazel, wrote a column for the New York Amsterdam News. She was a very good-looking woman. Her husband, Ralph, looked like Cab Calloway.

Recent events have caused me to remember a social gathering, party held in Harlem, a few steps from Alexander Hamilton's home, and around the corner from Yolanda's fathers Brownstone, where, Yolanda and I met "Bumpy" Johnson. Ellsworth Raymond "Bumpy" Johnson was at that time the Black Mob Boss of Harlem. "Bumpy" made his reputation by successfully waging a mob war against German Mob Boss Dutch Schultz. At the party I was told that the "Bumpy" in his name resulted from his reputation of killing people, not because of a bump on his head. Quite a few Harlemites compared him to Robin Hood. "Bumpy" would talk to young blacks about "staying in school". "Bumpy's" personality was more like a business man with a legitimate career than a mob boss. A wag once commented "Bumpy worked in the streets, but was not of the streets".I assumed that accounted for his presence at the party Yolanda and I attended. This was the Harlem I remember, everybody knew each other, rich/poor, educated/uneducated, hustlers/regular folks, celebrities/non celeberities.

Yolanda changed me for the better more than anyone else did during my young adult life. I tingled when she said "yes" to my marriage proposal and was relieved that her parents didn't nix our plans from the beginning. Even though I would be away at the University of Michigan for the next two years, I believed that we would stay together. I suspect, however, that her father reasoned that our engagement wouldn't survive a two-year separation.

Cecil Marquez divorced Yolanda's mother and married a woman whose name also was Gloria. She was sigificantly taller than Marquez, who was a little over five foot tall, a factor that undoubtedly contributed to his Napoleonic complex. He was bright, ambitious, and quite wealthy. He was part-owner of a Harlem hospital, owned an apartment building on Riverside Drive, as well as other real estate holdings, and had a forty-five-foot boat, which he would occasionally transport to Conn., near another house he owned in Pound Ridge, a very exclusive community in upstate New York, near Greenwich, Connecticut. He put his older brother through dental school. He often took large groups of his family to various expensive New York restaurants for holiday celebrations.

Yolanda and I were included in many of the family outings. We once enjoyed a festive Thanksgiving Day dinner at Tavern on the Green, a popular Midtown restaurant, while I was at Columbia. They brought a turkey to the table and you could carve off as much as you wanted. It must have been one of Marquez's favorite dining spots because nearly all the waiters knew him.

I couldn't afford an engagement ring, so Yolanda provided a diamond stone; I furnished the setting. We spent a great deal of time together before I went to Michigan. She promised to visit me as often as possible. During our separation, we knew that her dad and other forces would test our commitment to one another. Upon arrival, I soon realized that the glamour and trimmings of big city life that we enjoyed in New York would be nonexistent in the suburban town of Ann Arbor. Still, I had challenges, intellectual and otherwise, to confront, a degree to obtain, and a totally different kind of environment to explore.

CHAPTER 6

"A journey is like marriage. The certain way to be wrong is to think you control it"

JOHN STEINBECK

I left New York in the winter of 1949 with Yolanda Marquez still controlling my heart, but with my mind focused on capturing another prize: an electrical engineering degree from the University of Michigan. Phase II of my educational journey began in Ann Arbor, where I hoped to list on my résumé a Bachelor of Science in electrical engineering degree alongside my AB in mathematics from Columbia. I wondered whether this midwestern locale would affect adversely the psyche of a young, inner-city black.

Back then, the population of Ann Arbor and the University of Michigan each was thirty thousand. Our football stadium then had a seating capacity of ninety thousand plus and since almost every home game was sold out every year, the attraction of the university's gridiron squad obviously extended well beyond city limits. Nearly everyone on campus went to the home games. On weekends the team was out of town, many of the students would play tag football on the campus lawns. When I was there, the university was the town's lifeline. It still is.

Not surprisingly, Michigan offered a different lifestyle than Columbia, but in one way, it was the same. Though the "Whites only" or "Colored only" signs of the South weren't displayed on either campus, neither Michigan nor

Columbia did much to eliminate the racial taboos of that era, especially as they applied to housing accommodations. I discovered that my first day on campus, thanks to Val Johnson, a well-intentioned friend and Michigan alumnus.

I met Val at a social event at Smith College before I enrolled at Michigan. Val, who graduated from Michigan the year after I arrived, was an interesting person, very savy, very political and very ambitious. By political, I mean, he was a good athlete who pushed himself to be a Michigan track star. He did that only because he wanted to become president of the Michigan student body. He believed that the athletic credentials would enhance his popularity and electability. He was right. In 1948, Val achieved his goal and became the first black person elected as president of the University of Michigan's student body. Val knew many of Michigan's black and white athletes. In fact, most of his close friends were white.

I told him of my plans to enroll at Michigan when we met at the Smith College social event, and he arranged for two of his white friends to be my roommates. However, when I arrived on campus, I was reassigned to a room with two other black students in another part of the dormitory.

Years later, a story appeared in a few New York newspapers published about Val Johnson threatening to commit suicide by jumping out of the window of the United Nations building because he didn't get a promotion he thought he deserved. That was sad. Val thought that because he had skills, doors would open, that the white world would welcome and embrace him. The difference between him and me was that I knew those doors wouldn't necessarily open. I had no illusions that whites would automatically afford me the same opportunities as my white contemporaries.

Black women students at Michigan also discovered that they wouldn't be allowed to share bedrooms with white students, except in unusually rare cases. An adherence to rules regarding color can backfire or cause administrators to commit–at least in the eyes and minds of black folk–comical violations of the university's unwritten race codes. Case in point: Jean Drew, mentioned in the previous chapter, enrolled at Michigan as a graduate student the year

I arrived. Jean's uncle, Charles Drew, was the director of the first American Red Cross blood bank, ; Jean looked white. When she arrived on campus, the university's administrators saw this person with a white face had applied to live in a black house and said, "You can't do that. We will put you over here." And that's what they did.

During my first few months at Michigan, it became clear to me that if I stayed in the dormitory, eventually, I would "starve to death". I went to bed hungry every night and yearned for more food after each cafeteria meal. Then one day, my childhood friend, Lester Florant, also a Michigan graduate student (electrical engineering), suggested that I move into one of the university's six co-ops, where he lived. Lester said more food was available in the co-ops, and that was all I needed to know. I couldn't wait to move in. Owen House, the house where I lived had thirty-five students living in house but fed about seventy-five. The other houses varied in size; the women's houses tended to be smaller. The rates were the same. Then students living in the six co-ops paid about three dollars per week for the room and six dollars per week for meals.

Under the co-op rules students weren't allowed to choose their roommates, so Lester and I were never roommates. The process of getting in was very democratic—we drew lots. One of my housemates was Mexican. He and I used to simulate bull fighting in the living room of the house. Another housemate was a Polish fellow named Robert Zajonc, a refugee from World War II. Our co-op sponsored him, paid his tuition, and let him live in the house at no charge. He eventually got his PhD from Michigan and became an eminent psychologist. In 2002, a Review of General Psychology survey ranked Bob as the thirty-fifth most cited psychologist of the 20th century. I got to know Bob pretty well.

Later that year, when Lester and I returned to New York for the Christmas Holidays, we were invited to a Christmas party at a mutual friends home.Both Lester and I were friends with Ozzie Buckmire, who had a much younger sister Sybil. When Lester and I arrived at the party, there was Sybil, all grown up;, Lester was smitten. Within a year after Lester graduated from the University of Michigan, I received a wedding invitation announcing their pending marriage, during the coming Thanksgiving Holiday. I was still driving my 1936 Ford Station Wagon with over 200, 000 miles on it. I decided to drive my car to New York for the wedding. A once in a decade (30 plus inches) snow storm was predicted for my drive to New York. I had arranged to drive two fellow New Yorkers there, primarily to help with the costs. We had planned to make the trip without stopping overnight. The weather prediction was an understatement. The first day we had only gotten as far as Pittsburgh Pa. That was when my two passengers left and took the train to New York. I continued on alone to the Pennsylvania Turnpike. About sixty miles later on the Turnpike, my car gave up. I was fortunate to be picked up by a couple driving "a late model car" to New York, and would not accept any money for driving me. Another instance of human kindness I experienced in my life. For football fans, that snow storm has been credited with the University of Michigan's invitation to the Rose Bowl that football season. Michigan blocked a punt by Ohio State and kicked a field goal, in a shortened "end zone" dictated by high mounds of snow.

Prior to my arrival in Ann Arbor, Langston Hughes(a former Columbia student in 1921) was invited to speak to a group that I joined upon my arrival. Hughes grew up in a series of midwestern small towns, and was apparently more attracted to the black people and neighborhood of Harlem than to his Columbia studies.

Hughes later received a degree from Lincoln University in 1929, an historically black university. Thurgood Marshall, the supreme court justice was a classmate at Lincoln. Langston Hughes' life and work were enormously influential during the Harlem Renaissance of the 1920-30's. His poetry and fiction portrayed the lives of working-class blacks in America. Hughes arrived at Michigan to promote his book "Simple speaks his mind". I was the only one in the group who owned a car (that 1936 Ford Station wagon with over 200, 000 miles on it), therefore I was asked to pick up and return Hughes to the airport and drive him around Ann Arbor to the various events to which he was scheduled. Hughes, of course gave me a signed copy of his book, and I followed the series as it flowed from his pen. I continue to admire Hughes as one of the early prominent black writers as a source of inspiration.

A few of my housemates were from India. They had the shock of their lives when they tried to get a summer rental in Dearborn, an all-white neighboring community. Welcome to America.

Al Burton, a civil engineering student, who was a Tuskegee Airman during World War II, was my roommate for a year. Al and his wife, Vashti Burton later became God Parents to my son Brian. We both moved back to the New York City area and the families have remained close. Al and I called each other "roomie". We painted our college room dark green, with dark shades, to enable us, to sleep during the day, if we wanted to, then we would stay up after midnight studying while listening to the "clear channel" radio station from Nashville Tenn. playing jazz. Al loved boats, which he owned and maintained himself, for most of his life, after graduating from Michigan. Al past away recently, and is survived by his wife, Dr. Vashti Burton and son, Mike.

Each co-op resident was assigned an in-house responsibility. Marvin Epstein, a Cleveland native, chose to clean the toilets because he could do that late at night. A journalist major, Marvin decided that it was easier to transition from his evening editing duties with the newspaper to his house duty job with the toilets. I suppose either job, at times, could be quite messy. Marvin and I became good friends. I started off as a cook and it was great fun. I was cooking for seventy-five people. Sometimes, I'd take a pound of butter, throw in some potatoes, some meat and a lot of other stuff. I felt that what ever I tossed in the pot turned into a tasty meal.

The co-op pantry was established on an honor system, which meant each student paid whatever the posted price was for each food item he chose from the pantry. Nothing was under lock and key. We had a policy called "guffing," which meant that certain foods, such as potatoes, milk, bread, peanut butter, sugar, and salt, were free, but meat items, such as hamburger, steaks and beef, could be purchased.

A few months later, I became purchaser of the food and commodities for all six houses, so instead of cooking for about seventy-five people, I was buying food for approximately three hundred. The greater responsibility awakened the entrepreneur in me and I so began demonstrating the instincts of a seasoned negotiator. I knew everyone wanted more meat, so I devised a way to make that happen. In those days, food markets had just begun to sell prepackaged meats. Before then, you'd go to the market, tell or show the butcher/salesperson how much meat you wanted, and he'd cut it, slice it, and wrap it up and give it to you.

People weren't as affluent as they are now, and I noticed most people ate meat only on weekends, and the leftover meat would stay in refrigerators the rest of the week. Since meat was not as attractive after a few days, the markets had no choice but to dispose of it. I made most of the large purchases for the co-ops from an A&P market near the campus. After watching them throw large batches of meat away every week, I decided to make the manager an offer he couldn't refuse. I told him that I would come in every Saturday night and buy all the leftover meats they had at a greatly reduced price. He agreed.

From then on, we had meats on the guffable list, available at any time at the same price that I had paid for it. Our co-op families and friends were delighted that they could purchase beef, steaks, and every other meat for ten cents a pound! I was a big hero in all the houses after making that happen. I also decided to put cookies and candy on the guffable list at wholesale prices. Let's say you could buy a candy bar for five cents at the store; you could get it for two cents on the guffable list.

While my co-op colleagues viewed me as someone to praise and pamper for my work as a purchaser, my fiancée back East had decided I was someone to let go. Yolanda dumped me by phone, no less. She came to visit me once during my stay at Michigan. Months later after her visit, she hit me with a "Dear John letter" over the phone! I don't know what led to her decision, but I think it had something to do with her mother remarrying and moving to Virginia Beach, Virginia. With her mother moving South, Yolanda was forced to stay with her father.

I believe he coaxed her into breaking our engagement. He didn't see me as a good enough catch. She told me that he once said, "He's never going to be able to afford you, so drop him." She asked me to return the diamond stone that she had provided for the engagement ring, but I sent her the entire ring. We kept in touch for many years and I received a nice, long letter of congratulations from her when I was appointed to the board of directors at Chase Manhattan Bank.

Yolanda's father also divorced his second wife, Gloria, and for many years, she dated Dennis Baron, whom I met at Columbia. Occasionally, when I saw Gloria and Dennis during visits to New York, she'd tell me that Yolanda should have married me. Yolanda's father made a similar statement when I ran into him at a party in Teaneck, New Jersey, many years later. He said, "I was wrong. You should have married my daughter."

With my long-distance love life in shambles, my engineering classes, combined with my thriving side career as an entrepreneur, were welcomed distractions. The co-op provided me with a truck and I really enjoyed my weekly trips to the farms to buy fresh produce, though at times, some farmers were puzzled by my presence. There were people in some of the rural areas of Michigan who had never seen a black person, "up close and personal". Some would ask, "Are you an American?" They were, however, always friendly and cordial.

Founded in 1817 on a forty-acre slice of rural America, the Ann Arbor-based campus has now developed into a splintered educational facility on 871 acres, composed of four sections (North, Central, Medical, and South). In contrast, Columbia, founded in 1754 as Kings College, is situated on a thirty-two-acre plot in upper Manhattan, which is a twenty-minute subway ride from Times Square, one of the world's most famous entertainment centers and an easy walk from my Harlem community. Though Ann Arbor was but a sleepy community when compared to New York, it grew on me and I found myself enjoying campus life there much more than I did while at Columbia.

During one return trip from the farm area, a train wreck occurred not too far from where we were. The freight train was loaded with tons and tons of cabbage. A train official told us that the wreck had made the cabbage unsalable, so we could help ourselves to as much as we wanted. We loaded the truck with cabbage several times and our co-op residents and friends ate cabbage for weeks! The frequent trips to the farm area also afforded me considerable time to think about many things, including what Otis Redding so accurately described in his ballad, Pain in My Heart, that just wouldn't let me be. Something was missing in my life.

Barbara Van Dyke, a twenty-year-old graduate student and Alabama native, was the housemother at one of the women's co-ops when we met. She chaperoned about thirty students, some of them older than she was. She didn't skip any grades in elementary school; she just started early. Barbara's parents, Dr. Henry and Bessie Van Dyke, were raised in different Michigan towns—her mother in Allegan and her father in Three Rivers. Both earned B.S. degrees from western Michigan colleges. Henry also earned an M.S. from the University of Michigan and a PhD in chemistry from Michigan State University. Bessie got her M.S. from Michigan State University. Neither could find a job in the North, so they moved to Montgomery, Alabama, where they were hired as schoolteachers. Barbara had two siblings, Jacqueline (Jackie) and Henry Jr.

Henry Sr. taught chemistry at Alabama State before becoming the Head of the Chemistry Department and Bessie taught in the Alabama school system. Barbara's brother, Henry Jr., started elementary school when he was six years old. Her parents couldn't afford a babysitter, so Bessie put four-year-old Barbara in class with Henry Jr., and they were assigned to the same classes throughout elementary school. Barbara was able to keep up, so no one complained. She finished high school when she was sixteen and graduated from the University of Michigan with a degree in history when she was twenty.

We began dating soon after we met, but because of earlier commitments, each of us went to our college prom with someone else. Incidentally, Duke Ellington's orchestra provided the music that night. Barbara went with Jim Williams, one of my housemates, and I went with a friend who was attending Ohio State University. Barbara had her own room in the co-op and could come and go as she pleased. She didn't have to "keep hours," as they called it back then. Now it's called having a curfew. We spent a lot of time together, but I also had occasional weekend dates with two other women, one in West Virginia and the other in Indianapolis. I suspect that Barbara knew I was dating other women, but she never said anything. Maybe that's why an announcement appeared in the newspapers shortly after I drove Barbara and her brother to Montgomery for the holidays.

Henry Jr., who became a playwright and was the author of two books, was drafted by the Army and spent a tour in Germany. He stopped in Ann Arbor on his way home to see Barbara. She asked me to drive them to Montgomery, which I did. We rode in my 1936 Ford Station wagon, which had two hundred thousand miles on it. I spent a few days there and then drove back to Michigan by myself. Actually, we stopped on the way to Montgomery and stayed overnight in Nashville with a friend of Barbara's father, who was head of the Tennessee State University's chemistry department. I made the same overnight stop when I returned to Michigan. Part of the time, I drove back in a rainstorm with faulty windshield wipers, kept the driver's side window rolled down, and used my hand to keep the windows reasonably clear by using my hand as a windshield wiper. When I reached Nashville, the friend of Barbara's father had my wipers replaced at the university's auto repair shop.

A few weeks later, an announcement of my engagement to Barbara was in the New York Amsterdam News, a black New York weekly newspaper. I didn't know how it got there, but Barbara did. She said her mother placed it. For a while, I didn't know what to do. I was twenty-five years old and knew that my family wanted me to get married and that her family wanted her to get married. I did love her, but I wasn't in love. We were very compatible. We got married.

With the wisdom that sometimes comes with hindsight, my being married at this juncture of my life was a positive. Up until this point in my life, I had no one depending upon me. My father sent money home to his father well into his married life. I believe I was about 12 years old when this practice stopped. When I was in college, my father told me that "I would not have to do that for him", unless there were extrodinary circumstances. This remittance was the single thing I remember my parents arguing about. Prior to my marriage, I had no sense of anyone being financially dependent upon me. I made decisions based soley on my own needs and desires. In my mind, marriage required a major transformation in my thinking. When our four children began arriving, as planned, the sense of financial and human responsibility increased tenfold.

Prior to our marriage, Barbara, and I, dicussed what each of us expected from the other in our marriage, including the number of children we wanted, and if we could financially support each of them through college.

In my first employment as a professional engineer, I was not "dating" as many of my colleagues were. I was more able to concentrate on the professional side of my life rather than the social side. Barbara's parents were very supportive of my career, on the numerous occasions when we needed "family" care for our children, when I or Barbara and I travelled for business needs. Philosophically, Barbara's parents, especially her mother and I were often on the same page.

I stopped going to classes just before we were married and started looking for a place for us to live. I settled on a town nearby which had Quonset houses. Each unit had a kitchen, bedroom, and bath. I spent much of my time making repairs and cleaning the place we would call our home. My father's wedding gift to the newlyweds was one hundred dollars, and that took us through the first few months. Without a job, it was for me a time of doubt and high anxiety.

Someone in Michigan's administrative office called and told me that even though I had passed all my exams, I would not be allowed to graduate if

I didn't return to class. I ignored the threat. While we were in Montgomery rehearsing for the wedding, I received another call from Michigan. This time, I was told that I would be allowed to graduate. I was quite relieved, but I didn't participate in the graduation ceremonies because they were held the same weekend of our marriage, which took place in Montgomery Alabama, Barbara's hometown.

When we returned from the wedding, I began my search for employment while Barbara pursued her master's degree at the University of Michigan. Thanks to a quirk in the laws that governed Alabama's segregated school system, Barbara's graduate school expenses (tuition and room and board) were paid by the state. As her landlord, I collected the rent. Alabama wouldn't allow black graduate students to attend the University of Alabama. Since the state had no black graduate schools, it agreed to pay all expenses to any black student who was accepted at a graduate school outside the state. Put another way, the state of Alabama during that time paid black students not to go to the University of Alabama. That worked out well for Barbara and me.

At this point, I will pull out of my story, a thread that to some of us who enjoy, as I enjoy, potato chips, may be of interest.

One of the undergraduates living in the Co-Op house that Barbara Van Dyke was the House Mother, was another Barbara, Barbara Wolfinger, in the field of physycology. She was dating a graduate student Mike Helfgott (PhD) in physycology. Upon graduation, they both joined Dr. Ernest Dichter's firm. Dichter, an Austrian born, American Phychologist, and marketing "Guru" in the field of Motivational Research. Dichter believed he was able to "mobilise and manipulate human needs and desires, as they exist in the consumer". Dichter was among the first to utilize "focus groups" in research.

As told told to me by Mike, and Barbara, in the beginning of Dichter's career in the U.S., Dichter contacted Proctor & Gamble, as well as several other comsumer products companies. Dichter told them, that he, Dichter could increase their sales of one of their products sufficient enough that the "six figure" payment to him would be easily justified in terms of cost. Dichter would not revel how, until Proctor & Gamble executed a contract with him. After many months of negotiations, Proctor & Gamble agreed to Dichter's terms. The product that Dichter had selected was Rinso, the soap powder. After P & G agreed to terms, Dr Ernest Dichter simply told P & G to change Rinso from a white powder to a particular shade of blue. And it worked! Proctor and Gamble achieved its improved sales targets.

Dichter repeted this scenario, at least twice, with other comsumer products.

A 2013 N.Y.Times magazine article on "How the Processed-Food Industry Creates and Keeps Selling the Crave", cites a 24 page report prepared for Frito-Lay by Dr. Ernest Dichter. The report states . . . The company's potato chips were not selling as well as they should, for one simple reason: while people like and enjoy potato chips, they feel guilty about liking them. Dichter advised Frito-Lay to move its chips out of the realm of between-meals snacking and turn chips into an ever present item in the American diet. Dichter suggested avoid using the word "fried" substitute the more healthful-sounding "toasted". He also suggested repacking the chips into smaller bags, and making the chips much less greasy. Dichter said that the "more anxious customers, the ones who have the capacity to control their appetite, will select the smaller pack. Dichter advised the increased consumption of chips in small bags as a part of the regular fare served by restaurants, and fast food establishments.

As I said, for me, the coating of salt, the fat content that rewards the brain with instant feeling a pleasure, the sugar that exists, not as an additive, but in the potato itself, all of this makes the Potato Chip the "Best Addictive Food"

. . . . SOUND FAMILAR . . .

All my classmates had found jobs before they graduated, but neither I nor Clay Holland, the other black graduating engineer in my class, were as fortunate. During the summer after graduation, I did land a construction job with Michigan Mold & Plastic, a company in a town not far from Ann

Arbor. Basically, I spent the summer pouring concrete. If my efforts to land an engineering job had failed, at least I knew I would be able to make a living as a laborer.

CHAPTER 7

"If necessity is the mother of invention,
Discontent is the father of progress"

DAVID ROCKEFELLER

"Computers are good at following instructions, but not at
reading your mind"

DONALD E. KNUTH

In 1951, a new wave of engineers knocked confidently on the industry's doors in search of entry-level jobs. I rode that wave, though I felt at times like a surfer without a surf board. The doors that had opened widely for my fresh-faced colleagues with similar University pedigrees were closed to me. My credentials were fine, but my fresh face was the wrong color. I couldn't get a job in the industry. I tried to exude confidence, but evidently, I needed more. Few blacks had scaled the barriers that loomed before me.

I knew virtually no other blacks who were trying to do what I wanted to do, except my childhood friend, Lester, and Clay Holland, my engineer classmate at Michigan. Neither could find a job. It took Lester six months of beating the bushes before he finally got a job at General Cable. Later, he was hired by Allen B. DuMont's company and subsequently worked for Lockheed.

Frankly, I was steeped in anxiety. I was fresh out of college, married, and didn't have a job. The major engineering companies were hiring, but they just weren't hiring black engineers. Finally, Uncle Sam came to the rescue. I landed a job with the Detroit Tank Arsenal, a U.S. government facility that designed and developed tanks. The Arsenal, located in Warren, Michigan, Detroit's largest suburb, was built in 1940 by Chrysler Corporation. My job paid three thousand one hundred dollars, per year, a typical middle-class salary at the time. The Arsenal was the nation's first manufacturing plant built for the mass production of tanks. Located on 113 acres, it was also the world's largest tank facility, surpassing the largest German facility, which was built during World War II. It was constructed to survive attacks by the most powerful weapons of that era. (Detroit News.com, 12/12/2008)

The Arsenal had designed an orientation program that allowed its new engineers to rotate through each branch of every division in which engineers were employed. It took a year to cycle through the program. My intent was to stay focused on an engineering career, but that changed near the end of my rotation when I worked in the Arsenal's Research and Development Division (R&D).

That's when I learned of the Arsenal's plans to use computers, the latest in the changing world of technology. I was fascinated by the potential use of computers in solving complex mathematical problems. I spent long hours in the R&D offices and much of my spare time with the subcontractor, the University of Michigan, absorbing as much as I could about the computer field. The first commercial digital machine was delivered the year I graduated. When the orientation program ended, I got what I wanted: a job with the R&D division. I was the only black engineer in the Research and Development Division. Almost all other professional blacks at the Arsenal worked in the laboratories. Ed Richardson, who became my mentor, worked in one of the labs that specialized in batteries. Ed, who was about ten years older than I, was a chemistry major at Wilberforce (Ohio) College.

During my training period, in addition to meeting and becoming friends with Ed Richardson, I began a friendship with Gene Derricotte, who I had met briefly at the University of Michigan. A friendship which continued well into my personal and professional life. Gene also worked at the Arsenal. As a part of a foursome, which occasionaly included Gene's brother Bruce and Joe Jennings, Gene and I began to play golf on Sundays at the University of Michigan's golf course. Gene played football at Michigan from 1944 to 1949 (with a World War ll interruption as a Tuskegee Airman). Gene was the Defiance Ohio High School Class Valedictorian, excellent student, and a star athlete. Gene was an outstanding player on the 1947 Michigan Football Team, (which was Coach Fritz Crisler's last "single wing" team), and the 1948 Team, both teams were undefeated, and ranked number one in the nation in the A.P. poll. The 1947 Michigan Football Team is considered by many to be the Greatest U of M football teams of all time. At the end of that football season Notre Dame was ranked ahead of Michigan.Both were undefeated. Many noted that every southern A.P. voter had voted for Notre Dame, which at that time was not integrated, as opposed to Michigan's three star players, Derricotte, Len Ford, and Bob Mann, who were black, both Len Ford (outstanding defensive end with the Cleveland Browns, and Bob Mann with the Detroit Lions) went on to play professional football. Gene sustained a career ending injury during training camp after being selected in the first round by the undefeated league defending champion, the Cleveland Browns. I was on the Michigan's Golf Course with Gene when the then Athletic Director Fritz Crisler suggested to Gene that he consider returning to Michigan and receive an advanced degree. Gene took Crisler's advice, and became a Dentist. When my oldest son Erik was born, Gene Derricotte became his God Father.

The Battery Lab. also had a couple of "characters". Two of these "characters", were a small man, named Merrill, and a much larger man, who formally played as a lineman on a college football team, Hawthorne Lee. Both men were "sports nuts", and hung out together. Merrill would frequently bait

Hawthorne. Merrill would look up some obscure sports fact, then bring the conversation around to the circumstance that gave rise to the sports fact. A sports fact which to the average person would seem unlikely. Then Merrill would say "I bet you", this comment based on his knowledge of the obscure fact. This went on, time after time. We in the audience would always recognize, with barely concealed laughter, what was unfolding. Hathorne Lee would almost always "fall" for this "set up". This was one of the lighter moments of my then uncertain professional life.

As an R&D trainee, I worked for a man named Bill Mazur, who seemed to like me. He's probably the reason I was assigned to R&D. I remember his name vividly because when I lived in New York in the 1940s, a sportscaster there had the same name. Bill Mazur was from Cicero, Illinois, a town south of Chicago that was notorious for its nastiness toward Negroes. During my life I've met many people of different ethnicities, who looked upon me as a man, not a Negro, colored person. Bill was among them. He was three inches taller than I, maybe 6-4, a big burly guy, dark hair. He could have been mistaken for someone from the Middle East. He had no problem working with or socializing with me and he paid no attention to the racial mores of that era.

For example, while on assignment for the Arsenal at the Aberdeen Proving Grounds in Maryland, Bill took me to a known-to-be segregated Baltimore restaurant for dinner. We had no problem. A few weeks later, I went to that same restaurant alone and was shown the door instead of a table. When I was with Bill, we were never refused service at any restaurant he chose. Just by watching him, I learned so much about how to manage and interact with people.

The R&D's major mission was to use the new technology to improve the tank as a weapon on the battlefields of the Korean War (1950-53). The engineers at the Arsenal were responsible for improving the entire tank system: batteries, fuel consumption, and so on. I was assigned to the team responsible for improving the accuracy of the tank guns. Our Army tank commanders in Korea concluded that the firing accuracy of our tanks was ineffective because of–among other things–stabilization problems. Put simply, the tanks had to stop before they could shoot. We were working to design a tank that could shoot its main gun (cannon) while it was moving.

The tank commanders on the Korean battlefields knew that at one thousand yards, the coaxial machine guns had the same trajectory as the cannon. They would start firing the machine guns at nine hundred yards, and then raise the sight incrementally until they reached the target, and then pushed the button to fire the cannon. Our job was to stabilize the tank so that its cannon could be fired more accurately while on the move.

Before I arrived at the Arsenal, the research branches of several companies/institutions, including the Massachusetts Institute of Technology (MIT), Westinghouse, Ford Instrument Division, General Electric, Michigan University's Willow Run Laboratories, Chrysler Corporation, Minn-Honeywell, and others, were under contract with the Arsenal to produce a sophisticated stabilization system that would control the guns and keep them aimed at the target while the tank bounced up and down on muddy or uneven terrain. The Army now uses several labs, including the Ground Systems Power and Energy Lab (GSPEL), which can simulate any road condition or off-road terrain found anywhere in the world today.

Though I was a recent college grad, my assignment was to check in occasionally on the contractors to–and I quote–"supervise what was going on." I had to sign off on whatever they were doing. This sign off responsibility, I believe resulted in the contractor "putting up" with all the "dumb questions", that I asked. Having math and engineering degrees proved to be invaluable assets in many ways. In those days, most electrical engineers worked for companies that generated power. The rage at that time was servo-mechanisms, which was a self-correcting system that used negative feedback to make corrections. Securing the title, servo engineer, became my top goal—until I began making regular trips to the Willow Run Laboratories, where computers were used to simulate stabilizing the tank guns.

Subsequently, we built a simulator that allowed us to put the tank personnel with responsibility for sighting the gun in the same environment as if they were in the tank. We'd then simulate all the tank motions, with the gun moving up and down to learn how to keep the gun on target. We also learned from the British. Their centurion tanks were stabilized, so we borrowed some of their technology and brought it to the United States.

John Sheldrick and I and two other engineers at the Arsenal incorporated the British tank stabilization system for a US tank which needed to be tested under field conditions, The site selected for these tests was the army's Camp Irwin in the Mojave Desert in California. Since at the time there was no operating manual for the stabilization system, each of us had four month stints providing technical support and maintenance during the testing period, Barbara, my wife, was two months pregnant at the time, so we decided to drive from Detroit to California for my four month stint. We wondered about both sleeping and eating accommodations on the drive to California on Route 66. The "GREEN BOOK" came to our rescue. The "GREEN BOOK" was a publication listing places nation wide that would accommodate Negroes. It has since become the subject of a movie.

We were the people designing the system, and we didn't have "how-to-fix-it" manuals to use when something went wrong. We'd go wherever the tanks were being tested, with spare parts and other equipment to fix the problem. Once, I had to check out a classified gyro from the quartermaster and believe it or not, they wouldn't let me turn it back in. When I brought it back, the person said, "We have no record of you taking it out. You can't give it back because you never got it!" This went on for several months. I kept trying to turn it back in, but they kept saying I never checked it out. I finally ended up burying it in my backyard. If somebody were to dig up this classified item fifty years later, he or she probably would ask, "How did this get here?"

This may be a little snobbish, but let's say that I had greater exposure to the evolving high-tech world than some of my contemporaries. Through my queries to the researchers I learned that just about the entire auto industry didn't have a firm grasp of the physics of the problem. I'll explain what I mean in the form of a joke. They hadn't established the standards to determine the quality or comfort of the ride in a vehicle. They had what was called a calibrated "ass-ometer." A person would sit in the vehicle and say, "The ride's OK." That's very subjective. It took researchers much, much later to come back and say, "You can write equations for what happens between the shock absorbers and the springs in the vehicle." At the time, they didn't have that ability in the general automotive field. The Arsenal, General Motors, Ford, established computer labs to address the problem. The computer world then was in its infancy.

Since Bill Mazur neither understood nor was he interested in working with computers, it was decided that I'd work with the University of Michigan's Willow Run lab. So there I was, a wet-behind-the-ears Michigan grad, pestering people in the forefront of this computer technology with questions. We paid their bills, so they were obliged to respond. I was going back-and-forth to the lab in Ann Arbor, talking with their researchers and observing their experiments.

The Willow Run lab had developed twenty-six nonlinear differential equations that would describe the suspension system of a tank and its impact on the gun. They had an analog computer that simulated the motion of the hull of a tank while traversing smooth or rugged terrain.

Though I had never used a computer, and didn't know much about computers when I joined the Arsenal, I felt comfortable, indeed, at home with this new technology. In my short time on the job, it became clear to me that analog computers were fast and accurate machines that, when properly programmed, would provide the data sought. I often stressed that point with my bosses. My ability to explain technical concepts in easy-to-understand-fashion enhanced my value and endeared me to the Arsenal's top management. My value probably spiked even higher when my boss learned that Ford was interested in hiring me. Ford offered me a job. I believe the head of R&D began considering me for a promotion when he learned that other organizations were interested in hiring me. He began making me feel that I was someone he didn't want to lose. I had no interest in leaving the Arsenal. Ford Motor Company wouldn't hire me when I got out of the University of Michigan. Neither would General Motors. At this point, in my career, I would not have gone to work for either GM or Ford because their bias toward black engineers was about the same.

I don't mean to wave my own flag, but I had confidence in myself. I also dressed the part, acted the part, and might have seemed a bit of a showman while explaining my high-tech toys, including the oscillograph, a variation of the oscilloscope, which measures current or voltage as a visible wave form on a small fluorescent screen. Allen B. DuMont, Lester's former boss, was a renowned electronics engineer, scientist, and inventor. He designed and mass-produced practical oscilloscopes and called them oscillographs. DuMont also improved the cathode ray tube in 1931 and later manufactured and sold the first commercially practical television set to the public in 1938. (Wikipedia.org/wiki/Allen B. DuMont)

DuMont's early oscillographs had two- to three-inch screens, but I got one for the office that was as big as a twelve-inch TV screen. I used it to paint a picture of a tank, and the analog computer would simulate the vehicle going over various terrains. It was more a showmanship thing than a useful training aid, but frankly, it was one of the reasons my superiors became receptive to my suggestion, which was to set up our own computer laboratory at the Arsenal. They wanted to feel comfortable saying that we had the same technology at the Arsenal that the contractors had. We eventually aquired two computers, an analog and a digital computer.

We started with an analog computer because the digital computers at that time were not fast enough for our application. Once the industry enhanced the speed of the digital computer, the R&D chief officer authorized me to buy a digital computer and named me director of the newly formed Arsenal's computer section. I wanted to buy the computer instead of leasing it because I didn't want the government to take it away from us if we ever had to tighten our financial belt. That's when my work at the Arsenal turned into a fun job.

In 1952, the Army began shipping the M48 Patton Tank to the Korean War zone. With kudos to the Arsenal, the M48 replaced the M46 in Korea with the following improvements: (1) new hemispherical turret, (2) new designed hull, and (3) improved suspension. For the next several years, we continued to monitor and improve the M48. Indeed, from 1952 to 1959, the Arsenal built nearly twelve thousand M48s, the third and final model of the tank that was named for World War II hero George S. Patton. We never came up with a way to stabilize the M48's tank. That was finally done forty years later with the Abrams tank, named for Gen. Creighton Abrams, Commander of U.S. military forces in Vietnam (1968-72) and former Army Chief of Staff.

From our experiences in using and maintaining the computers and other equipment during computer tank simulations, I knew that a "how-to-book" was needed. I commissioned the University of Michigan to write a book about how to apply computers to resolve issues involving the accuracy (or lack thereof) of the tank gun on the battlefield. The book, entitled Applying Computers, published in June 1959, was prepared by Irving J. Sattinger, who headed the Special Projects Group at the Willow Run Laboratories at the University of Michigan. When we started on the project, I said to Sattinger, "Let's go to all the top computer facilities in the country, to Boeing, Cal Tech, and just talk to people in their laboratories." And that's what we did. We got most of the information we needed. Those visits also opened all kinds of future business opportunities for me. The people we interviewed were giants in their fields.

When we completed our fact-gathering visits and interviews, Sattinger and I met frequently to collaborate on the manuscript. I would talk about how the material, illustrations, schematics, and cartoons should be presented and how the chapters should be structured. I created all the cartoons in the book. The more we worked, the more Sattinger became uneasy about the absence of recognition for my input. When the manuscript was nearly done, Sattinger said, "Why don't you become coauthor? Many of the ideas are yours."

We presented the idea of making me a coauthor to his boss at the University of Michigan, and he said, "We can't do that, even though it's true. It's the reputation of the university at stake. You paid for it, but we're the experts, so even if you contributed, we don't want the world to know that."

I'd prefer not to believe that I wasn't made a co-author simply because my fresh face wasn't the right color. I'd rather believe that as an academic university, Sattinger's boss believed that Michigan's reputation rested on successfully tackling trailblazing achievements without including non-staffers as authors. Sattinger compensated for my omission as a coauthor by citing my role on the acknowledgments page. It reads:

This book contains material and ideas gathered from many sources. In particular, I would like to acknowledge the important contributions made by Mr. Thomas Wood, Chief of the Computer Laboratory at the Ordinance Tank-Automotive Command, under whose aegis this book was prepared. In addition to initially recognizing the need for a book intended primarily for the user of computer facilities, he suggested many ideas concerning the form and content, which have been adopted. He carefully reviewed and criticized the manuscript throughout its preparation. The interchange of ideas required to clarify our concepts of computer use was of great assistance.

Another important source of information and ideas has been a series of discussions which Mr. Wood and I held with members of the computer staffs of a number of industrial and government organizations throughout the country. These discussions were helpful in formulating and confirming basic ideas on the subject. Too many individuals were involved to permit naming them all.

I.J. Sattinger

Head, Special Projects Group

Willow Run Laboratories

The University of Michigan

Ann Arbor, Michigan

Applying Computers was among the first books published about the computer field, which then was still in its infancy. Though I wasn't listed as a coauthor, I felt good about making such an important contribution. I don't remember the name of the first book, but near its end the author predicted that compilers would never exist, but of course, a year later, FORTRAN, the first compiler, became available. Compilers reduce mathematical expressions to programs.

Before I became director of the Arsenal's computer division, I took computer courses at night at Wayne State University. Arvid Jacobson, my Wayne State professor, reminded me of my Stuyvesant High English teacher, Mr. Lowenthal. Though it wasn't listed in their syllabus, each man made "lessons of life" an integral part of their curriculums. Jacobson often said, "The most difficult thing that you have to wrestle with in your business career is the conflict between your personal ethics and what may be asked of you to do in business." He was right, of course, but during my first years in the workforce, I learned, too, that the racial climate of that time was equally troublesome for young black professionals on the move.

Case in point. I was elected chairman of the Midwest Simulation Counsel. I believe the person who nominated me for the position was Dr. Robert Howe, a University of Michigan professor. There was also an Eastern Simulation Counsel and a Western Simulation Counsel. As a director, I was expected to attend a national conference of the three simulation counsels, along with the Association for Computing Machinery, which at that time, was the umbrella organization for almost all computer software and hardware organizations.

The site of the 1953 meeting—the Shamrock Hotel in Houston, Texas—created the dilemma. Legal racial segregation in Texas and other southern states was in full effect. So, I asked my secretary, who was white, to call the hotel and let them know that I was a Negro—that's what we were called at the time–and that I'm coming there to attend an event and wanted to know if that would be a problem. My secretary told me they said, "We don't discriminate and therefore, there wouldn't be a problem." A week later, the hotel manager called back and said, "There is a problem; it's against the law."

I said, "Well, I'm chairman of one of the discussion groups and I'm coming to the meeting." The manager said, "Here's the solution. You can't stay here, but if you stay with your group while you're in the hotel and don't try to use the facilities of the hotel independently, you'll be fine." I said, "Fine."

I stayed with a friend in Houston and attended all the sessions at the hotel. I knew only a handful of people attending the conference, so there were times when I was alone in the lobby or while leaving a meeting. During the opening reception, I sensed someone following me in the lobby. When I moved, the shadow of the person following me moved.

I ran into Jerry, the salesman, who earlier had sold me an analog computer. I don't remember his last name, but he worked for Electronics Associates, which then was a major manufacturer of analog computers. While chatting with Jerry, I turned around and saw that the person following me was a police officer. He probably wondered what a lone black man was doing at this reception.

When he realized that Jerry knew me, he walked away. Near the end of the conference, the fellow who ran the analog computer facility at Wright-Patterson Air Force Base in Dayton, Ohio (unfortunately I do not remember his name) said, "Tom, where've you been, we never see you after the meetings?" I told him about the arrangement with the hotel manager, that I could attend the meetings but couldn't stay at the hotel or use its facilities because of the state's racial segregation laws. He looked at me dumbfounded and said, "I'm from Texas and I should have known! Honestly, I've never looked at you as a Negro, when I'm with you in meetings or socially. I see you as a colleague."

He was truly apologetic. Later, at the closing session attended by about five hundred representatives of the nation's fast-growing computer industry, he told them about what had happened to me but never used my name. Since I was the only black member in attendance, they knew who he was talking about. He wrapped it up with this: "I want the governing body to pass a resolution that says we will not have any meetings at any facility that will not accept all our members."

Quite a few members from the South objected to the proposal. One southern member said, "That's a social issue and we're a technical organization. We don't want to get into social issues." After a twenty- to thirty-minute discussion, the motion was passed. In subsequent years, the meeting has been held in Las Vegas and I believe it's been there ever since. The computer industry's decision to change the venue of its annual meeting was a small step toward combating the racial barriers of the South, but a step nonetheless.

When I look back on my Detroit work years, I can say without hesitation that the managerial experience I gathered there was invaluable. My decision to establish roots in the computer world, which was something many people didn't understand at the time, surely gave me an edge. I doubt if I would have been a standout and gained the working supervising experience, had I went to work for a major New York engineering firm or General Motors. Being snubbed by the industry's private sector might have been a tender mercy in disguise. It surely was a case of a negative that turned into a positive.

Still, I reached the point where I knew it was time for me to drive away from the Motor City. I had begun to channel my mother's thoughts and concerns regarding the education of my children. There were no white/colored signs posted on stores in restaurants, but racial barriers were present everywhere and they were just as debilitating. Blacks couldn't eat in most restaurants and the schools were segregated. In some department stores, blacks weren't allowed to try on clothes. We lived in Detroit, a big city in the Midwest, but it might as well have been any southern city.

Living in the Detroit area, I felt that I would be helpless in trying to protect my young children from the "sticks and stones as well as words" of racial discrimination that can break the spirit of young black children. I felt, that although "far from perfect" by any standard, the New York area would provide more of a shield for them until they became adults.

Levi Jackson, my Michigan next door neighbor and good friend, shared with me one of the most hypocritically inspired acts of racism imaginable. It involved an Ivy League organization. In the late 1940s, Levi became the first black captain of Yale University's football team, and a campus hero. After he graduated and became one of the first black executives hired by the Ford Motor Company, the Yale Club of Michigan sent him an invitation each year to attend its annual meeting, which was held at the Grosse Point Yacht Club. One year, he decided to go, but they wouldn't let him in. He asked them, "Why did you invite me if you weren't going to let me in?" They told him, "Because if we didn't invite you, people would think that we were prejudiced. We thought you'd have sense enough not to come." (smile)

Levi was a Hillhouse High School (New Haven, Connecticut) football and basketball star when we first met. His team played in the preliminary game when I played for Columbia vs Yale in an Ivy League basketball matchup. Unlike many jocks, he had no illusions, no fantasies about his abilities, he was an outstanding football player. Levi was the quiet type, soft-spoken, and he never looked for the limelight.

Personality-wise, Levi reminded me of a twenty-five-year-old pastor I met during the 1954 Christmas season in Montgomery, Alabama. The clergyman, who had then been recently named pastor of the Dexter Avenue Baptist Church months earlier, presided over the wedding ceremony of my wife's sister, Jackie, and her fiancé, Bill Williams, both graduates of Michigan State University. Looking back, it became part of one of my most memorable Christmas seasons.

I spent quite a bit of time with the pastor during the rehearsal breaks. I was Impressed with his worldview of the U.S. problem with race, his "non violent" approach ,and his never stop trying Attitude.

A year later, when the 1955 Montgomery bus boycott became national news, a family member reminded me that the pastor leading the bus boycott was Martin Luther King Jr., the same man who had married Jackie and Bill Williams, the same man I chatted with daily for several days.

The year-long bus boycott was a successful protest of the policy of racial segregation on the city's public transit system and one of the seminal events of the Civil Rights era. It began the Monday after Rosa Parks was arrested for refusing to surrender her seat to a white man, and it led to a United States Supreme Court decision that declared Alabama's law that segregated buses "unconstitutional." Dr. King arranged for middle-class blacks with cars to drive along the bus routes and pick up the lower-income blacks who needed round-trip transportation to work, grocery stores, or social events. Some wealthy white women also supported the protest by driving their maids to and from work. In my opinion, the bus boycott would have failed if members of Montgomery's black middle class hadn't supported the boycott by trans-porting low-income blacks to their destinations. Many of them risked loss of jobs and their lives by supporting the boycott. They are among the unsung heroes of that movement.

Later, the University of Michigan Hospital became an unsung hero to the Wood's family. Barbara experienced a difficult health crisis during Barbara's first pregnancy. She developed toxemia, a serious illness that some-times occurs in pregnancy. High blood pressure, swelling of the hands, feet, and face are some of the symptoms. If the condition worsens, the mother could slip into a coma and the baby may be stillborn. We were on the road quite a bit during her pregnancy. We spent four months in California, drove back to Michigan, then went to New York, and then back to Michigan.

Thankfully, Barbara recovered, but she was hospitalized for some for-ty-five days in the University of Michigan Hospital. The health insurance that

I had covered only ten days. I owed the hospital over fifteen thousand dollars. My annual salary was approximately five thousand dollars. Our doctor, at tht University Hospital, knew my situation and called me into his office. He said, "We know you can't pay this bill and if we insisted on you paying it, we know it would ruin your life. We've made arrangements to take money out of a special fund we have for this type of situation. You won't have to pay anything."

At the time, that was the best gift I'd ever received, but it didn't alter my plans to move on. I promised myself that when Kay, our first child, attended kindergarten, we wouldn't be in Detroit. With or without a job, the Wood family would start anew elsewhere.

CHAPTER 8

"Computers are getting smarter all the time, scientists tell us that soon they will be able to talk to us, by they, I mean computers, I doubt scientists will ever be able to talk to us"

DAVE BARRY

Before I left the Detroit Tank Arsenal in 1959 to work for International Telephone & Telegraph (ITT), I had decided that the technical field of the computer world was not the place I wanted to be. At the time, 45 percent of IBM's workforce was comprised of technical personnel, but the better paying careers were in management or sales. That's where I wanted to be.

However, neither IBM nor any of the other major computer companies considered me worthy of employment in management or sales. Even Electrodata, which had become a division of Burroughs Corporation, wouldn't hire me. Since I had purchased the Arsenal's first mainframe computer from Electrodata, I'd hoped my application would open a door or two at that company. Electrodata's sales team did have Gloria Bullock, a black mathematician, on its staff, but she sold products to engineers and scientists, not the public. Soon after Burroughs purchased Electrodata, Gloria was transferred from sales to the education department. One thing was clear: at this time many corporations were reluctant to assign qualified blacks to prestigious positions that required interaction with the public, even if they had convincingly demonstrated the ability to function effectively. Consider the air travel industry, for example.

Back then, all major commercial air travel was first class. The planes were propeller driven; the big jets came later. One or two airline companies began hiring blacks as pilots. Before each flight, pilots walked down the aisle to greet passengers. On one of my flights, after a black pilot greeted his passengers, about a third of the passengers left the plane when they realized that a black man would fly the aircraft. Other industries experienced similar reactions, as blacks slowly acquired skilled/managerial positions in industries throughout mainstream America.

My career search ended with a technical managerial position with ITT. Several friends and coworkers called me crazy for turning my back on the Arsenal job (GS-13). The head of the Arsenal was a GS-15, just two grades ahead of me. I was told that job security for a black manager in private industry would be nonexistent. I left anyway. My stint at the Arsenal strengthened my optimism about succeeding in the emerging computer world, despite the racial barriers.

I felt that competence trumped skin color in my first excursion into the workforce in Detroit, where my boss picked me to head a computer division that I had convinced him to create. Those assets, combined with the four years of management experience that I acquired at the Arsenal, I believe made me an intriguing hire for ITT, where I quickly became my boss's boss's boss. Before I explain that, stay with me as I share a brief history of the company.

ITT was cofounded by brothers—Sosthenes and Hernand Behn of St. Thomas, Virgin Islands. They ventured into telecommunications by purchasing the Puerto Rico Telephone Company in 1920. With the quick purchase of telephone patent's and other smart acquisitions, including the Cuban Telephone Company, the brothers edged past American Telephone and Telegraph (AT&T) in stature by providing the first worldwide system of interconnected telephone lines.

I became an ITT employee just after British-born Harold Geneen became president and CEO. Under Geneen's leadership, ITT, then based in White Plains, New York, quickly emerged into a multibillion-dollar conglomerate, deriving its wealth from hundreds of acquisitions of diversified industries, including telecommunications. Its sales grew from about seven hundred million dollars in 1960 to more than eight billion dollars in 1970.

Before taking the helm, Geneen was the controller at Raytheon in Massachusetts. He was an accountant, a numbers person, and sometimes numbers people can see things that many of us don't see when looking at the same set of numbers. For example, he looked at the Hartford Insurance Company and determined that it had something like three to five times the monetary reserves needed with respect to what the law required as a reserve for an insurance company. Hartford's stock was selling low, which meant the value of the company was greater than its stock value. People generally don't consider big reserves when choosing investments. Geneen saw Hartford's poor earnings, bought the company, and sucked all that money out, which gave him a lot of money to play with tax-free. That was his big coup. Hartford, by the way, is still a part of ITT.

Another change Geneen made affected me directly, but it didn't really bother me. He decided to give every manager an IQ test. Several of my ITT colleagues with top jobs included two that hadn't gone to college. They were nervous about failing the test and losing their jobs. Geneen's modus operandi was to create separate companies to work on different projects. Once the project was completed, everyone that worked on it could be let go, except those who were on corporate payroll. After I took the test and passed it, I was placed on corporate payroll. I had become someone ITT wanted to keep, even if any project I worked on had been completed. That's why Geneen's requirement didn't bother me. Computer technology was in its infancy in the 1950s and people with my experience and expertise were rare.

Now comes the part where I became my boss's boss's boss. My first assignment was to oversee an ITT contract with the Systems Development

Corporation (SDC). A tall woman, whose first name was Adrian, was my first boss. I don't remember her last name. She reported to Arnie Siegel, an MIT fellow and genius programmer. Siegel reported to Don Combelic, the director of programming. For some reason, Combelic decided to move sideways into another division. Before he left, he named me as his successor. Neither Adrian nor Arnie expressed resentment or opposition to my two-tier promotion. I'd like to believe that Combelic recommended me for the job because I had acquired several years of managerial experience as director of the Arsenal's computer facility and at ITT, I was already supervising three hundred outside contract programmers under ITT's contract with Systems Development Corporation. A letter of recommendation submitted to Combelic by Dr. John W. Carr III, a pioneer in the computer industry, probably had some sway in Combelic's decision to make me his successor.

John, a North Carolinia native, held a Masters and PhD in mathematics from MIT. Among other achievements, he was president of the Association of Computer Machinery (ACM) in 1956-58; founder and first editor-in-chief of Computing Reviews; and recipient of the 1975 ACM Distinguished Service Award. He was an associate professor at the University of Michigan when I was the director of the computer division at the Detroit Arsenal. While I was attending a computer convention in San Francisco, John threw his arm around me and joked, "Let's go find somebody who'll take us to lunch." He became a good friend and mentor. I never saw the letter John wrote but I know it must have been glowing. Sometimes who you know can make a difference. Combelic had worked for John at MIT.

My primary job as director was to produce the computer programs for Air Force project 465 L, which was to control the flights of the Strategic Air Command (SAC). With three hundred SDS programmers and ITT's one hundred programmers, we produced the computer programs that tracked, monitored, and controlled the flights of B-52 airplanes, each armed with two atomic bombs, that made daily runs to and from the Russian border and other targets in the Eastern bloc.

The SAC project was not a war game. The pilots flew toward their assigned Soviet targets every minute of every day of the year with the understanding that if ordered not to return home, they would drop nuclear bombs on those targets. At the time, it was the largest real-time computer program control system in the world, and it included a computer diagnostic program that could determine which components in the computer were failing and would re-route the computer programs around the failing components. I have not seen any diagnostic program control system today with a better comparable feature, and the system was introduced more than fifty years ago.

It was a fail-safe system, and we, at ITT controlled the whole flight operation and lived daily with the understanding that a single miscalculation or careless mistake by either side might hurl our world into nuclear chaos, or worse—oblivion. Many youngsters on both sides of the Iron Curtain went to bed in fear of the possibility of death by nuclear destruction during the Cold War era, which often was defined as a prolonged state of military and political tensions between the free world and communism. In Teaneck, New Jersey, where I lived, bomb shelters were sold.

The Cold War grew out of the split of the wartime alliance between the U.S. and the Soviet Union, which occurred a year or so after Nazi Germany was defeated in World War II. Their relationship was dubbed "cold" because no major fights occurred between the two superpowers, but there were regional battles in Korea, Vietnam, and Afghanistan that were supported by the rival major powers.

ITT got the SAC contract because it was a telephone company that had a message switching computer system. The 465L project had computers in Spain, Massachusetts, California, Florida, and Hawaii, all connected by phone lines to the mainframe in Omaha, Nebraska, SAC headquarters, where we had two 7090 IBM computers, then the largest in the world. Latched together, they were powerful enough to run the whole system. They were serviced by ITT's message switching computer system. We called the message switchers "computers"; today they are called servers. It is like the Windows operating system in your computer. It shifts you to other programs, online, email, and so on. It allows users to perform multiple tasks.

Shortly after I became Director of Computer Programming for the SAC project, I received a rather sharp "dressing down" by a Mr. Gaffny, the Director of Personel. The "dressing down" resulted from my granting six of my programming staff a vacation (with pay) for the period from Christmas until after Easter. Unknowingly I had broken a number of ITT personel rules. I felt that I had saved ITT a significant amount of money in making the vacation grant. The Director of Personel had other thoughts. My actions resulted from a "delimma" I inherited when I became Director of Programming. The division had been given an "impossible" task, to produce a simulator for the actual computer, well in advance of the arrival of the actual computer, which was July. The computer programmers needed to check out their programs as they were written. After delivery of the actual computer, there would be no need for the simulator. In this case, the creation of a simulator for the actual computer was the kind of task that one could not just add staff to speed up. The maximum size of the group was six. I told the six people in the group "that if they completed the simulator by Christmas, I did not want to see them again until after the Easter holliday.

The group finished the simulator by Christmas!

I solidified my value as director during an important SAC conference I attended about the project by catching a significant error during the presentation. I noticed that instead of two computers latched together to handle the traffic, there was only one computer displayed. Someone omitted one server in the display! I reported the mistake to my boss and in the process learned one of the key elements of "team" management. My boss thanked me and then let his boss know that "We" discovered that a server was left off during the conference.

In hindsight, after ITT signed the contract, it soon became clear that in its proposal to the U.S. government, ITT had completely underestimated the computer programming that was needed for that kind of control system.

In ITT's intial prosal ITT estimated that the staff required to produce the computer programs at approximately 10% of what it actually required. Eventually, when I joined ITT and after my multi level promotion, I had one hundred programmers in house, working directly for me. Plus an additional three hundred more System Development Corp. programmers off site but close to the ITT location. I supervised the entire project.

At another high-level conference that focused on cost-cutting, I was humorously chastised for giving a presentation that prevented any layoffs in my group. A two-day review of personnel was conducted by an Air Force general officer, who was head of the ITT division. He annoyed many of us by allowing his little dog to scamper around the room during our reports. He let the dog run everywhere, but no one complained. The general asked each presenter to describe the mission of its division and for a breakdown of personnel and responsibilities in each section. The first presenter was the high-powered manager from the hardware division. He occasionally drum-rolled his fingers on the table and seemed more concerned about impressing the general than he was about preventing layoffs in his section. The general slashed eight people from his design section and six people from the analysis section. I was the director of the programming division and was scheduled to face the general the next day.

I went back to my office after the session and spent the entire night searching for ways to convince the general that I needed everyone I had in my division. By the next day, I had broken down every job and showed that I had 7/8 of a person for one job, 3/4 of a person for another, but never more than a complete person for any job within my division. I made it so the general couldn't cut any job in my division without eliminating the task. I could tell that the general didn't know what to say, so he didn't say anything. I didn't lose a single position. My boss came over to me laughing and said, "Great presentation, but don't do it again." I think that's what the general told him, so he told me. I don't remember my boss's name, but I knew his boss's name was Martin Dubilier.

Martin, a Princeton and Harvard Business School graduate, was president of International Electric Corporation, the division of the ITT that I worked for, he was also an eminent scientist in his own right. He was twelve years old when he invented a rust-resistant train track. Six years later, he invented a low-voltage flash bulb that eliminated the need for battery packs. Martin's father, William Dubilier, was a renowned inventor with more than three hundred patents.

During one of our infrequent meetings on business matters, Martin and I discovered that we had a mutual friend: Norman Skinner, my Stuyvesant and Columbia classmate. Norm was Martin's roommate at the Harvard Business School. They became close friends, but not close enough for his family members to ignore the racial taboos of that time. "I asked Norman to be in my wedding, but that idea was nixed by my family," Martin said.

We are all flawed, some permanent, some temporarily, some partial, some wholly, some flaws seen, some flaws unseen, some flaws dictate the direction of our life, some flaws do not.

Fame whether sought after, or not, can be destructive.

In my opinion, this was the case with Norman Skinner and Val Johnson (previously mentioned). Norm, was my close friend for more than two decades.

If fame is a significant pillar in one's economic well being, fame can make for an unstable foundation.

Clive James, the Australian author, critic, and broadcaster remarked in his major documentary series "Fame in the 20th 'Century" that, "Achievement without fame can be a rewarding life, while fame without achievement is no life at all". Fame, simply put, is name recognition, not necessarily achievement. One can achieve in one field, and have name recognition in several other fields.

Norman Skinner was black and a high profile athlete in Stuyvesant High School, and Columbia University.He had excellent grades which enabled Norman to enter and graduate from the Harvard Business School.

Norman made many close friends during his years at the Harvard Business School. However, upon graduation, he was not able to enter the work force at the level his classmates with similar grades entered.As an example, Norman's room mate and classmate at the Harvard School of Business, Martin Dublier, upon graduation went to work at the prestigious McKinsey& Co., a business consulting firm. In Norman's mind this was totally unexpected, and confidence shattering. Norman continued the single life style of some of his single Harvard classmates, apartment in the "village", sports car, etc.Soon the financial pressure led Norman into a number of "questionable"financial deals. After the first questionable deal folded while I was living in Michigan, I suggested that Norman spend time with me and my family until things return to "normal". After the second and third "questionable" deal folded, neither I or our other mutual friends (including Martin Dublier) could locate Norman. After moving back to the New York area, I accidently met Norm in mid-town Manhattan. We were glad to see each other, and arranged to have lunch in a few days. We met for lunch, Norm acted as if he had just left his office to have lunch with me, and suggested we return to his office which was on Madison Ave nearby. Upon entering the office complex, the receptionist said in greeting Norm, "Norman how are you, we have not seen you in months".We then went into a very spacious office.Knowing Norm, I knew that this was not his office.I said to Norm "This is me!, We both come from Harlem". "We both have had "hard times", You do not need to pretend with me". I later found from other mutual friends that this "charade" was a "reenactment" Norm and I have not seen each other since.

That day, was one of the saddest days of my life.

I quickly learned that most of the people who worked for me at ITT were better programmers and far more experienced in programming than I. In fact, three of my programming staff, who I later joined in a barrier-breaking business venture, were truly gifted scientists. They were: George Morgenstern, an eminent mathematician; Sheldon Best, a major contributor to the first successful High Level-Language FORTRAN compiler; and Arnie Siegel, whose major achievement in the world of technology was the

Automatic Program Tool (APT). Indeed, Arnie's APT was the genesis of today's automated assembly line production process.

George could solve complex mathematical problems in his head. He worked at Raytheon before he came to ITT. He was an extrovert, a talker, the most colorful of the three and a very bright guy, sharp on his feet. He also was a Brooklyn rabbi and an orthodox Jew. His father was not orthodox, but his grandfather was. George reverted. In fact, he was ultraorthodox. He observed all the rules. He had to be home by sundown at the start of the Sabbath, and wouldn't work on the Sabbath. He wore a yarmulke, a skullcap worn by Jewish males in the synagogue and the home and observed the dietary rules. Occasionally, I would eat kosher with George, but he could not go out to non-kosher restaurants with me.

Sheldon and Arnie were intellectual introverts, with minimal people skills and hardly any interest in activities outside their scientific fields. They were programming geniuses and scientists, who made landmark contributions during the infancy of the computer technology era. Working with an IBM team led by John Backus in late 1953, Sheldon helped develop the first successful High Level-Language FORTRAN compiler, a milestone in the history of computing. The team's work made it easier for the entry of mathematical equations into a computer.

On the importance of the development of FORTRAN at the time, Backus said, "I guess the best analogy comes from the development of mathematics. Mathematics, you know, started with arithmetic, and then it got into slight abstractions, like simple algebra, simple equations. Then it got into questions of the structure of algebraic laws for the operations of arithmetic. What we've been stuck with in programming is analogous to the arithmetic stage. "What I'm trying to do is move from that hideously complicated manipulation of numbers up to abstractions, where you have structure and you can reduce a whole set of rules to one simple rule. If I succeed, hopefully, we'll have an intellectual foundation for a lot of new computer designs." Sheldon wrote the part of the FORTRAN that handled the mechanics of the assigned subscripts to the variables, which was a very difficult part. He wrote it while he was working in the MIT radiation lab.

FORTRAN means formula translation. If you can develop an algorithm, or a recipe, for doing something, you can solve any mathematical problem. It was proven centuries ago by mathematicians that if you can add, subtract (which is negative adding), multiply (which is multiple adding), shift left, shift right, you can solve any problem. The process is called numerical analysis.

As a section leader, Sheldon was almost as close to a pure academician or research person that I've known in the computer field. He would stay up all night, solving problems in astronomy. He'd sit at his desk for thirty-plus hours, not getting up, working on whatever job that he was assigned to do. He was held in high esteem by his fellow computer scientists. He was from the Midwest, went to the University of Illinois before MIT.

Arnie developed APT (automatic programed tool). It was the first successful attempt to use a computer to control a machine tool. The problem that Arnie solved was this: As the aircraft industry's aircraft got faster and faster, the industry began using precious metals, such as titanium, lithium, and so on. The industry's machinists began making costly mistakes using the ultra, lightweight, but very high-priced precious metals. Using mathematical principles, Arnie developed a tape that fed into a machine tool that repeatedly produced whatever shape you wanted with the accuracy you wanted. Though he solved a major industry problem, Arnie never made a penny from his computer program (APT) because his research and work was accomplished through an MIT fellowship that was underwritten by the Air Force.

Without my knowledge George, Arnie, and Sheldon concocted a plan that they believed would allow each of us to prosper as partners of our own computer company, with me as the chief executive officer. I'm pretty sure the idea was spawned when Sheldon learned that Roy Nutt, also a member of the team that developed FORTRAN, had formed Computer Sciences, which was the first computer programing company to go public.

Their plan to leave ITT and to form a computer firm fell on fertile grounds because I had thought often of doing just that. They didn't see having a black boss in an independent business as a deterrent. I was a bit older than they were, and they looked up to me and were convinced that together we could create something special.

In my time as their boss at ITT, they impressed me as people who harbored no racial bias in their hearts and really didn't see any in the outer world. I think they knew it was out there, but they weren't really exposed to it. They saw me functioning, they saw me bringing the business in for ITT, so they probably minimized the impact. Keep in mind, this was a few years before the Civil Rights movement's "March on Washington," before Martin Luther King Jr. spoke so eloquently to the nation about wanting his children to be judged by the content of their character, not by the color of their skin.

CHAPTER 9

*"Do not go where the path may lead, go instead where there is
no path, and leave a trail"*

RALPH WALDO EMERSON

We came close to landing a major contract shortly as we started the computer programming company. Wright Patterson Air Force Base wanted to modify Arnie's Automatic Program Tool (APT), which was considered a major achievement in the technology industry. Arnie's APT was designed to be used on the 7000 series IBM machines, which were the size of a 30 foot x 40 foot room and had to be air-conditioned. Wright Patterson wanted to modify the APT so that it would work on non air conditioned midsized computers.

I learned that the Wright Patterson official handling the request for proposal was the same person that had let the contract to MIT under which Arnie produced APT. I contacted him, and Arnie and I went to see him. He was ecstatic to see Arnie after so many years. He told us that a key criterion for getting the contract was that the program must be designed to run on any midsized machine available. He said he had allocated five hundred thousand dollars for the program and asked us to submit a bid. I submitted a 230, 000-dollar bid, less than half of what he had allocated. We really thought we had it locked! Guess what? IBM bid twenty thousand dollars, stole the contract, wrote the program for one of their machines, and told Wright Patterson that they weren't going to share the program with its competitors.

They simply delayed access to the program to other computer companies. Welcome to the real world.

That was our introduction to a no-holds-barred business tactic. It's a cutthroat game. IBM was known for doing things like that in those early days. For example, if IBM believed that a competitor was preparing to introduce a new machine and that people might buy it, IBM would announce that it also planned to launch a new machine which would be better. Even if IBM didn't produce it, people didn't dare switch to one of IBM's competitors. Then IBM would delay and delay and delay. That's a tactic IBM used to keep people from buying somebody else's product.

It's the same philosophy of those with patent pending and copyright pending inventions or creations. IBM used that tactic frequently and very effectively.

IBM mainly was in the hardware business, but it also produced software. That changed, however, after the New York IBM manager, who was a fellow Stuyvesant High alumnus, filed an antitrust suit that forced IBM to unbundle; that is, sell some of its computer properties rather than rent those properties. The company chose to stay primarily with the hardware business and leave much of the software business to others. That proved to be a bad move. Here's my rationale.

Compare what you invest in a CD player to what you invest in CDs. The cost ratio is probably 10 to 1, 30 to 1 or 100 to 1, depending on how enthusiastic you are as a collector. Also, consider one's experience with razor blades. Now compare what you spend to buy a razor to what you spend buying razor blades. Same thing is true with computer programs. Eventually, the programs are going to cost more than what you've invested in the hardware. In my opinion, IBM made the wrong decision, and now, it's basically out of the hardware business, and mainly selling software.

Sheldon, Arnie, and George weren't the only ones who believed that I was talented enough to become the head of a mainstream U.S. company. My father believed it, too. I wished that he had lived long enough to give me a congratulatory hug for becoming the first black CEO to take a company public, selling an over-the-counter stock. He almost did. Kidney disease put him in the hospital in November 1960. I was at his bedside at four o'clock in the morning when he died. Later that morning, I learned that John F. Kennedy had been elected the thirty-fifth president of the United States. Weeks later, I, became the CEO of Computronics, a New Jersey-based computer programming firm.

My partners and I agreed that our firm's name should be linked to the emerging high-tech computer industry. I came up with the Computronics name and that suited them just fine. Of the four partners, George and I were the company's people persons; Arnie and Sheldon were the scientists extraordinaire. My partners had asked me to become the CEO mainly because they saw me as a effective manager;and they believed I would be able to raise the capital necessary for the start-up. They believed that I could get contracts for our fledgling company.As a result, I made most of the decisions. I believe I could have demanded 50 percent of the company stock and let them divide the rest three ways. Most companies were not structured with four equal partners. In those days if you could sell, you could form a company because there weren't too many people that had the technical knowledge and ability to sell the product. Because I was black, I wanted to avoid any possible conflicts down the road, so I insisted that we become equal partners.My thinking at that time was, that I wanted each of the partners to be effected equally by any decision made in the future.

The compatibility and working relationship I enjoyed with George, Arnie, and Sheldon at ITT remained solid in our new roles as equal partners of our own company. However, some adjustments were needed. Other people had handled the so called "mundane" tasks associated with operating a business when we worked for ITT, which provided office supplies, including pencils, papers, desks, and office furniture. ITT also had personnel and business sections to pay the employees, arrange travel, and pay the bills. We realized that operating a company successfully would involve more than selling a product.

Nobody said, "Do this, do that," but it didn't take long for each of us to step up and assume responsibility for the things that had to be done. It was an easy transition because each of us assumed the roles we had at ITT. I was their boss and they did the technical work. No urgent meetings were called, and no panicky situations arose. Without discussion, we quickly developed a self-organizing system.

I was the CEO and sales arm of the company "the rain maker". Arnie assumed duties that frankly I felt were beneath his status as a partner, but he seemed to like it. Essentially, he became the company's executive vice president. He set up a one-man, human resources department, and assumed responsibility for the payroll. When we needed to hire additional support staff, Arnie took charge of that, as well. Even when my friends or other partners' friends were being considered for jobs, Arnie decided who to hire or not to hire. I'd huddle with Arnie and our accountant, Morris Zimmerman, of Anchin, Block & Anchin, who provided and completed all the financial forms that were required when accounting reports were due. I didn't get involved in a lot of the internal housekeeping functions. Arnie did that.

George gave up his duties as a programmer to handle the people involved in the technical side of the business. He became the supervisor of programmers. I wanted George to help with marketing and he tried, but it didn't work. In my opinion, George was an orthodox Jew with a fatal flaw, he wanted all Jews to conform to the orthodox doctrine. Whenever we interviewed a potential customer who was Jewish but not orthodox, George would try to convert him on the spot.

I'd say, "George, leave the guy alone!" I could tell that in some cases, the person didn't want to hear that kind of talk. Once, when I was eager to rush home to watch a television episode of Roots, George chided me, saying, "You mean you have to watch national television to know where you came from?" I said, "George, I know where we came from. Our history was handed down from generation to generation." George and I had our fun.

Though he was a partner, Sheldon was heavily involved in the actual programming work, but that was his personality. He was like a foreman, who preferred to be in the trenches with the workers. Even as a partner, he'd pull all-nighters searching for a solution to the latest technical problem confronting the company. Each of the partners had an all-in commitment to the company and that paid off.

Martin Dubilier, my boss at ITT, gave us our first contract, a contract worth fifty thousand dollars. Soon after that, I secured a contract from RCA to provide a significant portion of the software for their 300 series computers. A bit later, George nailed down a two-year deal securing a contract to do programming for the Israeli Missile Defense System. The Israelis asked us to send orthodox Jewish programmers only. We sent eight or nine people to set up and maintain their system for two years. I guess the Israelis believed that since our programmers were orthodox, they wouldn't reveal any Israeli secrets. I never knew what they did, but one of them, Monroe Weinstein, came back with a wife. Weinstein was comparable to George in terms of mental acuity. He didn't stay with us long after he returned. I believe he formed his own company.

Almost all of the startup money for the firm came from my friends and business associates in Detroit's black community, one group, was led by Dr. Charles Wright, who founded the Museum Of African History, the largest Black History Museum in the U.S. ouside of the one at the Smithsonian in Washington D.C.. The other Detroit group was organized by Joe Jennings, who's friendship I enjoyed until his recent death, here in Palm Coast Florida. My friends in the Detroit area knew me as an adult, as a successful manager at the Detroit Tank Arsenal and they provided generous support. I received very little support from Harlem, my hometown community, I believe the reason, was because folks in New York knew me as a high school and college student, not as a businessman.

We were profitable six months after the company was formed but developed a cash flow problem only because we routinely had to wait up to six months before receiving payment for our services from the U.S. government and several other customers. I went to several banks including the Chase Manhattan Bank hoping to receive an injection of cash through a loan, but the loan officer at Chase offered a better solution. He said, "You don't need a loan, you need more equity in your company. I'll put you in touch with some people who might be able to help." He sent me to Laird, a Wall Street firm, which was run by a group of young investors. Those young people passed the hat and gave me more than one hundred thousand dollars to invest for them in Computronics stock. I was in my mid-thirties at the time, the average age of members of the Laird firm was twenty-five and they already were millionaires.

An interesting incident occurred during my quest for an "accounts Receivable" loan of $50, 000 (a high end car loan today - $ 500, 000 todays dollars) I said that I was seeking a $50, 000 loan, but first I needed to use the toilet. The bank officer started to give me directions—down the hall, left at -etc—then he hesitated and said "You want a loan of $50, 000 —the rest room is right here, (about ten yards away), I went through an unmarked door in to a bath/toilet suite with all the amenities of a high end hotel – interesting.

We hired Sam Pierce's firm, Battle, Fowler, Stokes & Kheel, to handle our legal work during those early years. Sam, a Phi Beta Kappa and my role model, had a huge address book, which he used, routinely, to touch base with political friends and other social contacts, so he wouldn't have to ask them for favors out-of-the-blue. Sam was a bright, likeable, outgoing, and gregarious kind of guy.I met Sam as a teen-ager through his brother Chet. Chet was at Harvard during my years at Columbia. Chet became the first black to play football on the playing field of a predominately white university in the south, when Harvard played The University of Virginia in 1947.Chet later became the President of the American Board of Pyschiatry and presently a portrait of Chester Pierce hangs in his undergraduate hall at Harvard. Sam Pierce his older brother was able to use his connections to bail us out of a jam with RCA, one of our major customers.

We did a lot of software work for the RCA 301, a midsized computer. In those days, companies that produced mainly hardware had small programming staffs. Among other programs, Computronics wrote FORTRAN for the RCA 301. RCA, which owned NBC, wanted to showcase its computer capacity while linked at remote locations. Thus, during the 1964 presidential elections, Computronics was given the task of writing the computer programs that NBC used to predict the outcome of the 1964 elections. The input came from the NBC studios in New York; the computer was in Camden, New Jersey, connected to NBC by telephone lines. It was the first time a computer was linked to telephone lines in a commercial venture.

In the course of our computer business relationship with RCA, there was a dispute about a payment of thirty-five thousand dollars to us. We thought we were right, and I'm sure they thought they were right. I didn't want to sue because I thought that might be bad for business, and RCA, which owned NBC, was one of our best customers. But thirty-five thousand dollars was a lot of money during that time, and I didn't want to just let it go. I told Sam about the problem and he found a favorable solution with a telephone call to NBC president Robert Sarnoff, his college friend.

Sarnoff and Sam were friends and classmates at Cornell. Sam tells Sarnoff that one of his clients is in a dispute with RCA about payment, but the client doesn't want to sue RCA. Sarnoff asks, "What's the number in dispute?" Sam tells him, and Sarnoff says, "Done." Problem solved without litigation. That was the kind of influence Sam wheeled through his connections, and the first of many legal "difficulties" from which he rescued me.

Sarnoff was a pioneer in integrating television shows. During his tenure, NBC was the first network to allow a black singer, Nat King Cole, to host a program, and in 1965, Bill Cosby became the first black actor to play a leading role in an hour-long prime-time series, I Spy. Sarnoff, the oldest son of RCA founder David Sarnoff, became RCA's chairman and CEO when his father retired in 1971.

The search for new clients kept me quite busy and often on the road during my first few years as Computronics' CEO. Then another emotional loss slowed me down. Two years after my father died, my mother became seriously ill. I tried to put her in a nursing home in Teaneck, New Jersey, but it only accepted white patients. A nursing home in nearby Englewood, New Jersey, that was integrated accepted her. Before leaving on a short business trip, I visited her, just to let her know I would be out of town for a couple of days. On my way back, Frances, my sister, called and told me that our mother might not be with us when I returned. When the plane landed, I went directly to the nursing home. My sister, my wife, and a minister were waiting for me outside her room. As I approached her bed, she looked at me and said, "I've been waiting for you to come back." Then she closed her eyes and died. Several doctors told me that sometimes a dying patient can will themselves to stay alive for long periods of time to say goodbye to a loved one. It was an indelible experience.

As the singular "Rain Maker" for the company, my marketing efforts produced enough programming contracts to keep the Computronics staff of a little over one hundred busy.

A Smithsonian publication in the summer of 2019 puiblished an article on the Apollo Program. The article covered not only the technical aspects of the Program, it covered the importance of the Program. ; "In 1999, as the centuty was ending, the historian Arthur Schlesinger Jr. was asked to name the most significant human achievement of the 20th century. Schlesinger said "the one thing this century will be remembered for 500 years from now :This was when we began the exploration of space.He picked the first moon landing, as the most significant event of the 20th century.

One of the more personally challenging and satisfying contracts I negotiated for Computronics, involved JFK's space program. In a 1961 address to Congress, President Kennedy vowed to put " . . . a man on the moon and return him safely to the earth" by the end of the 1960s. I knew that computer programming would be an integral part of the Apollo mission and that my background, which included the construction and operation of simulators, might help Computronics become a partner in our bold venture to the moon.

The Apollo Program was the U.S. human spaceflight program which succeeded in landing the first humans on the moon and returning them safely to earth. The mission was accomplished when Neil Aemstrong and Buzz Aldrin landed their Apollo Lunar Module on the moon and walked on the lunar surface, Michael Collins remained in lunar orbit in the Command Module, and all returned safely to earth.

Landing on the moon was a result of the massive commitment of funds and technological achievement made by America "not at war". At one time, the Apollo Program involved over 400, 000 people supported by over 20, 000 companies and universities.My company COMPUTRONICS was very proud to be a part of the effort.

The Apollo Lunar Module was designed to descend from lunar orbit and land two astronauts on the moon surface and then return them back in orbit to rendezvous with the Command Module.The contract for the Lunar Module was awarded to the Grumman Aircraft Corp.

The Command Module, a conical crew cabin, designed to take three astronauts from launch to lunar orbit and back to earth. North American Aviation was awarded the contract for the Command Module.

In 1962, North American Aviation, which was based in Downey, California, was a major manufacturer in the aerospace industry. It was involved in the creation of several historic aircraft, including the T-6 Texan trainer, the P-51 Mustang fighter, the F-86 Sabre jet fighter, the X-15 rocket plane, and the Apollo Command and Service Module.

I traveled to NAA's headquarters to chat with a fellow whose last name was McIntyre. He told me they needed a simulator, which would help the astronauts experience the conditions they would face in outer space. Because I had built a simulator for the Detroit Tank Arsenal, I knew the problems; I talked his language. He hired us as consultants with the task of writing the specifications for a simulator for the Apollo command module, which would be used to carry astronauts from earth into orbit around the moon. Grumman Corporation was the prime contractor for the Lunar Excursion Module (LEM), which took the astronauts from the lunar orbit to the surface of the moon and back.

We told NAA officials that digital computers had gotten faster in recent years, and that they should be used on the simulators instead of analog computers. They agreed. When NAA signaled its readiness to let the contracts for the simulators, we contacted the eight firms competing for the contract to build the simulator. LINK, the premier firm in the simulation of aircraft business, which was based in Binghamton, New York, was our primary target.

Arnie, Sheldon, and I worked all night on a proposal for LINK to hire our firm to write the programs for the simulator. Ed Link, founder of Link Aviation Devices, Inc., had created the LINK Trainer, which was used to teach new pilots how to fly by instruments. More than a half million U.S. pilots, as well as pilots from many other nations, were trained on LINK simulators.

Because of its relatively remote location, Binghamton, New York, I chartered a plane to make the pitch. Each of us gave solid presentations. LINK's chief technical officer liked our plan and promised COMPUTRONICS the contract to write programs for the simulators for the Apollo module if they had the winning bid. Then he said, "We already have the contract for the LEM module, why don't you start on that immediately." We did.

Our specialty was real-time programming, which meant through simulators, the astronauts would learn what to expect during their space flight. We were proud to have received commitments to write the programs for the Apollo Command and Lunar Excursion Modules and confident that we were the best real-time programmers in the business.

I established an office in Los Angeles. NAA assigned a former test pilot, whose first name was Francis, I don't remember his last name, as a member of our simulator crew. Someone told me an interesting story about Francis. He was a test pilot for the X-15 rocket plane—one of the first aircraft to break the sound barrier—until a tragic accident ended his flying career prematurely.

Evidently, he wanted to impress his girl friend, who was watching from the ground, as he flew an X-15 at a test facility. He made an unplanned trip in the aircraft with just a protective bubble on his head, without the full protective suit, thereby leaving the rest of his body exposed. Somehow, he was accidentally ejected and much of his body was badly injured and much of his skin stripped away. He was lucky to survive. His new job with TAW, was to test how realistically the simulator approached actual conditions, a much safer task.

We had urged LINK officials not to use a "new computer", mainly because it takes a while to work out bugs in a new system. We recommended the Control Data Corporation (CDC) computer, a respected firm with an established record of success. I suspect that because of some prior business relationship, LINK president Lloyd Kelly didn't take our advice. He chose not to go with CDC.

LINK contracted Computer Control Company (3C)–with its new computer–to control the LEM simulator. We had 3C ship a prototype of its computer to our office, in Teaneck, New Jersey, so we could test the computer programs. We used techniques to ensure that our programs were functioning properly, and we were confident that they would continue to do so when they were linked with 3C's computers at the testing site in Cape Canaveral, Florida. However, they did not.

We knew our programs hadn't caused the malfunctions that were occurring during the test, runs. 3C officials swore that their computer was not the problem. They were blaming us and we were blaming them. Fistfights erupted between the hardware and software personnel. Amidst the strife, I met with the head of 3C's company in his Massachusetts office. I said to him, "You know that your machine is not working and our computer programs are working". Why do you keep accusing our work of being the problem?" He said, "I thought I would accuse you, you would accuse me, and the customer would not know who to believe. It didn't occur to me that no one would believe you or your company because you're a Negro. I did what I had to do to save my company." Bottom line? Lloyd Kelly sided with 3C.

After that meeting, LINK's chief scientist couldn't look me in the eye, and the other LINK people, who had worked with us, couldn't understand why Kelly made the decision. That's when I realized that even people who are not prejudiced will resort to biased tactics if it's to their advantage. Still, I'm quite proud of the role Computronics employees played during the early phase of our country's historic venture to the moon. We wrote the programs for the LEM simulator that was used to train the astronauts for their journey from lunar orbit to the surface of the moon. I was disappointed and saddened when we did not get to write the programs for the Command Module simulator, though it had been promised to us.

I don't believe Kelly was an engineer, and he didn't impress me as a computer-savvy administrator. Discarding the advice of his chief scientist, Kelly used a hybrid computer–an analog system using digital techniques–to activate controls in the Command Module simulator.One can interchange "hardware" and "software". As a "hardware" company, 3C, tended to use more "hardware" rather than "software" in its simulator design. As the respective names imply, the "hardware" is more bulky and more difficult to change than the "software" as a simulation usually requires. When it was completed, many of the engineers working on the project, nick named the Command Module simulator "The Train Wreck". The nick name followed when it was eventually displayed at the Smithsonian. The LEM simulator was controlled by a single digital computer, of a single file cabinet size, which was neatly attached to the simulator. The computer controlled all the gauges inside the simulator, such as altitude, pressure, speed, and so on.

Both simulators were displayed in the Smithsonian in the 1980s, but the Command Module simulator has been moved to the Smithsonian's storage facility in Suitland, Maryland. The difference between the two simulators is striking. Had Kelly allowed us to fulfill the contract as promised, the Command Module simulator would not have resembled an unfinished jigsaw puzzle, a "train wreck" as many called it. Perhaps not wanting to explain the reason the LEM simulator was technically superior to the Command Module simulator, Kelly wasn't truthful in his description of the sequence in which the two simulators were completed. In his memoirs, he said that after the Command Module simulator was completed, Link turned its attention to the LEM simulator. I believe that any rational person looking at the evidence of the date's would come to the conclusion that this is a blatant lie.

Our company completed its work with the LEM simulator before 3C began its work with the Command Module simulators. Why did he lie? I believe, he lied because he didn't want to explain why he chose not to hire my company, Computronics, which already had demonstrated the most efficient use of advanced technology in its work on the LEM simulator. We would have done the same with the Command Module simulator. Kelly wanted to show improvement from the Command Module simulator to the LEM simulator, but that wouldn't be possible if the public knew that LEM had been completed first. He didn't want to respond to the obvious question, which would have been, "If you already have benefited from the advanced technology used in the LEM simulator, why go backwards?" Or, "If you have a car, why go back to a horse-and-buggy?"

The Cape Canaveral experience was the culmination of a series of racial incidents during my involvement with the space program that caused me pause, and made me wonder if blacks would ever be accepted as equals at all levels of mainstream America. Senseless harassment of our employees had been a nagging issue throughout our work with the space program. Once, we had a dozen programmers working on the LEM simulator at McDonald Douglas in St. Louis. Two of them were black. The hotel manager phoned me and said, "Mr. Wood, I'm doing you a favor by letting your Negras (a variation of "Negroes" with a southern accent) stay in our hotel."(I am sure that it was beyond his imagination, that the person he was talking to was a Negra-smile.)A few weeks later, Arnie sent a black woman programmer to St. Louis.

One of our white male employees picked her up at the airport. That prompted a second call from the hotel manager. He said, "I thought I was doing you a favor by letting your Negras stay in my hotel, but miscegenation is something we cannot stand." Our entire crew was thrown out of the hotel. That same crew left St. Louis and worked on the programs at Cape Canaveral, where the fistfights occurred.

The 1963 March on Washington, D.C., where Rev. Martin Luther King Jr. delivered his landmark "I have a dream speech" provided the camaraderie and inspiration I needed to counter the impulses that the Apollo experience had stirred within me. I found some comfort knowing that the 250,000 mostly black people who had gathered at the Lincoln Memorial that August 23rd shared my pain during those troubling times in a racially divided America. I wanted to bring my family with me to the March, however I felt that there would be violence by those who opposed the March, and I went alone. I was wrong the March was peaceful.

On the flight from New York to Washington, I met Basil Paterson, who became a New York State Senator in 1966 and one of four black men who controlled Harlem politics in the 1950s and 1960s. Former New York mayor David Dinkins, Congressman Charlie Rangel, and former Manhattan Borough president Percy Sutton were the other three.

I was moved emotionally by gospel singer Mahalia Jackson's rendition of I've Been Buked, and I've Been Scorned. Her powerful voice seemed in harmony with my inner thoughts, brought us to our feet, and tears to many eyes, including mine. In describing Mahalia's impact on most blacks in the audience, Lerone Bennett, Ebony magazine's editor, wrote, "There is a nerve that lies beneath the smoothest of black exteriors, a nerve 300-years old, throbbing with hurt and indignation. Mahalia Jackson penetrated the façade and exposed the nerve to public view . . . the button-downed men in front and the old women in the back came to their feet screaming and shouting. They had not known that this thing was in them and that they wanted it touched. From different places, in different ways, with different dreams, they had come and now hearing this song, they were one."

Organized by A. Philip Randolph, leader of the Brotherhood of Sleeping Car Porters, the event became the platform for Dr. King's message of hope. As Dr. King was about to end his speech, some reports say Mahalia Jackson, who stood nearby, urged him to share his dream, which he ad-libbed. Dr. King's "dream" speech is considered one of history's most galvanizing and important speeches. From ground level, I stood on the first step on the left side of the Lincoln Memorial by an evergreen, facing the front. I was a little taller than everyone around me, so I had a very good view of Dr. King, who was about fifty feet away, half the length of a basketball court. I listened in awe, as Dr. King shared his vision of an America free of racism. My kids used to call me stone-faced because the dad they knew rarely showed emotion. They should have seen me that day.

As I watched Dr. King deliver his speech, I was reminded that in 1954 his presence had made our family gathering for a December wedding one of the most memorable yuletide seasons I ever had as an adult. Nine years later, I stood before an older version of that young pastor, his persona magnified by his aura of greatness. I was profoundly moved and proud to be a part of an important moment in American history.

I also remember seeing Henry Green Parks Jr., of H.G. Parks, Inc.. He took his company (after Decisions Systems "over the counter offering") to become the first black corporation to be listed on the New York Stock Exchange. At the time, Parks was one of the nation's most successful black entrepreneurs, I didn't really know him. With only two helpers, Parks started his company in Baltimore, Maryland, and turned it into a multimillion-dollar business with three hundred employees, a processing plant, and annual sales of fourteen million dollars.

Buoyed, by the March, I returned to work eager to start anew. Despite the setback in Computronics' space venture, I wasn't ready to raise a white flag. I saw great potential in our computer firm, as did others. I recalled an earlier proposal, made by Bill Paley, the legendary CBS founder, that promised to make us rich. Paley dabbled in the analog computer business in the 1960s, while he turned CBS, then a small, radio network, into one of the most powerful radio and television networks in history. Paley's advisor told me that he wanted to provide Computronics with an unlimited amount of money, whatever we could justify, with one catch: he wanted 80 percent of the company.

With hindsight, providing us with all the money we would need, I'm sure Paley also would have opened doors to us that I wouldn't have been allowed to enter without him as an escort. I believe my partners and I would have become instant millionaires had I accepted Paley's terms. The downside? It would have been like going to work again for ITT, and I just didn't want to "hoe that row" again.

I was encouraged when I learned that Computer Sciences, cofounded by Roy Nutt and Fletcher Jones, Roy one of Shelton's and Arnie's friends from MIT, recently had become the first computer firm to trade company stock to the public on Wall Street. Despite the troubling setbacks, I believed Computronics would be next.

CHAPTER 10

*"My philosophy is don't complain,
Don't explain, and above all, don't whine.
You can't be a leader, if you whine"*

TOM WOOD

*"Discrimination has a lot of layers that make it tough for
minorities to get a leg up"*

BILL GATES

As Computronics' CEO, the search for new business was my front-burner priority. But thanks to Computer Sciences' successful venture onto Wall Street, securing funds that would allow us to make a similar move loomed as an achievable goal. A breakthrough in my hunt for a reputable investment banker came in a return phone call from Shields & Company, requesting I return for a second interview.

As I shook hands with the three interviewers, I realized that one of them had been my seatmate on a recent flight from California to New York. I don't recall his name, but during that flight we talked about business, our families, and life in general, but I did not try to sell him on anything. Our conversation was cordial, mainly social. I believe I must have impressed him, and I've always suspected that his input into Shield's decision regarding Computronics was favorable.

As the three representatives and I were returning to Shields' office from one of our lunch time meetings, I recognized a long time school friend named Teddy standing in the shadows at 40 Wall Street. He was obviously high or intoxicated and obviously panhandling. He stared at me and I'm sure he recognized me. First, I wondered, "Should I stop?" Then I said to myself, "I can't walk by this guy, he's a childhood friend." I excused myself from the group and said hello to Teddy. We talked for a bit, then I returned to the Shields' group. By that time in my life, I'd had my share of setbacks, but, I'd also been lucky. I turned and looked back at Teddy and said to myself, "There but for the Grace of God go I." I've often wondered if that brief encounter with that childhood friend helped persuade Shields to roll the dice with Computronics.

Ultimately, the final decision to grant us the 1.7 million-dollar offering—a lot of money back then—was made by Cornelius Shields, a prominent yachtsman from Larchmont, New York, who was then in his 80s. The offering was guaranteed, which meant that Shields' firm would pay our company and all the people who were selling the stock whether the stock was able to be sold to the public or not. That's why you want a reputable company as your underwriter. I'm sure he knew the obstacles that our black-run firm would encounter in this stock sale. Apparently, he took steps to counter a possible racial backlash. Shields made his decision less than a year after Martin Luther King Jr. delivered his "I have a dream" speech. I think he just felt that the time was right to do the deal. Here's why I say that.

Normally, if you're trying to market something, you want the person who knows the company and the company's product to talk to the people charged with selling the company's product. It's like selling cars. You have the person who knows all about the car, talk to the salespeople. He's the one who can best explain to the salespeople the points of the car to emphasize and the points to avoid. Accordingly, Computronics' president normally woiuld have met with, and talked to, the salespeople, but Shields didn't ask Computronics black CEO to do that. He must have known the risk of revealing that the president of the company selling its shares was a black man, and decided not to take that kind of risk.

I can not be absolutely certain of this, because these kind of records are not, and were not kept by race. I believe with a significant amount of certainty that when "I took Decision Systems "public", it was the first time a company with predominately black ownership placed it shares on a American organized stock market.

The company's name, Computronics, had worked for us just fine for four years. However, when Shields learned that the National Cash Register Company (NCRC) already had trademarked the name "Computronics" in six states, we knew the company's name had to be changed. Our investment bankers wanted us free to sell its shares in all fifty states.

Hence, in 1964, Decision Systems was born. I came up with the name because I thought that it described more accurately what we were about. Our programs were making decisions that were fast enough to make changes in the way machines operated.

Of all the cliffhangers or near disasters I experienced up to that point this one topped them all. The problem involved two troublesome Computronics stockholders, one I knew quite well.

Beauregard Stubblefield was never a close friend, but we had socialized over the years on several occasions when I lived in Detroit. Still, I was hurt deeply when he publicly questioned my integrity, as we transitioned from Computronics to Decisions Systems. The other stockholder, whose name I don't remember, sent me on a frantic day-long scramble with stops at a home in Manhattan, to a Wall Street post office, and, finally, to Shields' New Jersey office, armed with a certificate that was needed to close the deal.

Stubblefield was among a large group of Detroit blacks who invested in Computronics' stock when the company was formed. My partners and other business associates assumed that most of my financially successful Harlem friends and associates had helped launch Computronics. Not so. A tight-knit group of Detroit blacks, who either worked with me, knew me as an adult, knew me as a successful businessman, or as a friend, were my early investors.

Stubblefield, a PhD from the University of Michigan, in mathematics, was an interesting fellow. He worked for me at the Detroit Tank Arsenal, and I brought him along with me when I took the job with ITT. I stayed with his relatives in Dallas when I attended the national simulation and computer conference at the Shamrock Hotel in Texas. Stubblefield then worked for me later at Computronics, he and his wife lived around the corner from us in Teaneck, New Jersey. But we really weren't close friends. Stubblefield bought five thousand shares of Computronics stock when it sold for two dollars a share. Our relationship became complicated after he saw me in my office huddled with Shields & Company underwriters. He wanted to know what was going on.

I told him that rules governing this type of transaction prohibited me from discussing it with him. Anyone who violates the rules might be charged with insider trading, which occurs when a stock trade is influenced by the "privileged possession of corporate information that has not yet been made public." One of the more publicized cases of insider trading involved Martha Stewart, a well-known entrepreneur and businesswoman. In 2003, Stewart was arrested and later convicted of insider trading for using information that she had received, that was not public information. She served five months in prison, five months in house arrest, and two years on probation.

Stubblefield persisted, saying, "I'm your friend, you can tell me," but I refused, remembering how I'd been burned in the past by a friend, who also said, "You can tell me," and so on. I didn't want to be accused of insider trading and land in jail. Stubblefield went to Detroit, called a meeting of Computronics' other Detroit shareholders, and said to them, "Tom is cheating us."

When I discovered what he had done, I flew to Detroit to talk to the shareholders. Stubblefield wasn't there, but his lawyer did attend the meeting. Stubblefield must have been afraid to face me. After I talked to the shareholders, they all agreed to stay with me. Then Stubblefield met with the underwriters and told them I was cheating him. The underwriters agreed to sell a portion of his shares in the public offering, and he received one hundred thousand dollars out of the public offering. Stubblefield sold some of the Computronics shares that he initially paid ten thousand dollars for all of the shares. I just couldn't understand why he did it. Distraught by his actions, I remember at one point, I cried. That's something I hadn't done for quite a while.

The other troublesome shareholder also had worked for me at ITT. I didn't really know him, and we didn't hire him at Computronics. One day, he told me that he had run into some financial difficulties and wanted to sell his shares. I told him that was fine, but he must get that certificate to me by a certain date. If he stated in the prospectus that he plans to sell, he must sell by that date; he can't change his mind. He swore that he would get it to me in time. That was the last time I took someone's word for something of that importance.

During the next few weeks, he was traveling, and I was traveling, and neither of us contacted the other. The week before the offering was scheduled to take place, still no certificate. Finally, I reached him by phone and he said, "I changed my mind, I don't want to sell." I guess he figured that the company stock was going to take off like a rocket. I said, "You can't do this, you have to sell!" He said his mother had the shares and she's the one who's making the decisions. Two days before the offering, Charlie Jaffin, my lawyer, and I visited the mother at her New York apartment. We talked to her for maybe two hours. She finally agreed to give us the certificate but said her son had it. I told her we must deliver it to the underwriters in two days. She called her son and he promised to send it to her by overnight mail.

The day of the offering, we arrived at the mother's house in the early morning, still hoping that I would have the certificate and be at the underwriters' office in New Jersey by 10 a.m. That's when we had promised to deliver the certificate, so the selling shareholders and Computronics would receive our checks. I'm not usually a person given to emotion, but when his mother opened the door and said she didn't have it, she sensed my anger. She said, "I told my son to send it by overnight letter, but it's not here." We raced down to the Wall Street Post Office, which is a huge cavernous place. Why I thought someone would give me the letter, I'll never know. I saw a black postal worker and told him my story. I figured he might be familiar with the importance of some of the Wall Street transactions. I told him the underwriters were at that moment sitting in their New Jersey office, waiting for this letter to complete a major transaction. The postal worker sees a black guy, who says he's the company's president, accompanied by a white guy, who says he's the company's vice president, something I'm sure he doesn't see every day. He decided to help.

The postal worker goes through all the mail but doesn't find the letter. Then he said, "Let me check one other place." He goes to a room where the mail is stored before it's sent back to the sender due to a wrong address. He found the letter. I could not believe it; the son had put the wrong address on a letter sent to his mother!

Two hours after the closing time the underwriters are still waiting. Then the postal worker said, "I can't give the letter to you because it's not addressed to you." I called the mother at work; she takes a taxi over, , and then says, "Before I give you the letter I want you to give me money for the taxi driver." I laughed in disbelief, and quickly gave her the money. We were more than four hours late, but the underwriters were still sitting there, waiting. Finally, I relaxed and breathed easier, grateful to have survived another nerve-racking cliffhanger.

Almost immediately, after going public, the company's shares jumped from nine dollars and fifty cents into the 30-dollar to 40-dollar range. As I recall the numbers, and these are approximations, one million dollars of the stock went to Computronics, and each of the partners received one hundred thousand dollars, which was a lot of money in 1964.

The desire to excel using our creative skills often kept our programmers in the office into the wee hours of many nights in search of a better mousetrap and prompted me to place a few more phone calls and take a few more business trips in search of our next contract. After losing the Apollo Space program job, I had trouble landing the more lucrative contracts. Then an opportunity arose. Job Corps, a U.S. government plan that offered young people, ages sixteen to twenty-four, access to the workforce through a vocational and education training program, was introduced. The program was launched in 1964 during the start of President Lyndon Johnson's administration. Johnson appointed Sargent Shriver as director of the U.S. Department of Labor program.

The Job Corps center contracts were awarded to companies in partnership with colleges/universities. It took me a year and a half to convince officials at Howard University, an Historically Black College/University (HBCU), located in Washington, D.C., to join us in partnership to seek a ten million-dollar contract to operate a Job Corps center.

With Howard University as our partner, we spent more than a year negotiating with Job Corps to teach computer programming to students in the inner cities. The Job Corps project was something I really wanted on a personal level, not just as a business success. We were pursuing it during the Civil Rights era, and I knew the opportunity would be especially beneficial to promising young blacks and other underserved communities. I thought the timing was right. I hired Ed Richardson, who had worked with me at the Detroit Tank Arsenal, and was then working in the computer division of RCA, to write the proposal. Ed was a much-valued mentor during my first few years at the Arsenal, especially regarding administrative rules and organizational processes. When he saw me stumbling about, he'd said, "Here kid, do this, don't do that." Ed touched all the bases in our proposal regarding the Job Corps project. I thought we were well-qualified and well-suited, a sure thing for the contract. But we didn't get it.

The administrator of the program in that area said to me, "I'm not giving you a contract." He said the contracts were earmarked for the major companies, such as AT&T, General Electric, and others. Political reasons, I suspect. That's another thing that disillusioned me and helped me realize that no matter how good we might be, we weren't going to get an opportunity to participate in some ventures. Losing the Job Corps contract was especially troubling to me because our proposal was designed to teach inner city kids how to write programs for computers in the 1960s. That was revolutionary for that time period. If we had succeeded, I'm sure a larger percentage of blacks would have found jobs in the computer industry.

During this time, I received another piece of "bad news". Al Liebowitz, the "over the counter" trader who "made the market" in our stock, called to let me know that our stock was in decline. "He made the market" is a Wall Street term which means Al bought stock when someone wanted to sell and sold when someone wanted to buy. He was a middle man. Al told me, "There's a rumor on the Street that's driving your stock down."

I said, "Tell me what the rumor is, and I'll see what I can do."

He said, "The rumor is the president of the company is a Negro and that's what is driving the stock down."

I said, "Well, that's true."

There was nothing I could do about it, except hope that the downward spiral soon would end. I wanted to believe that investors would conclude that if they gave us a chance, they would be rewarded in the long run. We were a reputable firm with super-talented programmers. Investors surely would see that. Then again, maybe they wouldn't. I wondered if I was destined to find and travel a different career path. The history of racism in America was then–and still is–an on going reality.

There was one investor in Decision Systems who's loss I did not find out until much later. His loss was a suprise to me, as I did not know that he was an investor. That investor was my twelve year old "God Son" Gregory Florant, who used his accumulated savings to buy shares in Decision Systems.

This was his introduction to the "ups and downs" of Wall Street which sometimes are based on non-financial factors.

Some of the most insidious examples of bias I encountered as a CEO were perpetrated by a few white colleagues who hid their bias behind hypocritical smiles. Fletcher Jones was such a person. Fletcher was a west Texan. Roy Nutt, his partner and Arnie and Sheldon (two of my partners) had worked together at MIT. Fletcher and his partner, Roy, formed Computer Sciences, which was based in California. It was the first computer programing company to sell its shares to the public through the stock market. Roy was the inside guy for their company; Fletcher was the salesperson and a frequent traveler for his firm, as I was for mine.

My partners and I once traveled to California on a courtesy visit to chat with Fletcher and the Computer Science staff, but Fletcher wasn't there. He knew we were coming. Why would he take a pass on saying hello to his longtime friends? I didn't read too much into it at the time. Later, it all came together. A contract administrator that I worked with at a California company, told me that Fletcher had been "trash talking" against me.

"Fletcher Jones was in here last week telling us whatever you do, don't give your business to the nigger," the contract administrator said. I assumed he had volunteered the same advice to others many times, and that he might have been the source of the "rumors" that caused our company's stock to decline. I never told my partners what the contractor had said. Fletcher, Roy Nutt, and Sheldon, and Arnie were very close friends.

The Apollo fiasco, combined with the Job Corps rejection, rattled my self-confidence. As a leader, I faced a dilemma. If you're an offensive lineman in football and you can't handle your defensive opponent, you're not going to go back to the huddle and tell the quarterback, "Don't direct any plays to my side because my opponent is kicking my butt!" If you do that, the quarterback loses confidence in you. If you're the quarterback and you say to your teammates, "I can't throw a 30-yard sideline pass," your team mates will lose confidence in you. As CEO, I wasn't going to burden my employees with an unsolvable problem.

I began to wonder if being the "black" boss of any company was worth pursuing. The obstacles were great; the resistance, cunning and tenacious. The LEM/Command Module APOLLO fiasco happened because I was black. Excellence just wasn't enough. Some companies were willing to give us a chance, but those who didn't give us a chance, controlled a sizable chunk of the computer business.

One must not forget that in 1960, when my partners and I left ITT to form COMPUTRONICS, the United States was legally segregated by race in the southern states, and "de facto segregation existed in most of the remaining parts of the U.S., including New York City where I was born, as well as New Jersey where ITT was located.

In 1959, a young black engineer left the Midwest, and moved to New Jersey with his family. He decided to buy a home in Teaneck, primarily for its proximity to his new employer, and very importantly, Teaneck's excellent school system. Within two weeks of moving into his home, one or more of his "Good, Mannered, Respectable, Law Abiding neighbors", painted "nigger" on his garage door. For blacks, this was not an isolated occurrence.

That young black engineer, was me!

This scenario or a facsimile thereof has taken place too often and in too many communities in the non legally segregated northen United States.

In 1996 I had a similar experience, when I moved to Florida. I bought a house in a upscale, gated, ocean front community. Just as in New Jersey, one or more of the "Good, Mannered, Respectable, Law Abiding" neighbors staged a reenactment of what happened there. This time it took the form of a "Huge Rotting Dead Fish" on my doorstep.

It took the "March on Washington" for jobs and freedom in 1963, and other significant events to begin to end segregation. The March moved the U.S. Congress to pass the Civil Rights Act of 1964, that outlawed discrimination based on Race, Color, Sex, or National Origin. The "March" where

Martin Luther King standing in front of the Lincoln Memorial gave his historic "I have a dream" speech to an estimated 300, 000 people, of which 75% were black.President Kennedy proposed Civil Rights Legislation in 1963, it was opposed by a filibuster in the Senate by Senator Strom Thurman.After Kennedy was assassinated, President Lyndon Johnson pushed the bill through Congress, and signed the bill on July 2 1964.

The problem that legal and sometimes "de facto" segregation posed for me, as the sales arm of the company, "the rain maker", was that I could not legally operate in the American south. Also because of "de facto" segregation in parts of the north, I faced prejudice in pursuing business, taking customers to lunch, staying in hotels, and something one from the north does not usually think about, transportation, taxi's, etc.

And interesting aside; I was able to obtain a contract with the Pentagon in Arlington, Virginia.The Computronics staff that worked under the contract in the Pentagon were white, and could fuction in that environment.I on the other hand, had to stay in hotels in Washington, D.C. and could not entertain my client in Virginia.

A large portion of the computer business originated in Texas at the Manned Space Center (which was legally segregated). There I could not function at all.

The racial problems that I encountered, with few, and one notable exception(Fletcher Jones of Computer Sciences), came from customers and potential public shareholders, not from members within the computer industry. Almost everyone I encountered within the computer community was supportive, but competitive as necessary.

You don't always know why a stock declines, but I knew why ours did. I didn't blame myself, and I didn't complain or whine. You can't be a leader if you whine.

I began slowly to move away from Decision Systems emotionally and later, physically.

Other segments of the business community welcomed me warmly. As a black CEO, I was a rarity in that world, and one of a kind as head of a computer firm. Luckily, a business organization that was formed to help young white executives to connect and learn from each other had opened its doors to people of color. I accepted an invitation to join.

*"There is not an American in this country free,
Until every one of us is free"*

JACKIE ROBERTSON

CHAPTER 11

"Don't worry when you are not recognized, but strive to be worthy of recognition"

Abraham Lincoln

This bit of good fortune came my way as I neared a birthday milestone. Shortly before I turned forty, the Young Presidents' Organization (YPO) invited me to join the then-budding group of young white executives. The honor materialized as I wondered whether I should remain on the career path I had chosen. My involvement with YPO became a useful distraction from my duties as a CEO, but also provided tips on how to be a more effective young leader of a midsize firm.

I joined the organization in the mid-1960s, when the age limit for membership was forty, and the organization had about two thousand nationwide members. The other eligibility requirement was that each member headed a company with net worth of three million dollars. By 2010, the net worth assets requirement had risen to ten million dollars and the age limit was forty-five. YPO is now a global network of twenty thousand young bosses in more than one hundred countries. Its founding mission: Better Leaders through Education and Idea Exchange.

YPO was founded in 1950 by Raymond Hickok, who was twenty-seven when he became head of the Hickok Manufacturing Company of Rochester, New York. He replaced his father, S. Rae Hickok, who died of a heart attack in 1945. The family's three hundred-employee company special-ized in making belts, jewelry, cuff links, wallets, and other men's accessories. In his first few years on the job, Hickok struggled because he didn't have anyone to provide feedback on being the man-in-charge. He began attend-ing meetings in the Rochester area with other young executives who were in the same predicament. Through those brainstorming sessions, he sensed the need for an organization that would help young bosses deal effectively with the problems of running a major corporation by sharing their experiences. Hickok launched another successful marketing ploy also in 1950—the S. Rae Hickok Professional Athlete of the Year Award.

The Hickok Belt, which became a major event in sporting news, was presented each year (from 1950-1976) to the pro sports world's athlete of the year. The trophy was an alligator-skin belt with a solid gold buckle, an encrusted 4 carat (800 mg) diamond and twenty-six gem chips and valued at more than ten thousand dollars. Rocky Marciano, Sandy Koufax, Mohammad Ali, Willie Mays, and Jim Brown were among the recipients. (Wikipedia).

Once a year, YPO hosted what it called a University for Presidents conference for which they invited prominent government leaders, such as the U.S. Secretary of State and Secretary of the Treasury, as well as the heads of Fortune 500 companies, as guest speakers/lecturers. Several other major meetings were held throughout the year in various major cities. Occasionally, guest speakers included scholars in various fields, but mainly they were busi-ness types.

Corporate heads generally are workaholics with A-type personalities. They frequently neglect their wives and families by spending late nights at the office and often weeks on road trips, always in search of more funds or better deals. Hickok structured YPO guest speaker/lecturer activities into more of social events by including the wives in all events, instead of having the men gather for business functions, while the women spent the day taking tours, the YPO included the wives in all events including business, and social activities. There were parties every night. I had never been in an organization that held such elaborate affairs. Formal dancing, costume parties, and other upscale activities were included on the agendas in Las Vegas, New York, and San Francisco.

The history behind how I became the YPO's first member of color–which was told to me much later–somewhat diminished the joy I felt when I was selected. Turns out, I was chosen under duress. In the story that I was told, YPO brought in a black professor from Case Western University in Cleveland as the guest speaker at one of its functions. However, the professor was excluded from almost all social activities. Father Theodore Hesburgh, a YPO member and President of Notre Dame for thirty-five years (1952-1987), learned of the exclusion of the black professor from social functions and that YPO had no black members. Hesburgh gave YPO's leadership an ultimatum: "Get some black people in here or else I will expose you." They went looking.

Barry Gordy, founder of Motown, which was based in Detroit, and I were the nominees considered for membership, mainly because we were the only black heads of companies that met YPO's requirements. Two YPO committee members came to my house in Teaneck, New Jersey, I surmised, to make sure "I could eat with a knife and fork". Well, I guess it's normal to interview a prospective member to determine if he would fit in. I don't know if Gordy was interviewed. I believe Earl Graves, founder of Black Enterprise magazine, and Faye Wattleton, who in 1978 was named the first black president of the Planned Parenthood Federation of America, eventually became YPO members years later.

I was introduced as a new member of YPO in the 1960s at a meeting of the New York chapter. No formal speech was required, just an informal chat about my family and business. The national organization also sponsored "University of Presidents," annual events that lasted for a week and included intense sessions for the men and extracurricular activities that included the wives. The first University of Presidents conference that Barbara and I attended was held in Phoenix, Arizona, and there was a stir. Evidently, they were expecting a darker-skinned black, because they couldn't find me. I guess I didn't stand out in the crowd. I heard someone say, "I'm glad they got a light-skinned one."

Since we weren't aware of seating arrangements, Barbara and I stood near the entrance, until someone from the New York delegation caught my eye and beckoned us to their table. The New York group welcomed us warmly and made us feel at ease. However, Howard "Bo" Callaway, a Georgia politician and U.S. Secretary of the Army under President Nixon, approached me and said, "You know, we don't have any problem with you, but we don't want those New York Jews shoving Negras down our throats." That turned me off, but that was Bo Callaway, a southern eminent upstanding citizen, whose family owned Callaway Gardens in Pine Mountain, Georgia.

Though it was designed to help our nation's young presidents, I believe that business leaders of any age and from any country would profit by attending YPO's roundtable business sessions for a few years. Its mission is to educate through an exchange of ideas, and from my perspective, its mission was accomplished. Indeed, many of the members of my era were among the wealthiest and most respected business leaders in the world. Of course, we had our share of controversial and shady characters, as well. YPO members in the New York chapter of my era included:

*Steve Ross – A Brooklyn, New York native, Steve began his business career in the mid-1950s while working for his father-in-law, Edward Rosenthal, director of Riverside Memorial Chapel, then the nation's largest funeral company. Steve soon became the president of Kinney and moved the firm from downtown New York to Midtown at Rockefeller Plaza. He expanded into the world of entertainment, purchasing Warner-Seven Arts film studio and record business in 1966. In 1972, Steve was appointed CEO, president, and chairman of Warner Communications. With Steve at the helm, Warner Communications later merged with Time, Inc., in a fourteen billion-dollar deal, which then created the world's largest media and entertainment company. Ross became a TAW stockholder.

*Roy M. Goodman – Roy was the grandson of Israel Matz, the founder of Ex-Lax company, and leader of the liberal Rockefeller wing of the Republican Party. He was the person who beckoned Barbara and me to sit at his table during our first YPO meeting. Roy was a member of the New York State Senate for thirty-three years (1969-2002) and served several terms as Chairman of the Senate Committee on Investigations, Taxation and Government Operations. A Harvard alumnus with a Bachelor of Arts degree (1951) and master's in business administration (1953), Roy became president of the United Nations Development Corporation in 2002.

* Bernard "Bernie" Cornfeld – Many 0f the U.S. soldiers were stationed in Europe after World War II and Bernie, also a World War II veteran, used his salesman's charm to convince many of them to buy securities in Investors Overseas Services (IOS), his mutual funds company, based in Geneva, Switzerland. Bernie was a stutterer and didn't relate well to large groups, but with smaller groups of five, ten, fifteen people he was mesmerizing. In 1962, IOS launched its "Fund of Funds," which meant investing in shares of other mutual funds, and the stock took off. Bernie earned more than twenty million dollars in the first few years. Bernie's favorite sales pitch, "Do you sincerely want to be rich?" became a by word for his success. Bernie's company raised more than 2.5 billion dollars in ten years, earning him more than one hundred million dollars.

* Eli Black – Eli was a Polish-born immigrant who began his investment banking career with Lehman Brothers and soon after worked as a finance officer for the American Seal-Kap Company, which made caps for milk bottles. Eli renamed the company AMK Corp., after its ticker symbol. He was thirty-three when he became Chairman and CEO of AMK in 1954. By 1967, Eli's company was ranked among the top 500 companies in America.

* William "Bill" Damroth – Bill joined his mentor, John Templeton of the Templeton Foundation, to form the Nucleonics, Chemistry and Electronics Fund in 1956. Templeton, who was considered one of the world's greatest investors, became a billionaire as a pioneer of globally diversified

mutual funds. Besides being fellow Stuyvesant High alums, Bill and I had much in common. We lived in adjoining New Jersey towns; he in Englewood, and I in Teaneck. Bill became interested in Africa. He passed the hat at a YPO meeting and collected one hundred thousand dollars from ten YPO members, including Time Warner founder Steve Ross. Bill also joined Decision Systems' Board of Directors, and by doing so, he demonstrated the value of Raymond Hickok's vision of young executives helping each other by sharing their experiences.

*Tom Bata – Tom controlled the Bata family's worldwide shoe organization during the second half of the 20th century. After moving his family from Czechoslovakia to Canada in 1938 to escape the growing Nazi threat, Tom created the Bata Shoe Organization of Canada. Tom Bata once told an interesting story of how his company entered the shoe manufacturing business in Africa. The international shoe industry became curious about establishing businesses in Africa about the same time as I did. Each sent representatives to Africa to assess the market. All save the Bata reps came away saying, "No one is wearing shoes... it's a lousy business." The Bata reps came away saying, "No one is wearing shoes . . . it's a great business!" They started by offering flip-flops, then added dress shoes and became immensely successful.

As a YPO member, I attended a YPO national meeting in Washington D.C. At that meeting I had an opportunity to meet, shake hands, and chat very briefly with Robert Kennedy. Robert Kennedy was an icon of American liberalism. By coincidence we were approximately the same age, and we both joined the Navy's V-12 program during World War II, he at Harvard, and I at Columbia. Our paths did cross again from a distance.

Robert Kennedy lived while in New York in the apartments above my office at 866 United Nations Plaza. I on occasion would see Robert Kennedy in his top down convertible car pass under my window.

Robert Kennedy in 1963 made, what looked at the time, an unsuccessful attempt to improve race relations in the U.S.

He organized a meeting with the novelist James Baldwin of "The Fire Next Time" fame, and others prominent in the black community. The meeting quickly developed into bitter conflict. The meeting illustrated to Robert Kennedy the depth of black feelings about the U.S. racial situation. I believe that the meeting became a positive turning point in Robert Kennedy's attitude about the civil rights movement. I believe the meeting also changed Kennedy's idea's about the "wait your turn" theory which some Americans had expoused. The exchange between Baldwin's brother David, and Robert Kennedy went as follows ; Robert Kennedy said "I'm Irish, my family 's only been here for two generations, and now my brother is President". To which Baldwin replied "we have been here for five generations, and there is nothing to show for it". I and a great many others believe this exchange eventually produced a positive change in prospectus about race issues in Robert Kennedy.

CHAPTER 12

"Success is to be measured not so much by the position that one has reached in life, as by the obstacles which he has overcome while trying to succeed"

BOOKER T. WASHINGTON

"Showing Up is 80 percent of life" is an adage attributed to actor/director Woody Allen, but some say it's a variation of a phrase that might have been borrowed from a pioneer movie mogul or a great thinker of an ancient era. Actor Marshall Brickman delivered the quote in Allen's movie, Annie Hall. Brickman and Allen wrote the Oscar-winning script, and the 1977 film also won Oscars for Best Picture, Best Director (Allen), and Best Actress (Diane Keaton).

During my career as a black entrepreneur–a rarity in the white business world in my day–a variation of the "Showing up" phrase became a part of my DNA. As I said earlier, whenever someone waved a dollar in the air, I was there. I believed it would be mine because I showed up to collect it. I would travel thousands of miles to gain the ear of any investor/banker/customer who'd hear my pitch.

Moreover, my status as CEO of Decisions Systems, our New Jersey-based computer firm, enhanced my profile considerably. During that time, blacks from various walks of life came to visit me, apparently believing I could help them do something similar or get something better. Bill Coleman,

Secretary of Transportation in the Ford administration, asked me to become a board member of the NAACP Legal Defense Fund, and I became a board member of the Urban League under Whitney Young. During that time, tennis star Arthur Ashe and I became members of the Sigma Pi Phi fraternity, the nation's oldest black Greek-letter organization. It also is called "The Boule." Notable members include W.E.B. Du Bois, an early Civil Rights leader, former Virginia Governor L. Douglas Wilder, and American Express CEO Kenneth Chenault. Ashe and I missed most meetings because of our careers. "The Boule" now has more than five thousand members in 126 chapters in the U.S. and the West Indies. The organization, founded in 1904, recognizes blacks who have made significant contributions to society.

I'd been anointed a bona fide success story and people tend to want to know you better when you've been dubbed "special." Some black people came by my office, apparently, just to gawk at me. Blacks weren't the only folk eager to take a closer look. Evidently, my name was added to several VIP-type mailing lists; and I began to receive invitations to high-powered business banquets and social events, one of which was signed by David Rockefeller, who was then chairman and CEO of the Chase Manhattan Corporation (1969-1980). David invited me to a luncheon at Chase's New York headquarters. I already had made plans to be in Africa.

I wasn't being capricious. I just didn't want to alter my travel. I figured there would be a lot of small talk, but nothing of significance would happen. Also, I knew that these luncheons usually served as window dressing, held only so organizers could report that several black businessmen were among the guests. But Bob Boyd, a longtime friend, then vice president of a Philadelphia bank, urged me to postpone my trip to Africa. "This is one luncheon that you'd better attend," Bob said.

Bob was among the few management-level blacks in the predominantly white world of business. He often informed other blacks about potential or actual management-level opportunities and would submit recommendations, if appropriate. Bob had heard that David Rockefeller's goal was to appoint a black person to the Chase Board of Directors. I changed my plans and accepted David's invitation.

David was the grandson of John D. Rockefeller Sr., cofounder of Standard Oil, and once controlled 90 percent of all oil in the United States. A world-renowned philanthropist, John, Sr. was the first American worth more than one billion dollars and became the world's richest man. Before his death in 1937, his fortune was estimated at 336 billion dollars. He was a small guy, a frail man, who paid others to fight for him during the Civil War. You could do that back then, if you had money. His philanthropic causes included the Rockefeller Foundation, which was created in 1913, and his financial gifts had a major impact on research programs in medicine, education, and science.

John Sr. spent the last forty years of his life in retirement at his estate, Kykuit, an enormous plot of property (1, 200 acres) in Pocantico Hills, New York. The New York skyline, only twenty-eight miles away, was visible from the estate. Each of his grandchildren, including David, had several acres and their own separate homes on their grandfather's estate, which included a nine-hole golf course, a movie theatre, numerous fountains and gardens, and a landing strip for the family's fleet of airplanes. Kykuit was the family's country club on steroids. David's siblings were: Abigail and John III (philanthropists), Laurance (venture capitalist), Winthrop (Arkansas governor), and Nelson (New York governor and U.S. Vice President under Gerald Ford). The Rockefeller estate, now an historic site of the National Trust for Historic Preservation, has been meticulously maintained for more than one hundred years.

I arrived at the Chase office at about 10 a.m., and spent a couple of hours in one of the big conference rooms, listening to bank officials elaborate on the intricacies of the banking business. Then David Rockefeller comes in and says, "Let's go to lunch." David was treated like royalty at any social gathering he attended. At political events, nothing happens until the President shows up. David exuded the same degree of gravitas. He was like a warm fireplace on a wintry night. Everyone, especially those on other boards, tried to get closer to him. Though he always had a bodyguard escort, there was an aura about him, even at board meetings.

I didn't know it at the time, but the Chase board meetings began with a luncheon. At lunch, the board members and I moved into this magnificent dining room where tables were adorned with sparkling silverware and exquisite china. I met C. Douglas Dillon, Secretary of the Treasury under President John F. Kennedy. Dillon was a member of General Motors Board of Directors. I also met and chatted with several other board members. I didn't engage in very much social talk, probably because most of the men were ten to fifteen years older. I was forty-four. The luncheon ended an hour or so later, then I left and went back to my office, which was on 49th Street and First Avenue.

About two hours later, David Rockefeller calls and says he would like to visit me in my office. When he offered me the position to be a Board Member of the Chase Mantattan Bank, I think my eyes might have sparkled and I felt even younger. David, who had a salary of a dollar a year, told me that all board members were required to purchase shares of Chase stock. He asked me if I needed help with that. I said, "No," but I probably should have said, "Yes."

Board members were expected to purchase one hundred shares, selling at that time at approximately eight hundred dollars per share. I bought ten shares. I've always tried to be fully black, both intellectually and personally, so I wanted to make sure David Rockefeller understood me as a person. I told David "I'm not a black leader. If that's what you're looking for, that's not me. I'm not someone who has a following or an audience. I'm just someone starting a business and I want to run that business. If that's the kind of person you're looking for, I will do the best I can."

He assured me that I was the man he wanted on the Chase Board of Directors. To prove it, he appointed me to several committees, including the

Executive Committee. He also nominated me to become a member of the Council On Foreign Relations.

Prior to my meeting with David Rockefeller I was aware that two publicly traded companies each had one black director, each of which I knew personally. They were Sam Pierce, my lawyer and long time friend, on the Board of U.S. Industries, as well as Asa Spaulding, of North Carolina Mutual Insurance Co., and my daughter Kay's uncle by marriage, on the Board of W.T.Grant.The appointment of Sam, and Asa to a U.S. corporate board was an historical event when it happened. However, when David Rockefeller appointed me to the Board of the Chase Manhattan Bank, one of the largest banks in the world, it started a movement, which continues today, to include blacks on major organization boards. Obviously this was not due to me personally, but it can be easily demonstrated that the trend, wave, occurred because of who made the appointment, not who was appointed. The stature of David Rockefeller in both the corporate world and in society made the appointment of black directors on corporate boards "not an outlier or anomaly". Today there are more than 100 blacks on various U.S. corporate boards.David Rockefeller's appointment of a black to his board of directors provided an example for other boards to follow, and they did. Very quickly General Motors, Prudential Insurance, CBS, ITT, and other organizations of similar statue followed, and as they say "the rest is history"

After joining the Chase Board, I received numerous offers to join additional Boards of Directors, almost all of them, I declined, due to the responsibility and time required of me as the "prime mover" of TAW.

Through my position as a Chase board member, I acquired access to a world of business I never knew. I began to see how things were done at the elite business level. For centuries in America, black people had been privy to conversations about business, politics and law—as slaves or servants—but we were invisible men and had no input in the decisions that were made. Finally, we began to have some input, some voice in the decision-making process, small though it was. At the time, I felt privileged to have been a pioneer with a semblance of power.

My association with David Rockefeller provided me more than a glimpse of the politics of the business world, as well as the lifestyles of the very rich and famous. David would host at least one board meeting annually at the family estate in Pocantico Hills, New York. I think David respected me for being down-to-earth and conservative in money and business matters. For example, I always took the subway to attend board meetings at Chase; most of the other board members arrived in limousines. To my knowledge, Bill Hewlett, of Hewlett-Packard, was the only other Chase board member who took public transportation to board meetings. Once, when Barbara and I attended a party at the Rockefeller estate, we arrived in a reasonably new Pontiac Grand Prix, which was quite impressive to me; most everyone else arrived in limousines.

I met John Johnson, founder of Ebony and Jet magazines, at one of David's parties at the family compound. Later, I met George H.W. Bush–a.k.a. Bush One–when he spoke to the Chase Board. About a week or two after we met, Bush called and invited Barbara and me to dinner that evening at his house. I told him that we were getting ready to have dinner at our home with my cousin Wendell Murray and his wife Nancy. He said, "Bring them too," and I did. George was a gregarious guy. We became friends. Later he, had dinner at my house. The two Barbaras had common interests, they both did needlepoint. The wives got along and George and I got along.

I also met Mobutu Sese Seko, who was president and military dictator of the Republic of the Congo (now Zaire) during one of my visits to the Rockefeller estate. Lunch was delayed because of Mobutu's late arrival. David sent a helicopter to pick him up at the airport, his entourage was too large–a second helicopter was dispatched. Dubbed as the archetypal African dictator, Mobutu reportedly embezzled more than four billion dollars during his three-decade reign.

Though David brought me into his inner circle of friends and business associates at Chase, he couldn't protect me from the occasional sting of racism that lingers still in workplaces at every level. Let me frame it this way. People who are not prejudiced themselves tend not to see the prejudice in their friends or colleagues. They're not sensitive to it. They say he or she didn't do this or that's not because the person was black, but because the person did something else. I think we are all that way. I don't believe David realized the extent of bias in the Chase bank at the Board level. Maybe he did, maybe he didn't, I don't know. I do know that in David, I never detected not even a hint of racism in his relationship with me.

I have David to thank for asking me to help baseball icon Jackie Robinson find someone to replace William R. Hudgins, who resigned as president of the Freedom National Bank. Robinson and several other investors formed the Harlem-based bank in 1964. Robinson was chairman of the Board of Directors.

I had met Jackie on numerous occasions at previous business functions in New York. I shook his hand several times, but, of course, he didn't remember meeting me. Charlie Jaffin, one of Sam Pierce's law firm colleagues, had been hired to manage the Freedom National Bank's legal work, so he was involved in the transition. I recommended Bob Boyd for the job. Yes, that's the same Bob Boyd who had pushed me to attend the Chase luncheon.

Bob was a three-sport standout with Loyola Marymount University (LMU) in Los Angeles and was named an all-pro wide receiver with the Los Angeles Rams (1954). He played varsity football; competed on LMU's boxing team; and won the 100-yard dash (9.8 sec.) at the 1950 NCAA National Championships in Track & Field. He joined the Rams in 1950 when Bob Waterfield was the Rams quarterback and Paul "Tank" Younger anchored the Rams' bull-elephant running game. Bob Boyd ended his pro career unexpectedly after playing only seven years. Soon after, he began a career in business as a co-founder of Imperial 400, a chain of motels in the USA.

Charlie chose to bring Jackie, Bob, and me together for a weekend visit in Princeton, New Jersey, his hometown. The social activity included attending a college football game at Princeton, Charlie's alma mater. The idea was to allow Jackie and Bob to get acquainted with a sports world activity as a backdrop. Charlie's plan went smoothly. Their similar backgrounds as black professional athletes allowed them to compare their experiences regarding the growth of the pro sports world as it was in the 1940s and 1950s to how it was in the mid-'60s. They jelled right from the start. When I asked Jackie what he thought of Bob, he admitted that their sports world connection made it easier for them to connect. Jackie added, "He's not just another jock. He's a very bright guy." Soon after we left Princeton, I learned that Jackie had hired Bob as president of the National Freedom Bank. I was honored to have been a part of the process.

The weekend also afforded me an opportunity to spend quality social time with my Brooklyn Dodger hero. The Dodgers were my team even before Jackie showed up in 1947. It was a big, big plus for me–and for so many other blacks–to watch him slide through one of our nation's most formidable racial barriers. Many blacks knew or had heard through the grapevine what Jackie had gone through before he reached the majors.

As a Second Lt. in the U. S. Army, Jackie was court-martialed for challenging racist comments made by investigating officers after a bus driver's complaint that Jackie had refused to ride in the back of the bus on an Army's segregated bus line. Nine white officers acquitted him of all charges. When Jackie joined the Montreal Royals, the Dodgers' farm team, for spring training in Daytona Beach, Florida, the state's segregation laws prevented him from staying with his teammates in a hotel. He stayed instead with a black family, which reminded me of what I had to do when Texas laws regarding public accommodations prevented me from staying with my computer group at our national convention at the Shamrock Hotel in Dallas.

Most blacks also felt his pain, as he silently endured racial slurs and taunts from fans, opposing players, and some of his Dodger teammates during his first year in the majors. Branch Rickey, the Dodgers' president and general manager, gave Jackie his full support, as did Dodger manager Leo Durocher, who issued a warning to some Dodger players who had threatened not to play if Robinson took the field. Said Durocher: "I do not care if the guy is yellow or black, or if he has stripes like a . . . zebra. I'm the manager of this team and I say he plays. What's more, I say he can make us rich. And if any of you cannot use the money, I will see that you are all traded."

Jackie's baseball skills diminished considerably in his final two years, probably because of diabetes. In 1955, his batting average fell below.300, to.256, and he stole only twelve bases. The next year, he finished with a.275 batting average and again had only twelve stolen bases. The Dodgers traded him to the crosstown rival New York Giants, but he instead announced his retirement in a Look magazine exclusive.

He was in bad shape during that weekend in Princeton. He limped noticeably, and I became aware of the scars, both internal and external, that he had collected during his life. Diabetes took away much of his sight in his later years, and heart disease slowed him even more. Jackie was fifty-three when he died of a heart attack at his Stamford, Connecticut, home.

Among so many other life-enhancing business and social experiences I still savor, I also have David Rockefeller to thank for that memorable weekend-long encounter with Jackie Robinson.

My connection to Chase and exposure to David served me well in the U.S., and during my work in Africa. Naturally, I'm grateful to Bob Boyd for pushing me to attend my first Chase luncheon. I didn't know it at the time, but several other black businessmen were invited to that luncheon. I was the only one to show up, and that, I believe, is how I became a member of the Chase board of directors. Who knows what would have happened if another black had shown up? Even though my first instinct was to skip it, I'm glad I showed up.

"I appreciate all that Tom Wood has done for the Chase Manhattan Bank"

DAVID ROCKEFELLER

CHAPTER 13

"We are all Africans."

Walter Cronkite,
CBS Anchor

I never liked the term "African American," the racial identity tag that the Reverend Jesse Jackson made popular in the late 1980s. It's a misnomer. I believe all Americans are African Americans. Some of us happen to be black. We all come from Africa. Humankind comes from Africa. It's the root.

We have known, for more than three decades that "homo sapiens" evolved in Africa some 200, 000 plus years ago and that all non-Africans descend from a small population that left Africa more than 60, 000 years ago. About 45, 000 years ago, the first modern humans entered Europe. That was the first wave, "Out of Africa", to enter Europe. The second wave to enter Europe, evolving from the first wave, came from Anatolia, what is modern day Turkey. The third wave to enter Europe, also evolving from that first wave, came from the Steppe, what is modern day Southern Russia.

Roger Wilkins, a fellow University of Michigan alumnus and friend, once said, "Whenever I go to Africa, I feel like a person with a legitimate place to stand on earth." Similar sensations saturated my being during my first visit to Africa in 1966 and conjures wondrous memories of time spent in Africa to this day.

Earle Seaton, a good friend and London-trained jurist, convinced me in the late 1960s to visit him in Tanzania, formerly known as Tanganyika. Earle and Lester Florant, my childhood buddy, were roommates at Howard University. Born in Bermuda, Earle earned a bachelor's degree from Howard, thanks to a full tennis scholarship. He also graduated from London University and later became a barrister and completed his dissertation in doctoral studies in International Affairs at the University of Southern California. Though he's not an African native, Earle became one of East Africa's most respected legal minds. He was with Tanzania's Ministry of Foreign Affairs when I saw him in Dar es Salaam. We explored potential ventures that Africa might offer.

President Mwalimu Julius Nyerere made Earle a judge before I arrived and later, he served as Tanzania's Legal Counsel to the United Nations (UN). A picture of Earle and Salim Ahmed Salim, Tanzania's ambassador to the UN, with several Chinese delegates, was on the front page of The New York Times in 1971 when the People's Republic of China (PRC) replaced the Republic of China (ROC) as the country's charter member at the UN. Earle was sent to the UN by Nyerere to facilitate the Chinese admittance to the UN. The Chinese had supported Nyerere's move for independence from Great Britain after Tanganyika joined Zanzibar to become Tanzania. Earle left Africa in 1972 to become the first black judge in his homeland, Bermuda. He later returned to work in Kampala Uganda for the British Commonwealth as an appellate judge.

I was forty years old when I walked on African soil for the first time and though I was still somewhat disheartened by recent business setbacks as Decisions Systems' CEO, it felt good to be in humankind's cradle, preparing to start anew. Earle saw Africa as the balm I needed to dissipate the pain that lingered. "America has a good reputation in Africa, and there are lots of opportunities," Earle whispered encouragingly, "and the commonality of being black will serve you well."

I began my first trip to Africa on a British Airways Jet. "The Comet", the first major commercial jet. Compared to todays jets, it had limited range.

We left London with stops in Rome, Benghazi, (yes Benghazi), Addis Ababa, Nairobi, and then Dar es Salaam, Tanzania.Dar es Salaam reminded me of the movie Casablanca. Dar es Salaam was then a ocean front, open air (almost no air conditioning) city. Many of the public spaces were populated with foreign nationals, freedom fighters, politicans, and exiles, mainly from southern Africa.Each group was organizing, plotting the overthrow of its colonial power.Their hope was to be on their way somewhere else, hopefuly their place of birth.It seemed to me that this was the case in almost every bar, or eating place. To my mind the atmosphere was one that a good movie or story can be set in. By way of illustration I will tie the threads of two real life stories to make the point, just as they were tied in real life. Almost all these characters, I have met and interacted with except two, Joe Louw, and Monteiro.

I met Marcelino dos Santos briefly on one of my 1966 trips to Tanzania. I remember him vividly, and I am sure he would not remember me. I believe Marcelino, at this writing is still alive.He is a colorful figure, a poet, a revolutionary, and an astute politician.He was one of the founders of CONCP(the conference of national organizations of the Portuguese colonies) at Casablanca in 1961.Marcelino is colored, mixed race, and as such felt that he would not be able to effectively rally the African population if he was the head of the liberation movement which was 95% black Africans. He therefore decided to recruit Eduardo Mondlane, who was almost a decade older than Marcelino. Eduardo Mondlane, a black Mozambican living in the United States, and teaching at Syracuse University in NY state to be the titular head of the independence movement. In addition Eduardo's cosmopolitanism and his marriage to a white American woman, his American education, made him suited for this role.The Portuguese responded by assassinating Eduardo Mondlane, in 1969 with a bomb in a chair in which Eduardo was sitting at a beach house on Oyster Bay owned by an American woman from Cleveland Ohio, Betty King, which was a week-end gathering place for we Americans. Mondlane had a favorite chair which he occupied in discussions with friends and supporters. I, on several occasions, sat in that chair. It is widely believed that the assassination was carried out by the Portuguese Secret Service (PIDE), and specifically by Casimiro Monteiro, born in Goa in 1920.He was also implicated in the assassination of Humberto Delgado, opposition leader to Salazar's government.

At the time I met Marcelino dos Santos he was living with Pamela Beira, whom he later married.Pamela was born in Johannesbug South Africa to white parents.She participated in numerous demonstrations, rallies calling for support of the African National Congress (ANC), she also worked for Helen Joseph, a veteran of the Anti-Aparthied movement. Pamela Beira, and Joe Louw were arrested in Jan 1962 by the South African Police under the Immorality Act, Joe Louw being a Colored South African.Joe Louw was sentenced and served 6 months in jail.Pamela left for Tanzania where she met Marcelino.Shortly after serving his prison sentence Louw received a scholarship to study at Columbia University in journalism. Upon graduation, Louw worked for Public Broadcasting Lab. He was following Dr. Martin Luther King in Memphis when Dr. King was assassinated.Joe Louw took the famous photograph of Andrew Young and others pointing in the direction of the shots which killed Dr. King.

As of this writing Marcelino dos Santos remains a powerful behind the scene presence in Mozambique, The university in the capital city is named for Edwardo Montlane.

I was also forty years old when I began to play tennis. In Africa in the places that I traveled, almost all of the major hotels where I stayed had tennis courts, or a tennis facility nearby. The pace of beginning a business in Africa was much slower than I had experienced in the U.S.. Often I found myself with only one, two, or in some cases no meetings in a day.As some one who beginning in high school and my years at college had participated in competitive sports on a regular bassis, I now had the opportunity to do so again. I began to play tennis, and usually took my Arthur Ashe Racquet with me on my trips to Africa.

I made several visits to Africa over the next eighteen months, studying the people and learning to appreciate the various business and tribal customs of the people I met. In my head, as well as my heart, I knew Earle was right, that Africa would be not just an oasis of opportunity for me as a businessman, but a place where I could help create a more prosperous future for the African people. However, the risks and obstacles would be numerous and formidable. Would I be perceived as another foreigner bent more on making a big buck, rather than a big, positive difference in their lives? Establishing trust and mutual respect would be essential to my efforts. Could I convince Africa's leaders to trust in me? Could I trust their leaders?. There was so much at stake.

I wanted to start changing America's perception of Africa as a perennial third world maze of countries incapable of advancing to a higher level. I had stars in my eyes. Tennis great Arthur Ashe summed up where I was in my life with this quote: "You get to the stage in life where going for it is more important than winning or losing." I was all-in on Africa, but I didn't go there hoping to be somebody. My objective was to do something special. I didn't want to start a business that would compete against Africa's small businesses or local governments. I wanted to introduce a private business operation that would address one of the continent's major needs. With assistance from sources in America, I believed I could establish a lasting service of value.

I chose the field of agriculture. I focused on finding ways to reduce the risks of Africans suffering with food-borne illnesses with the irradiation of their food. The paucity of refrigeration was a serious problem in Tanzania, where Earle was based, as well as in small villages throughout the continent. We, in America, had experienced similar problems decades before, and there are several countries in Europe that still have to shop for groceries every day. In Africa, the problem was more acute, so I decided that irradiated foods might be an effective solution. Food radiation reduces the number of pests, molds, parasites, and bacteria on many foods, but it does not make it safe from other organisms such as viruses.

Traditionally, we had used canning as a heat source to preserve food, but during my era, irradiation became an acceptable alternative. Radiation is produced by a radioactive substance–usually cobalt 60–or it can be generated electrically. The U.S. Center of Disease Control and Prevention (CDC) says it does not make foods dangerous. The CDC noted that NASA astronauts consumed irradiated foods without ill effects.

Irradiation is like canning or the pasteurization of milk. You can preserve milk by pasteurizing it. Homogenized milk is irradiated milk, but it isn't called that because of the public's concern about radiation. Canning preserves food stuffs. When you heat food, the heat kills the germs, and then you isolate it in a container where no new germs can enter. Irradiation does essentially the same thing, and it doesn't change the flavor of the food as much as canning does. But you can tell the difference. Irradiation might alter the flavor of T-bone steaks. I was convinced using irradiated food in Africa's developing countries would be a productive venture.

I saw value in introducing beef irradiation in Tanzania, which had one of the largest cattle herds in Africa. The herds walked long distances, just as U.S.-bred cattle had walked long distances many years before. Cattle herds in Texas had to be walked to Kansas City and other distant cities to slaughterhouses. They lost weight and had to be fattened. In Africa, there were no feed lots where cattle could be fattened along the way. Consequently, the herds were walked to market, slaughtered but lost value by the time they arrived.

My plan was to build an irradiation facility where the cattle were and then take the meat to market. I estimated that I would need about five million dollars to build the facility, but I knew I wouldn't be able to raise that kind of money in Africa. During my early visits, I became aware that many African businesses' did not have access to capital to buy equipment. I learned, too, that throughout the continent, if African governments, or individuals, wanted to buy a large or small product, they had to obtain a letter of credit, which meant that they, in advance, had to get a bank to guarantee to pay for the product, and then pay the entire amount when the product or services are delivered. Most people in the United States couldn't buy a house if we had to do that. We'd need a mortgage! But that's the way it was then and as of this writing, still is in much of Africa.

Irradiation was being used during the 1960s in several other countries, including Canada. Dr. John Masefield, a leader and innovator, is one of the most influential pioneers in the field of radiation sterilization. He was educated in engineering and physics in the United Kingdom. In 1959, John joined Atomic Energy of Canada and worked on the first industrial cobalt-60 irradiator in North America for the sterilization of medical devices. I got to know him when he was running an irradiation facility irradiating potatoes in Canada. I wanted to hire him to run the irradiation facility in Africa. John later won high praise and several accolades in the field, including the 2003 Kilmer Memorial Award for International Leadership for advancing the science and practice of radiation sterilization. He also became chairman of the board for the International Irradiation Association (IIA).

Before I began my search for U.S. investors for the irradiation facility, I knew I'd have to prove to the Africans that irradiated meat–which was still being tested in the United States in the 1960s–was safe. Tanzania's leaders wouldn't dare endorse the facility if it wasn't approved by the U.S.

The FDA decided that the tests that the Army had conducted to prove the safety of irradiated foods were not sufficient. FDA researchers found an error in the testing or believed that the data was incomplete. They never explained their decision; they just told the Corps of Engineers to redo the tests, which had taken twenty years to complete. That killed my interest in bringing the concept of irradiated foods to Africa. I wasn't going to wait twenty more years to find out if I could use the technique.

The FDA's decision took the concept of irradiated meat off my plate, but it didn't lessen my appetite to do business in Africa. Through my research on irradiation of food products I learned that leasing might also be a viable business venture in Africa, not only for me as an entrepreneur but for business-minded Africans. My primary goal was to start a business that would generate jobs and provide a path of success for those who might want to start their own business. For example, Africans, would—with a small down pay-ment—have access to equipment which would generate income, sufficient to make the lease payment plus return a profit and at the end of the lease, own the equipment.

For example, if someone discovered that there was a market for taxi service in certain areas of Africa, my company would lease a taxi to Africans who wanted to earn a living as taxi drivers. I envisioned business opportuni-ties through leasing equipment in other forms of transportation and in other industries, including agricultural, manufacturing, and communications. I had learned a great deal about leasing computers as CEO of Decisions Systems. The time seemed right. Destiny beckoned me to use my expertise to help expand economic opportunities—throughout the African nations.

My first opportunity for TAW to write a lease, occurred in Mexico, not Africa. Harold Epps, who had an office down the hall from mine in the United Nations Plaza building, had a number of connections in Mexico. I decided to start there. I wanted to use this opportunity to provide TAW with a "shake-out" operation for the African leasing. I arranged the financing with Bob Boyd's bank. Bob accompanied me on one of my trips to Mexico City to meet the proposed leasee. I met Don Gravito (I may not have the correct spelling) in Mexico with Hal and Bob Boyd. Don wanted to build an upscale apartment complex, and direct the net revenue to his two adult children. Don indicated, in his conversation with me, that he felt that his adult children would mis-handle any lump sum payment from him. Earlier in his career Don had organized and supervised a similar project.

Two problems confronted us. One : "Non-Mexican entities" were not legally permitted out right ownership of land.

Two : Arranging the construction financing. I decided to have TAW solve the first, and Don should solve the second. As such, Don put up a ten thousand U.S. dollar deposit to cover any TAW legal costs in solving the Non-Mexican entities" problem.

I hired Fred Rubenstein, a lawyer and a Cornell classmate of Dr. Meredith Gourdine. In his youth Fred had lived in Mexico, and spoke the language, as well as having legal contacts in Mexico.Fred's legal people came up with a solution to the "Non-Mexican" problem in the form of a long term lease.

Don insisted that he personally supervise the construction, as he had in previous projects.This was a mistake, for Don could not obtain construction financing beause of his advanced age.Therefore the first TAW lease did not occur in Mexico. What did happen, was that during my several trips to Mexico City, I became interested in Olmec Art and history.I visited the Mexican National Museum on almost all of my trips to Mexico City.What caught my attention was a collection of huge stone heads (4 to 6 feet) with what looked to me like, their hair in "corn rows" similar to those worn in Africa and the U.S..In the late 1970's.

I came across a book by Ivan Van Sertima entitled "They Came Before Columbus".Van Sertima was a professor of Africana Studies at Rutgers University in the U.S.. Van Sertima proposed that Africans arrived in the New World a millennia before Columbus, and were treated as God's by the indigenous people, hence the collosal heads.Intially Van Sertima's theory was dismissed by some scholars as "Afrocentric Pesudohistory" In response to the critics of Van Sertima, Clarence Weiant, an archaeologist replied"As one who has been immersed in Mexican Archaeology for some forty years, and who participated in the excavation of the first Olmec heads, I am convinced of the soundness of Van Sertima's conclusions". Many in the black community, both lay and scholarly gave creedence to Van Sertima's work.In 1970, Dr. Thor Heyerdahl in a raft called RA, built of papyrus, and based upon drawings from ancient Egpypt, crossed the Atlantic Ocean from Morrocco to Barbados, demonstrating that sailors could have sailed from Africa to the New World, by sailing with the Canary Current.The RA is now in a museumin Oslo Norway.A book "The RA expedition" and a documentary film, "RA", have been made about the voyages.

Leasing was somewhat of a fad during the 1950s. At the end of 1952, industrial leasing was a ten million-dollar per year business. By 1970, its annual volume had grown to twenty billion dollars. U.S. leasing firms had been operating internationally for many years, but mainly in Europe. Significant economic growth in Africa, however, was stifled by several worrisome problems, including shortage of capital, the constant risk of political upheaval, an unstable business climate and reams of red tape involved in political risk insurance from the U.S. government for exports to developing countries.

I suspected finding U.S. investors who'd consider giving a black person large sums of money to start a leasing company in Africa would be even more difficult than it had been for that same black person to raise seed money for a startup computer company that eventually had a public offering of its stock.

Turns out, I got lucky—again. It took me nearly two years of continuous travel on nonstop fund-raising junkets to raise the 10.8 million dollars needed to launch the first U.S. equipment leasing company to operate in Africa. Once again, if anyone waved a dollar at me or even showed a scintilla of interest, I'd track them down and hoped that I'd get the chance to state my case in person.

From my New York home base, I made numerous overnight trips to Chicago, St. Louis, Washington, D.C., and, at times, longer trips to Los Angeles and other West Coast cities. I attended seminars when I knew several top money people were guest speakers to set up meetings and appointments, and I'd occasionally travel to a town uninvited. I'd take a chance, in my travel to the city of a potential investor, call to let him know I was in town, and ask for a meeting. If he wasn't in, I'd leave my hotel number, and then sit by the phone the rest of the day, with my fingers crossed, waiting for a call back and hoping I'd get the chance to ask for big bucks. I wanted, indeed, I had to believe that another Cornelius Shields-type executive would look beyond my color and see a man of character, conviction, and competence and say, "Sure,

Tom, we'll take a chance. We'll invest a few million dollars in your company, with the understanding, of course, that we'll get much more in return."

I was motivated by the notion that if people believed you can make money for them, they'll give you a shot. The goal of the entrepreneur is to convince investors that he has a gold mine in a bottle that nobody else has, and that he'll let them in on it. This, of course, is the basis of scams, but it's also how early investors and stockholders in companies such as Apple, Microsoft, and Facebook became multimillionaires.

I was fortunate to have had Ed Irons, one of only a few black executives working at the United States Agency for International Development (USAID), as a financial mentor during the early phase of my hunt for funds. In 1964, Irons helped launch Harlem's Freedom National Bank, with Jackie Robinson as its first chairman of the board. I met Irons, who was a little older than I, when he worked for USAID, which was responsible for administering civilian foreign aid. He told me that USAID also guaranteed business investments made by U.S. investors in developing countries. Armed with that information, I moved forward in my search, which eventualy proved to be fruitful.

Prudential Insurance stepped up with a six million-dollar loan. Two major banks chipped in an additional 2.6 million dollars, which inspired Prudential to provide an additional one million dollars in equity. Still, we were 1.2 million dollars short of our established 10.8 million-dollar goal and had only a few months left to meet the deadline required to have the finance package complete. Smart investors don't give entrepreneurs unlimited time to start their business ventures. They set deadlines and if the deadlines aren't met, the deal is dead. Investors always include a line in the contract, which essentially says, "We can't let this commitment to loan you ten million dollars extend for ten or twenty years. If the deal isn't completed by the deadline date, we're out!"

Closing the African leasing deal became an all-consuming goal. Nothing else mattered. It became clear to me that my two-year stint chasing investors had taken its toll emotionally, as well as physically. I realized just how badly my relationship with my wife and family had deteriorated during a two-day stop at my New Jersey home when my eleven-year old son, Brian, who hadn't seen me in a few months, looked up at me and said quizzically, "I thought you were dead!"

His comment staggered me more than any comment I had ever received. But there was no time to make amends. My goal dangled before me—finally within reach. Herb Cummings, a close friend, joined me in my search for the final 1.2 million dollars needed, and frankly, I wouldn't have been able to close the deal without his input.

CHAPTER 14

"One can sit alone in an isolated room, and convince oneself of almost anything. The doubts and uncertainity begin when you leave the room, and enter the REAL WORLD"

TOM WOOD

Herb Cummings never met a person he didn't want to like or know better. He was all-over-you-friendly, an uncommon trait, I'd say for a multimillionaire. When he traveled with me to Africa, we'd occasionally mingle with the people in the streets or on walks through impoverished villages. Herb never hesitated to shake hands, hug babies with runny noses, or play with children.

I'd say to him, "Herb, why are you doing this? You might catch something." He'd smile while continuing to hold them as if they were his own. He had no qualms. He didn't do it because he was a liberal bending over backwards to show he's not prejudiced or to impress me or anybody else. This was Herb, showing love that came from his heart. I believe he truly loved Africa and its people.

His father, Nathan Cummings, on the other hand, was the hardnosed, sometimes ruthless patriarch and founder of Consolidated Foods Corporation, a Chicago-based Fortune 500 conglomerate, since renamed the Sara Lee Corporation. Though he never finished grammar school, Nathan Cummings was awarded several honorary degrees for his business and philanthropic achievements. He was the first born of Jewish immigrant parents who left Lithuania before the turn of the 20th century.

Herb was nothing like his father. He held no prejudices against black people or any people. He was Mr. Gregarious, the kind of guy who'd go into a bar at happy hour and know everyone's name before having one for the road. I'm exaggerating a bit, but you know what I'm talking about. He was someone who was eager to talk to people wherever they were and in whatever station of life they were. He was very frank, never devious. That's why he made us nervous during the arbitration.

I met Herb in the mid-1960s through Dr. Meredith Gourdine, who was an Olympic track star and gifted scientist. Meredith won an Olympic silver medal at the 1952 Helsinki Games in the broad jump, landing 1 1/2 inches short of grabbing the gold, which was won by fellow American Jerome Biffle. That loss haunted Meredith for the rest of his life. "I would have rather lost by a foot. I still have nightmares about it," he told The New York Times in 1998.

A Cornell University undergraduate, Meredith then earned a PhD in physics at Cal Tech and later pioneered the research of electrogas dynamics. He was responsible for the engineering technique called "Incineraid," which aided in the removal of smoke from buildings. He also developed gas dispersion techniques for eliminating fog from airport runways with a spray device. Meredith was the chief scientist at Curtiss-Wright Corporation from 1962-64.

He visited me several times in New Jersey when I had the computer company. During one of his visits, he admitted to me that he was envious of my daring venture into the business world. "If you can leave ITT and start your own computer business, I can leave Curtiss-Wright and start my business," said Meredith, who was then the Chief Scientist at Curtiss-Wright. Eventually, he did leave, establishing the Gourdine Laboratories, in Livingston, New Jersey, with a staff of more than one hundred. I helped Meredith and his assistant, Mel Packer, get started by providing them working space in the New Jersey office of Decisions Systems. I also became a member of Meredith's Board of Directors.

Meredith introduced me to Herb during one of his visits to my office. When Herb learned of my frequent excursions to Africa, he grilled me gently about what life was like there. Finally, he asked if he could tag along on my next trip, which became his first of many. Herb, who was a couple years older than I, was happily married to his wife, Peachy. They had three children, two sons and a daughter.

His love of Africa and international travel sealed our commitment to a lifetime friendship in short time. He was good company and always well-dressed and well-groomed. Herb was fashionably thin, had a little bit of white hair, and had the look and demeanor of a patrician. While in Africa, he'd sport a slight beard but would always be clean-shaven when he returned to the United States. He could fit in anywhere—in an impoverished village in Africa or in the upper reaches of society in Europe and America. He drank sparingly, loved classical music, and was a smoker.

Sometimes, when I stayed in Africa for extended periods, I'd say to Herb, "I can't get money to my wife. Would you give her five or ten thousand dollars to tide her over until I get home?" He'd make those loans to me without hesitation, and I always paid him back. It was a minor thing to Herb because it was pocket change, but to me it was a major thing. He once traveled with me on a business trip to Taiwan and on the way back we stopped in Hawaii, so that he could visit several places where he and his wife Peachy stayed during their honeymoon.

On one trip to Africa, Herb invited Bob Mayer, his brother-in-law, to join us. Bob spent most of his time buying African art from different countries. Bob later donated his collection to Morgan State University, a historically black university in Baltimore, Maryland.

Herb treated me like an equal though I was far from his equal economically. Through Herb, I met several of the world's richest families, including the Rothschilds, descendants of Germany's Mayer Amschel Rothschild, who established a small banking business in the 18th century. With his five sons, Rothschild's small banking business became an international family banking empire. By the 19th century, it was at its height. The Rothschild family reportedly possessed the largest private fortune in the world, as well as the largest private fortune in modern history.

Herb also introduced me to members of the Pritzker family, Chicago's leading collection of entrepreneurs and philanthropists. Eleven members of the Pritzker clan were on the Forbes magazine list of the four hundred richest Americans in 2015, including Penny Pritzker, an early supporter of Sen. Barack Obama's candidacy for the presidency. Each family member was worth more than one billion dollars. In his second term, Obama selected Penny Pritzker to be the thirty-eighth U.S. Secretary of Commerce. I don't believe Herb's father wanted him to invite me into their super wealthy world.

Occasionally, Herb traded on his father's name to gain entrance to some restaurants. Once when we were together in New York, Herb and Peachy invited Barbara and me to dinner at an exclusive Chinese restaurant in the theatre district of Times Square. The entrance was a plain storefront, and though nothing marked it as exclusive, it was known to be a dining haven for the wealthy and elite. There were no prices listed on the menu. The Wall Street Journal and several other New York papers published major articles about it when it closed. Though it was a "reservations only" place, Herb thought he could get us in without a reservation.

We were greeted by a Chinese woman named Peggy, the owner. Herb couldn't get a table—until he used his father's name. Then Peggy said, "Fine, you've got a table." If you weren't known to the woman, you couldn't get in or get a reservation. She didn't know Herb, but apparently, I was OK. As we were walking out, she whispered to me, "You can come back."

Herb had faith in me as a person and a businessman, and he shared my dream of starting a leasing company in Africa. He helped in every way possible and worked tirelessly to make it a reality. In our search for the final 1.2 million dollars, I realized that Herb was as determined as I was not to let this deal slip away. I learned of the extent of his commitment during a stop in New York. Out of the blue, Herb told me that he hadn't seen Nathan Cummings, his father, in more than two years and that he had made an appointment to see him that night at his spacious Waldorf Astoria apartment.

Remember King Edward VIII, the British monarch who abdicated the throne in 1936 to marry Wallis Simpson, a twice-divorced American socialite? Well, Herb's father bought the same fifteen million-dollar Waldorf Astoria apartment where the former king and his soul mate had lived during the early days of their controversial marriage. Once inside, it was obvious that Nathan Cummings' New York abode had been decorated and fit for a king. It was dubbed the "Royal Suite."

Herb misled me a bit when he said we would meet with his father that evening. As it turns out, our session was scheduled for, and began exactly, at 1 a.m., the next morning. Apparently, Herb's father squeezed us into his worka-holic agenda. We arrived at 12:45 a.m. and to my surprise, Mortimer Kaplan, a former director of the U.S. Internal Revenue Service (IRS), was just com-pleting his chat with Nathan Cummings. I wondered why Herb wanted me to go with him; he didn't tell me that TAW was the only item on the agenda.

When we entered the room, Nathan Cummings looked at his watch and said, "You've got twenty minutes."

Even with his son, Nathan Cummings was all business. Until that moment I hadn't realized Herb was really afraid of his father. In a quivering voice, Herb explained to his father that I wanted to start a leasing company in Africa. His father turned to me and said, "You want me to invest in this venture?" Before I could respond, he said, "I won't do it because you won't make any money. You will enable other people to make money, Africa isn't ready for you." He might have been prophetic on that point.

Besides being good company, I liked having Herb with me during my fund-raising venture for another reason. Despite my business achievements, I knew the color of my skin might be a turnoff to some potential investors. That's just the way it was, and in too many cases still is. Having a wealthy white friend as a board member and traveling companion might prove to be a difference-making asset. Herb gave me credibility, sad to say. We crisscrossed the nation, visiting investment banks, commercial banks, major corporations, and so on, with no luck.

With two days left before the deadline, I felt a great opportunity slipping through my fingers. Then Herb says, "I'll write you a check." With no promissory note or other binding contractual document required, he handed me a 1.2 million-dollar check and then left on a vacation to Mexico.

I had one more minor obstacle to overcome: getting the check deposited in a bank account. What happened next was hilarious, but also frustrating and typical of the racial double standards of American life during that era. When I went to the First National Bank of Chicago to deposit the check, the bank the check was written on, the bank teller and managers were incredulous. Their eyes danced with "how-could-this-be?" bewilderment. I knew what the teller was thinking: "How can this black person walk in here and expect us to believe that this is a legitimate check?" They kept me sitting around there for more than two hours because they had difficulty tracking down Herb, who was on vacation in Mexico. When they finally confirmed that it was Herb's signature on the check, their attitude changed dramatically. In the beginning, they had treated me like an imposter, or like someone who was there to rob the bank. A chat with Herb made me a valued customer, worthy of their respect, credible.

As a leasing company, TAW's raw materiel was money.

As a result, I felt that my objective, was to do business with a Bank officer that had a lending limit high enough that the Bank officer could handle TAW's loan needs without having to seek approval from a superior. It was fortunate that my/TAW's introduction to the First National Bank of Chicago was through Herb Cummings and (what is now) Sarah Lee Corporation. The good fortune resulted in the TAW account was given to a Bank Officer who had a lending limit, on his sole approval of $10 million. As such, I could over the phone, borrow for TAW $1 million, at a time, as long as I personally guaranteed the loan.

I'm sure Herb's last-minute personal investment was a spontaneous act of friendship and trust. In Herb's mind, it may have provided him with some leverage in my hiring considerations. It proved to be the first real test of our friendship and my business judgment. Herb's older son, Jim, had become a family problem, and without discussion, Herb turned to me for a solution. None of Herb's children finished college, though one might have started. I spent a lot of time at Herb's house in Chicago and got to know the family very well.

When my daughter, Kay, was preparing to go to the University of Michigan, Herb's daughter said to me, "I wish I could go to college." It was kind of funny to me. All of Herb's children were financially secure with the millions they received from their grandfather. Herb and his two siblings received significant sums when they were young, but the nine grandchildren got even more. Herb told me that their portfolios yielded more income than his because his portfolio was primarily in Consolidated Foods stock, while the grandchildren's stock was more diversified and had a greater yield.

They had little incentive to find meaningful work and seemed indifferent about pursuing a career that would require professional training at management level. Herb believed that I would provide the constraints Jim needed and that he would straighten out once he was under my influence. He asked me to hire him. After I interviewed him, I told Herb, "No." Jim didn't care about business or anything else, and that's why his father wanted me to put some constraints on him. I felt that he would have disrupted my whole operation if I'd hired him. That was the one thing I did that let Herb down, but I think it was a better business decision.

While Herb and I were in Rome, in early discussions of the deal with General Motors, Herb received a phone call, informing him that his wife, Peachy, had died. Herb's father, Nathan, learned of his daughter-in-law's death while vacationing with Henry Ford II, grandson of Henry I, founder of the Ford Motor Company, on a yacht in the Mediterranean Sea. Nathan's second wife, Joanne Toor Cummings, was traveling with them. Nathan married his first wife, Ruth Lillian Kellert, in 1919. She died in 1952. He married Joanne later. Herb invited me and TAW's entire New York staff to the funeral. Nathan Cummings might have expected to see me there, but the look he gave me made it clear that he hadn't expected seven other blacks to attend. But we were all there.

The staff came just for the funeral, but Barbara and I stayed a few days longer to attend a luncheon. Nathan spoke at the luncheon, and even though Herb's wife had just died, he denigrated and verbally abused his son constantly. He called Herb incompetent, said he couldn't do this or do that. I couldn't believe he would speak so harshly of his son publicly. It's one thing to do it in private, but it was astonishing for me to hear him trash his son that way, a day after Herb buried his wife. I cringed as I listened to Nathan's barrage of insults and wanted to get away.

I wasn't surprised when Herb told me of his plans to remarry awhile later, but I was stunned when he asked Barbara and me to accompany him and his new wife, Diane, on their honeymoon. We declined the invitation mainly because I believed it would have been inappropriate for us to tag along. I had met Diane earlier when she visited with Herb in Africa. She was a rail-thin model and a meticulous dresser. If Diane got even a small spot on her dress, she would change outfits completely. Herb's goal in life was to emulate his father, but not to be as ruthless as his father. Herb helped launch TAW, which represents my initials—Thomas Alexander Wood. I'm so grateful he did. His 1.2 million-dollar check made it possible for me to collect my first paycheck in more than four years and ended one of the more stressful periods of my life.

Shortly after this, to help with marketing in the French speaking African countries, I recruited Charles "CHIP" Bohlen, who was the United States Ambassador to France from 1962 to 1968, to be a member of the TAW Board of Directors. Ambassador Bohlen graduated from Harvard in 1927.

His great-great uncle was an American Civil War General, Henry Bohlen, the first foreign born (German) Union General in the Civil War.

CHAPTER 15

"When you start living the life of your dreams, there will always be obstacles, doubters, mistakes and setbacks along the way. But with hard work, perseverance and self-belief, there is no limit to what you can achieve"

ROY BENNETT

I've always tried to face the challenges—in my career and personal life—without fear or hesitation. Despite the racial barriers of that time, my philosophy was to move forward and never run away from a demanding job or task. Much of my attitude was formed from the encouragement I received during my childhood from my mother, an optimistic FDR Democrat. My mother's optimism wasn't normal for a black woman of her era. She believed in people. The opportunities that she had hoped I would experience as a preteen came to pass years later when I became a young man. That's when U.S. doors began to open to blacks, albeit ever so slightly.

My mother was a housewife, responsible mainly for maintaining the house and raising her children. My father, a Pullman porter and the family's breadwinner, was far more exposed to the sting of racism. He was a realist and much more security-oriented. For example, when I attended Columbia through the V-12 Navy program, some cadets were offered a chance to transfer to the U.S. Naval Academy, in Annapolis, Maryland. He wanted me to do that because he believed that a career as a naval officer would be much more comfortable and secure. I chose a different path.

My father never revealed his innermost thoughts or anecdotes about the difficult times he faced as a young black man in America. Sometimes, while watching him during a pensive or somber mood, I sensed the inner pain that he never shared. During my parents' era, most black people lived lives of quiet desperation. They were stifled by laws created specifically to oppress them in almost every way. American democracy at the turn of the 20th century used a system of gatekeepers that worked well for most whites. In my opinion the two main gatekeepers were the police, who enforced legal and de facto racial segregation, with an iron fist when necessary, and–though well-intentioned–schoolteachers. With some exceptions, they herded black teens into areas where they were rarely seen or heard.

From my view point, if and it is a big if, one does not count the treatment of the original inhabitants, American democracy's original sin is racism, and its impact on black Americans lingers still. It played the role in my decision to step down as CEO of Decisions Systems, which I headed for more than five years. Did I leave the firm because of the racial confrontations my company experienced while working on the Apollo Space program's LEM simulator? How many other Fletcher Jones-types were out there damaging my firm's business by telling contractors not to do business with "the nigger"? Should I have stayed awhile longer? Had I stayed, I probably would have eked out enough business to keep the business afloat. But for how long?

You don't always discover the source of a problem, but when I was informed of the rumor that had caused our stock to decline, it confirmed what I had already suspected: I was the problem. There was nothing I could do to stop the firm's downward slide. We had formed the nation's second computer company to offer stock to the public. Several other computer firms were created in subsequent years; none was headed by a black man. I couldn't change my racial identity. I had no choice but to consider other career options. I never told my partners at Decisions Systems the role that racism played in my decision to leave. I was probably too proud to admit that I no longer could do my job.

Before leaving Decision Systems, I made several attempts to hire marketing people, unsuccessfully. As I remarked earlier, in those days the field wasn't structured as it is today. People with the technical and marketing skills formed their own companies. As the industry grew, specialists in the various disciplines emerged. A good example is the development of the auto industry. It moved from handmade/custom-made productions to the assembly line.

To my dismay, Decision Systems collapsed not long after I left. It began a downward spiral because of who I was, but it may have happened, regardless. There's an expression that goes, "If you keep doing the same thing over and over and get the same results, why would you expect a different result?" That's the point; I didn't think conditions would change. I knew I was becoming bitter and I didn't want to become bitter. My father had a tinge of bitterness because he lived in the real world; my mother didn't. My mother used to say, "If the stove's hot, you take your hand off the stove." That's what I did. Other black strivers, including dancer Josephine Baker and writer James Baldwin, chose to pursue their dreams and continue their careers on foreign soil for similar reasons. You want to find a place where people will accept you at face value. I did not want my racial scar tissue, to become so thick, that I would become insensitive to the humanity of others.

My years with the computer firm were quite profitable, so I didn't initially struggle financially when I began my African career hunt. I sold my stock in Decisions Systems. The sale put me in a position of being suffiently affluent, that (unkown to me at the time) I was able to survive financially for almost five years without an income.This included the expense of maintaining a home, four children each with college level tuitons, as well as all the expenses of operating a business with office space and staff. I learned, however, that if you live off your savings for more than four years, make numerous round-trip visits to Africa, and don't pay too much attention to your expenses, the well could run dry. I did pay attention to my family's needs. Still, I had my share of worrisome moments.

Once, when I returned home from Africa, Erik, my older son, told me that he had been accepted at Phillips Exeter Academy, a private school in Exeter, New Hampshire. Erik had saved the funds needed for the application, applied himself and was accepted.

What am I going to tell him, "No, you can't go?"

He was fourteen at the time. We sat down with an accounting pad and estimated his first year's expenses. We totaled his tuition, room and board, and, of course, spending money. We came up with a number and we both agreed with the number. I wrote him a check which covered his expenses for one year. I told him he could spend it all tomorrow, just don't come back for more. I did the same thing each year with Kay, Vickie, and Brian when they went to college. Brian, the youngest, was the only one to run out of funds the last month or so; the others stayed within their budgets. I did the same thing with Barbara, my wife. There was no mortgage to pay, most major expenses were paid in advance. Barbara and I would decide what she would need to run the household. As I said earlier, I would try to return home every three months, but if I couldn't, I'd have Herb write her a check.

I don't believe my family was ever deprived. Nowadays, I'm sure many people would not approve of my corporate, head-of-the-household philosophy, but I got it from my father. My mother never knew how much money my father earned. I can pretty much figure out what he made because I know what Pullman porters earned during that time. I know how he accumulated ten thousand dollars on a one hundred dollars a month salary: the stock market plus tips. I knew it was all honest money. He used to tell me that he would eat at Father Devine's church diners because you could get meals for ten or fifteen cents. Whenever there was a family crisis, my father always came up with the money because he saved his money.

Barbara never knew how much I made. I believe that you can't run a business if you must sit down with your wife every month and discuss how much money you've earned or lost. If I did that with Barbara, we would have spent a lot of time negotiating because she wouldn't have agreed with many of the decisions I made. I might risk one hundred thousand dollars on one deal and one million dollars on another and she would have worried about whether she would receive her household money the next quarter. That's the way I ran my business and my life.

I wasn't a spendthrift, but if I wanted to buy something, I'd buy it. I didn't want a yacht, airplane, or any big-ticket luxury items. When I was Decisions Systems' CEO, I drove a Volkswagen for a while. My kids used to say to me, "Buy a Mercedes, Dad." I didn't; I bought Pontiacs.

During this period of my life I was asked to do something that gave me a great deal of pleasure.I received a telephone call from Jack Rohn, the Columbia University basket ball coach. Jack a Columbia basket ball player in the early 1950's who became the head coach in 1962 was selected coach of the year for the 1967-68 season, leading Columbia to a 23-5 won-loss record and winning the Ivy League Championship.Jack called to ask me to help recruit Heyward Dotson, a fellow Stuyvesant High School student, and outstanding basket ball player and an outstanding student as well.

Jack and I visited Heyward's home on Staten Island, spoke with his mother and explained to her the advantages of attending Columbia for a student athelete of Heyward's stature. I was told at a later date, that Jack and my visit made the difference in Heyward's choice of a college.

Heyward Dotson became one of the outstanding players on the Columbia Basketball team, along with Jim McMillian and Dave Newmark, both of whom played professional basketball. Upon graduation, Heyward Dotson chose a Rhodes Scholarship to Oxford instead of the NBA.

It is my understanding that, after his studies at Oxford, Heyward has led a "troubled life". I sincerely hope that the same kind of "thinking and actions" that effected Norman Skinner and Val Johnson did not contribute to his "troubled life".

I believe that Norman Skinner, Val Johnson, and Heyward Dotson, each believed that their achievements, academic, sports, etc would provide them with a "tailwind" when they entered the "real world", as their fellow white graduates with similar credentials enjoyed. This expectation, I believe was the root cause of the "troubles", much of which were of their own making. When I entered the "real world", I assumed that I would have a "headwind", due to my race, in any thing significant that I tried to do. This expectation kept me on a relatively even keel upon my entry into the "real world".

The thread linking, Norman Skinner, Val Johnson, and Heyward Dotson is to me very revealing. All three are black, athetically gifted, scholaticly gifted, with "stars in their eyes" when they left the confort of their university years and entered the Real World only to be disillusioned by racial attitudes in the United States which destroyed or limited their expected (in their own minds) careers. My friendship with Paul Robeson's son, reminded me of the similarities here and what happened to his father in his career.

Perhaps upon my entry into the real world, I sublimated, I love the "blues" and Fado music. One of the Webster dictionary's definitions of sublimation is "to express socially unacceptable impules, in constructive acceptable forms, often unconsciously". Music, and song down through the ages, has been a means for many oppressed peoples to call attention to, to protest, to communicate, to cry out to others their emotions about their prevailing conditions, to sublimate.

I believe Dr. Martin Luther King's non violent approach in the black struggle for human and civil rights served me well in my personal approach to the struggle.

In the contest between the non "violent approach" and the "by any means approach", my thoughts told me that if one choses the latter, you are really no different than the system and individuals you are trying to change.

One can disagree, firmly, without being a disagreeable person.

Many believe that Fado, "Portugues Soul Music", was inspired by African slave and Moorish songs, that Portugues sailors in the 1800's, expressed the pain of loneliness and danger at sea.Fado music speaks of fate, melancholy, longing and loss.

Blues originated in the U.S. deep south, by blacks with roots in African music and songs.The blues consisted of a narrative about slavery, racial discrimination, personal woes, lost love etc.

Wikipedia indicates that the blues form, sometimes characterized by the call and response pattern, the blue scale, blue notes, usually thirds, fifths, or sevenths, can be traced back to Africa.

Wikipedia also indicates that one of the earlist recorded references to "the blues"was writted by Charlotte Forten, then age 25 in her diary in 1862.Forten was a free-born black, schoolteacher in South Carolina when she wrote that she "came home with the blues" because she felt lonesome and pitied herself. Forten admitted being unable to describe the singing she heard, and wrote that these songs "can't be sung without a full heart and a troubled spirit". This full heart and troubled spirit has produced countless blues songs.

The blues and discouraging thoughts seeped into my mind when the irradiated foods project to reduce the risk of Africans getting food poisoning turned into a morass. At that time, I had reached the lowest point of my life. So much money and time spent, for nothing? I began to lose confidence in myself and to doubt my ability to support my family. I had a wife and four children to support, but no income. I hadn't collected a paycheck in more than four years. My only saving grace was that I had paid cash for our house in Teaneck, so there was no mortgage to pay. I also began asking myself the same questions that my Detroit friends and coworkers had asked. "Am I crazy? Why am I doing this?"

It's one thing to leave a career for a better one, but quite another to run a risky business venture in a foreign country. Finally, my plan for a leasing business in Africa became a reality. Thanks to Herb's TAW-saving contribution, I would collect my first paycheck in four-to-five years. I felt better about the path I had chosen, and I was convinced that I was moving in the right direction, toward something better, not just for me and my family but for the African people.

CHAPTER 16

"Africa has her mysteries, even a wise man cannot understand them. But a wise man respects them"

MIRIAM MAKEBA

Once the 10.8 million-dollar package was complete, the Overseas Private Investment Corporation (OPIC), an outgrowth of USAID, agreed to provide TAW's investors with financing guarantees, and political risk insurance. OPIC's backing was crucial; none of my major investors would have signed on without it.

OPIC's mission is to promote the development of U.S. companies that seek to invest overseas in emerging markets and analyze and manage the companies' risks, as well as support domestic foreign policies. Fortunately, we enjoyed the full support of Brad Mills, OPIC's director during our start up years. Mills, a Princeton graduate, knew the risks we would face operating a business in a foreign country, and he unhesitatingly encouraged our partners and investors to stay with us during difficult or stressful periods. Brad considered us "heroes" for pursuing the venture.

We launched TAW International Leasing, Inc. in 1970, in New York City. At its peak, TAW operated in fourteen African countries. We leased agricultural, manufacturing, transportation, and communications equipment in the Ivory Coast, Ethiopia, Zambia, Liberia, Gabon, Cameroon, Uganda, Botswana, Kenya, Mali, Upper Volta, Niger, Toga, and Ghana, and operated regional offices in Abidjan, Ivory Coast, and Nairobi Kenya, the last country to grant us a leasing license. One of TAW's initial lease agreements was to lease an aircraft to

Medecins sans Frontieres (Doctors without Borders).

Team TAW's upper management level consisted of CEO Wood, outside counsel Alan Dynner, the firm's attorney, and Samuel H. Howard, vice president and chief financial officer, Ernest Kalibala, manager for East Africa, and Mamadou Ba, manager for West Africa. It took Alan and Sam nearly two years to complete OPIC's application, which consisted of a maze of legal documents and paperwork. In assessing the process, Alan, a Yale law graduate, said, "It was a clever way to provide startup financing in African countries."

Sam spent most of his time structuring the financial and business relationships in each of the African countries that agreed to do business with TAW. Mamadou, a trilingual Guiniean investment expert and a former head of the central bank of Guiniea, managed the French-speaking countries; Ernie, a bilingual former U.S. banking manager, headed the English-speaking countries. Each shared my determination to make TAW successful.

Sam worked closely with Alan to negotiate financing and guarantee agreements with OPIC and our lenders. A graduate of Oklahoma State (BA) and Stanford University (MA), Sam also saved TAW a lot of money by refusing to let OPIC charge the company separately for each of the leasing agreements required in the fourteen African countries. He discussed his negotiations with OPIC in his book, The Flight of the Phoenix. Sam wrote, "We wanted to establish leasing as a business. It took over a year, but we were eventually able to obtain a blanket guarantee for leasing equipment with any country that had an OPIC arrangement with the United States."

A native of Marietta, Oklahoma, Sam was one of only a few people that I'd met who toyed with statistical data with admirable expertise while examining various business scenarios to determine profit gains or losses. For example, I might say, "Sam, what happens if sales in a particular country go up and the London Interbank rates go down?" I had an intuitive feel for what might happen; Sam had a quantitative feel and he was much more accurate than I was. Some people excel in mathematics or finance, but they have no heart for it. Sam had compassion for numbers; it's like a love affair. That's the kind of person you want in charge of the finance side of any business. He knew what the overall strategy was and excelled. Earlier, Sam worked as a financial analyst with the General Electric Company (1963-67) and served as a White House Fellow and assistant to U.S. Ambassador Arthur Goldberg (1966-67).

At the close of TAW's first year in business, the firm had five million dollars in equipment under lease. The second year ended with our African customers using twenty-two million dollars' worth of equipment, and the firm had helped more than sixty African firms start or expand leasing operations in forestry, tourism, construction, chemical processing, and transportation. No other foreign business firm operating in Africa could say that. Only four of TAW's one hundred-plus employees were based in the United States. Those based in Africa were native Africans, working in various positions, including managerial. We wanted more Africans in leadership positions, making managerial decisions.

On TAW's successful start, Alan said, "Tom came up with the idea of using what he called the 'full pay-out lease, ' which was a (different) form of financing. Instead of selling a truck, that is, TAW would lease the truck to an individual or business. The individual or business made payments, which included a sufficient amount to pay off the cost of the truck plus interest. At the end of the lease, the individual or business would own the truck."

Under TAW's leasing agreements, the lessee initially put up the first month's payment and then made monthly payments for the rest of the lease period. No other firms on the continent offered leasing opportunities comparable to TAW's. Other industrial equipment companies that operated in Africa tried to sell their equipment. If they offered financing, the business would have to obtain a "letter of credit" from a bank. In general, private companies couldn't persuade banks to provide such letters, which would guarantee payments, and some governments with access to credit declined because the commercial firms would not provide servicing.

Alan adds, "Tom wanted to provide both financing to African entrepreneurs and some expertise through American-trained Africans or black American businessmen, who presumably would be able to connect culturally and emotionally with the people that were getting the leases. This was really an idea which I thought was amazing and very progressive. Nobody had ever done anything like it before."

TAW was the only leasing company doing business across Africa and the only foreign firm whose offices were manned almost entirely by Africans. Mamadou, a former officer of the World Bank, headed operations in the French-speaking African countries. In my opinion, the African leaders in the French-speaking countries were better administrators than those in the English-speaking countries. Before independence, they were a part of the French government. Their countries' representatives were sent to Paris like state representatives in our country are sent to Washington, D.C. Some of the poorest Africans in French-speaking countries spoke French. However, most Africans in the English-speaking countries were given more freedoms, but they weren't given the language.

Kalibala, a longtime former banker with Manufacturers Hanover, oversaw operations in the English-speaking African countries. Ernie was among the first wave of black lending officers hired by major U. S. financial institutions. His father, born in Uganda, earned a PhD from Harvard. Ernie's father and Ralph Bunche, former U.S. ambassador to the UN, were good friends. When Idi Amin seized power in Uganda, he considered making Ernie's father president. Instead, Amin made himself president.

Having bilingual and a trilingual staff in leadership roles served us well. Other U.S. firms doing business in Africa had few African managers. African businessmen were in a new arena, as was TAW for that matter. I knew we had to understand and be sensitive to, Africa's politics, viewpoints, and culture, and we were. With Mamadou and Ernie as regional managers, we quickly resolved communications differences before they morphed into major problems.

We chose the Ivory Coast as our first leasing site, primarily because it had a strong central bank with a common currency that was transferable in all the African French-speaking counties. Its status as the business and financial center of French-speaking African countries also was a notable asset. The country had very good hard wood, but it needed heavy equipment such as bulldozers and tractors to convert the natural resources into commercial products.

We also leased smaller items, including copiers, business computers, musical instruments, nail-making machines, bakery equipment, buses, trucks, and an office building. In Zambia, we entered a partnership to grow green vegetables and fruit that were earmarked for the European market. In Kenya, we established a unique clinic nursing home operation in the village of Embu, which is sixty miles from Nairobi. We also leased other equipment ranging from aircraft to bowling alleys. We leased only equipment that a customer could use to produce income. For example, the taxicabs we leased were not for personal use, only for business.

Kenya was the last country that agreed to grant us a leasing license and we might never have gotten it if we hadn't received a little help from a very powerful and influential friend. We established an office in Kampala, Uganda very quickly, thanks to Kalibala, who was born in Uganda and raised in the U.S., but Kenya's government officials ignored our requests for a license. I soon realized that a license would be granted only if a substantial under-the-table payment was made. My philosophy in Africa was that I was there as a businessman. I wasn't going to offer bribes or get involved in any form of corruption to get business. David Rockefeller, Chase Manhattan Bank's CEO, helped me resolve the Kenya problem without abandoning my principles.

With hindsight, I believe that Ernie Kalabala's choice of a second in command, may have been a factor in TAW's inability to obtain a licence to do business in Kenya. Ernie picked a man from the Luo tribe, because Ernie felt that he was the best of the people available, without heavily weighting the political considerations. The Luo at the time, were the fourth largest tribe in Kenya, the Kikuyu were, and presently are the largest tribe. Jomo Kenyata was Kikuyu, and the first President of Kenya, and was in office when TAW applied for a business licence. The Luo were not removed by the British, as were the tribes in the "white highlands". The Luo were active in the "Independence Movement", but were not generally involved in the Mau Mau uprising. The leading Luo political leader, Oginga Odinga, left Jomo Kenyata's political party (KANU) and as a result, the Luo became politically marginalized under the Kenyata presidency. It may be of interest to know that President Obama's Kenyan father was a member of the Luo tribe. Many believe this was the source of his "problems" in Kenya.

Ernie also hired Roble Olhaye as the TAW accountant for East Africa. Roble, a man from Djibouti, who after the arbitration ended, became the Ambassador from Djibouti to the United States and the United Nations, where he became the longest serving Foreign Ambassador to the United States until his death in 2015. As such he was the "Dean of the Washington Foreign Diplomatic Corps". Roble was a fellow of the Association of International Accountants (UK) and a member of the British Institute of Management.

Djibouti is located in the Horn of Africa, and with its neighbors is considered to be the land known to the Ancient Egyptians as "Punt" meaning "God's Land".

David Rockefeller had planned a multi-country tour of Africa during the time I was expanding my leasing business. Before he went, he asked if he could do anything for me while he was there. I did not want to accuse the Kenyan government of soliciting a bribe. I told him that Ernie, my associate, was having trouble getting a business license in Kenya. I told David, "Ernie knocked on the door of their office, but he was turned away, by someone saying, 'No license, no license.'" David knew precisely what the problem was.

I met David after he arrived in Nairobi at a cocktail party given by Mwai Kibaki, Kenya's finance minister, who later became president of Kenya.

While talking to Kibaki, David signaled me to join them. He then asked Kibaki, "Why hasn't Tom received a leasing license?" Kibaki screamed across the room to one of his under-secretaries, who approached nervously. Kibaki asked, "Why hasn't Mr. Wood received his license?" His deputy kept his head down, mumbled something to Kibaki, then Kibaki turned to me and said, "Meet me in my office tomorrow morning and you'll have your license."

David invited Ernie, his wife, Evelyn, and me to a reception given in David's honor by Standard Bank, which had numerous branch offices throughout Africa and Europe. At the time, Chase owned 10 percent of Standard Bank. More than two hundred people attended the reception. David seemed shocked and visibly embarrassed that the Nairobi branch of a banking institution partly owned by Chase had not invited a single other black person to his reception. Ernie, his wife Evelyn, and I were the only black guests at the affair. David grabbed Ernie by the arm and kept him by his side throughout the evening. I believe David did not want to be photographed in an all-white environment in Black Africa.

During my many visits to Nairobi Kenya I had on several occasions experienced a pleasant surprise. These are two of them. I frequently stayed at the Hilton or Intercontinental hotel when in Nairobi. There was an Anglican Church between the two hotels with an imposing bell tower.I had walked past the church for several years on my way to or from the TAW office. For some reason, on this particular walk past, my eyes focused on the metal placque at the base of the bell tower. On the placque was an inscription which read

"THOMAS A. WOOD

MAYOR OF NAIROBI

1927-1929"

On another trip to Nairobi, I arrived early and was not able to stay at either the Hilton or Intercontinental. I was directed to an older hotel, the Norfolk Hotel. At the hotel, Dr. Louis Leakey was giving a series of lectures on "HOMO HABILIS" or (handy man). In 1962 under the supervision of Dr. Leakey, Ndibo Mbuika discovered the first tooth of HOMO HABILIS which lived between 2.1 and 1.5 million years ago. Attending a few of Dr. Leakey's lectures sparked my interest in early human development which exists today. After these lectures, I made several trips to Olduvai Gourge where HOMO HABILIS was found. One trip with Alan Dynner, another with Frank Savage, and also with my youngest son Brian. Dr Leakey's legacy results from his research of primates to understand human evolution.

During this period, at David Rockefeller's behest, I met with Anton Rupert, who had made a pitch to include Chase in a twenty million-dollar business venture that would liberalize or integrate black countries bordering South Africa without having to end apartheid in South Africa. If I approved of Rupert's proposal, Chase would be a part of the deal.

Anton Rupert a well respected Afrikaner billionaire, had the image in South Africa, as a "moderate" who would improve South Africa's international standing while maintaining South Africa's hard line system of Apartheid at home in South Africa. Rupert at one time was a member of the secret Afrikaner society the Afrikaner Broederbond.

I had lunch with Rupert, then the second richest man in South Africa, in Chase's New York office. We were joined by six or seven other highly-respected South African businessmen, including the heads of Ford Motor Company and IBM in South Africa. I was seated at the head table, next to Rupert, and there were at least twenty other people at adjoining tables. It was eerie from my point of view because the others at the meeting were seated on two wings of the table, but no one else spoke. They sat quietly throughout the lunch, just listening to our conversation.

Rupert knew of my equipment leasing companies in Africa and he invited me to stay with him at his home during one of my future visits. He also volunteered to show me South Africa. We began discussing his proposal. In a situation like this, I never initiate the conversation. I listen and then respond accordingly. For once, I was on the other side of the negotiating table; I was in the position of the buyer, not the seller. Rupert waxed on for about ten minutes or more about what he planned to do for the neighboring countries of South Africa. I kept asking him, "What are you going to do for the black South Africans?"

He danced around the issue, but never admitted there was nothing he could do to enhance the lives of black South Africans because it would have been against the law. Then he started telling me what he would do for the colored people in South Africa. I believe in anticipating my response, he glared at me then said, "You're not black!" I responded: "And you're not white!" "let's simply apply the conventional rules regarding race". Rupert was darker than I am. Still, I probably shouldn't have said that.

It's a sensitive subject for Afrikaans because many have black relatives in their distant past, but don't acknowledge them. It was an unkind thing for me to say and I believe he was insulted. He was very cool toward me after that and, obviously, he never followed up on his offer for me to visit his home and tour South Africa. Chase didn't make that deal, but later I learned that five other companies, including General Motors, agreed to invest in Rupert's venture.

By example and through conversations, I routinely passed on to my staff, Africans and Americans, without breeching any confidential information, what I had learned as a Chase board member. I also enjoyed sharing the TAW experience with my hardworking, talented, and dedicated staff, especially Alan, the firm's outside attorney, who often entertained us by telling a story, including a heartwarming story about his father.

Alan's father, Eugene, joined the Merchant Marines when he was thirteen; he went back to school much later in life to complete his education and curiously wound up receiving a Howard University bachelor's degree. Says Alan: "My father was working as an architectural consultant in Washington, D.C., while attending the University Without Walls. He hooked up with a Howard University professor and wrote his thesis on similarities between Mayan art and Chinese art. Howard officials liked his thesis so much that they told him, 'We're going to give you a Howard University degree. You earned it.' He accepted the degree instead of a University Without Walls certificate.

He started the program when he was seventy-two and completed it two years later. I went to his graduation and there he was, a little white face with white hair among a sea of young black faces. It was wonderful."

In setting up TAW to do business in Africa, my most personally emotional experience happened in Dakar Senegal. I had previously met Tom Roberts, a Harvard trained lawyer, living in Dakar. Tom knew almost all of the "players" in French speaking Africa. Tom had a law practice which included Pan American Airways and other American organizations doing business in that part of Africa. At Tom's suggestion, I visited the Island of Goree, and the "Door of no Return". Goree is a island of about 50 acres, one mile off the mainland of Africa. Goree Island is the closest point in Africa to the America's. As such, it became the point of departure for many African slaves bound for the America's. The island has over the years passed through many nations' hands, initially Portugal, then the Dutch, England, France, and Senegal. There has been some dispute as to how many slaves left from Goree bound for the New World, as compared to other locations in Africa. For many Goree Island has become a symbol of the "Atlantic Slave Trade", attracting such luminaries as United States Presidents Obama, Clinton, and Bush, as well as South African President Nelson Mandela, and Pope John Paul ll. When Pope John Paul ll visited Goree, he asked for forgiveness for any part that the church may have played on Goree. I really became emotional when I saw the groves made by the chains which bound the African slaves, as they passed through the "Door of no Return". A foot note—Tom Roberts became a shareholder in TAW.

Despite TAW's successful start, in the back of my mind, I feared that a misstep, financially or legally, might lead to a major setback in our risky leasing venture. To guard against that possibility, I began developing a fund-raising plan that would put Alan and me on the road again.

CHAPTER 17

"The entrepreneur seeks money, not to possess it,
But to use it"

TOM WOOD

As an entrepreneur, I bought money wholesale, , and then translated it into goods and/or services, and sold it retail, via a lease agreement. Money was my raw material, and as TAW's burgeoning leasing business grew in Africa, I always needed more.

TAW grew in spurts during the first two years and quickly improved the lives of those it touched. We routinely juggled negotiations with two, sometimes three countries at a time, while simultaneously pursuing additional partners and investors. In August 1972, General Motors became one of our highest profile partners by investing 1.2 million dollars in TAW.

The GM investment occured after a backburner idea I'd been brewing, moved to the front. Like most entrepreneurs seeking funds, I learned that if you can prove to a banker that you need a loan, you won't get it. But if you prove that you don't need money, a banker will gladly lend you money.

With TAW's ever-expanding African leasing business as an asset, several investment bankers I contacted indeed were amenable to my plan. I proposed fifty-two million dollars as a reasonable, rainy-day cushion. After I'd received pledges from several major banks to provide forty-six million dollars, in debt, I presented to Morgan Stanley, in my opinion, the premier investment bank on Wall Street, a proposal to raise the remaining six million dollars in equity. Bill Sword, a Morgan Stanley investment banker, liked the proposal and agreed to do it. He assigned one of his top people to begin negotiations. Morgan Stanley produced an "offering document" for the $52 million financing, which included the Gereral Motors investment. Word that Morgan Stanley had joined TAW in an international deal moved quickly on the business world's grapevine. Though prematurely, business colleagues readily extended congratulations. They knew that once Morgan Stanley made a commitment, the deal was done.

To be clear, at the time, the 10.8 million dollars we raised to form TAW and the fifty-two million-dollar rainy-day cushion were major financial transactions. Comparable deals into today's market would be worth about ten times as much. In context, in 1970 I would have needed about 108 million dollars to form TAW and close to 520 million dollars as my security blanket. Years later, I learned that my role in the Morgan Stanley deal was a source of inspiration for Reginald "Reggie" Lewis, then an aspiring black business-man. A Harvard Law graduate, Reggie was the first black American to run a billion-dollar business. With an estimated annual income of four hundred million dollars in 1992, he was listed by Forbes magazine as the richest black American in the U.S. and the first black to run a billion-dollar company, TLC Beatrice International Holdings, Inc.

Reggie was an admirer from afar. We met much later in the 1980s at a party in New York. I had followed his career closely and knew of his enor-mous success. I was truly surprised when he recognized my name. After the introductions, he looked at me again and said excitedly, "You're the guy who put together that 52 million-dollar deal with Morgan Stanley. I saw that, and it inspired me, made me believe that if you could do it, I could do it." When Reggie lived in Paris Reggie, became friends with Dominic Kanga, who was TAW's attorney in our French-speaking countries. They had become good friends.

I met Bill Sword through Charlie Jaffin. Bill lived next door to Charlie Jaffin, who was a member of Sam Pierce's law firm. In fact, when Sam Pierce took a leave of absence, to become the General Councel of the Treasury Department in Washington, Charlie did the legal work that took Decisions Systems, our computer company, public in 1964. Bill also knew fellow Princeton grad Brad Mills, OPIC's first director. The Princeton crew seemed to have been a close-knit group.

Not long after Bill produced an "offering document" and assured me that Morgan Stanley would provide TAW the fifty-two million dollars, I received a call from him. He told me that Herb Cummings, a member of TAW's Board of Directors, wanted to sell 1.2 million dollars of his company stock. Bill wasn't asking for my approval; I believe he called just to let me know that he was going to talk to Herb's father, Nate Cummings, regarding Herb's request. I was puzzled but not really concerned about Bill Sword's action.

It didn't occur to me, at the time, that Herb's chat with Bill would lead to the demise of TAW's deal with Morgan Stanley, but it did. After that call from Bill, The "offering went south" I never heard anything else regarding" the offering" from Bill. I had no choice but to assume that the deal was dead, but I didn't really know what caused its demise.I did not want to confront Bill with what I thought happened.

What I believe happened is this, Bill Sword was competing for the top position at Morgan Stanley, against one other person.As such he did not want to risk loosing Nate Cummings, Sarah Lee business, as a result of a situation between Herb and his father.As it turned out, that Bill Sword did not get the position, and subsequently left Morgan Stanley to form his own firm.

Herb had invested the 1.2 million dollars needed to launch TAW in 1970; I couldn't blame him. TAW wouldn't have existed if it weren't for Herb. I cut Herb a lot of slack because he was a decent human being and had done so much for TAW, and for me personally. He was flawed just as we all are. I knew Herb lived beyond his income from time-to-time. Once when we were in London, he decided that he had to have a Rolls Royce. He saw it in the showroom, liked it, so he bought it. During one period, he owned several residences, buying each one on the spur-of-the moment. He inherited much of his father's artwork, so whenever he needed money, he would sell a painting. I told Herb that I had gone to Morgan Stanley for the fifty-two million dollars, but he didn't tell me that he was going to talk to Bill about selling some of the 1.2 million dollars in stock that he had invested in TAW. I don't know for sure if Herb's phone call led to Bill's change-of-heart.

What I do know, however, is that when a firm like Morgan Stanley says it's going to do a deal, that deal gets done. As I said, here's what I suspected. Bill probably felt that he couldn't risk losing Nate Cummings as a client. Consolidated Foods, Cummings' company, was worth more than a billion dollars. My speculation is that Nate Cummings told Bill, "Don't do it!" Nate Cummings was known for doing that kind of stuff. He once fired the chairman of Consolidated Foods because the chairman didn't put his picture in the annual report.

Bill Sword also was a top official in the National Presbyterian Church. I've sometimes wondered if some level of spiritual remorse was behind his inability to explain to me why he decided to change his mind about honoring the deal that would have provided TAW with a fifty-two million-dollar rainy-day cushion. An out-of-the-blue dinner invitation that I received from Bill Sword years later confirmed my suspicions. When I arrived at New York's River Club, I was surprised to see Nate Cummings and among Bill's other guests Texas millionaire Ross Perot and Bill Moyers, former newspaper publisher and broadcast journalist.

As soon as I took my seat at the table, Cummings turned his back to me and engaged in conversation with Perot without once acknowledging my presence. My guess is that having me at the table was Bill Sword's way of needling Cummings.

Obviously, the fifty-two million-dollar cushion would have allowed us to weather any turbulence or obstacles with relative ease. Still, with GM as a partner, I was confident that TAW would help other international busi-nesses, including others in the United States, to view Africa as a continent with potential and worthy of development.

I set my sights on forming a partnership with a major U.S. auto man-ufacturer with a quality truck division. The trucks, tractors, and trailers that TAW would lease to the Africans would have to be durable, built to withstand the rigors of Africa's rugged roads and terrain. Before selecting GM, I met with the industry's primary manufacturers, including the big three—GM, Ford, and Chrysler.

Chrysler dropped out of contention very early. I decided that Ford had the best technical package, but GM had the best managerial package. I chose not to go with Ford because it didn't use a Ford engine in its trucks; a Cummings engine was used. I foresaw the possibility of another my-word vs. his-word confrontation, comparable to what occurred years ago during my Apollo space fiasco.

I suspected that if problems arose between the engine and the rest of the vehicle, Ford would say the fault lies in the Cummings engine, while the engine crew would point the finger at Ford. I wanted to have one person to confront. That's why I chose GM. It took a while to finalize the deal. We spent eighteen months in negotiations, and it was never a sure thing. I did not regret my decision to go with GM.

John Rock helped put the GM deal together. John and I were about the same age, young for the positions we held. John was considered a "maverick manager"; he operated like a troubleshooter but had no real title. I never saw his name on a masthead, but he had lots of power. Eventually, he became head of GM's truck division. People paid attention to him. My pitch to John was that American trucks would be far more efficient in Africa than European trucks. He thought I was an honest guy, he listened.

I told him that European countries are smaller, closer together. Their trucks are designed for one hundred- to two hundred-mile trips, not much more. African countries are much larger; many of their mostly unpaved roads stretch five hundred to one thousand miles. Where did the trucks in Africa come from? Europe. American trucks are more durable, built to travel for thousands of miles, from coast to coast. I believe John bought into my premise, that there was a tremendous market in Africa for American trucks. I told him that if GM became TAW's partner, I would buy four thousand GM trucks over the next five years. He liked my pitch and believed I could do it.

Working behind the scenes, John convinced GM's management to "do the deal." GM agreed to assist TAW in developing full-service maintenance, training, and parts facilities in Africa and sealed the partnership with a 1.2 million dollar investment in TAW. The GM deal linked TAW with a company which had the will and the resources to provide the initial service facilities, which cost anywhere from a quarter-million to a half-million dollars apiece. When you're setting up these facilities at scattered sites, it's an expensive proposition.

When the deal was finalized, USAID was embedded in OPIC, which was then headed by Brad Mills, a Princeton graduate. At the time, OPIC provided TAW's creditors with financial guarantees and political risk insurance to overseas investors. Brad fully supported TAW's leasing venture and he wanted to make sure GM did as well. He invited the GM top management, including the GM overseas head to his Washington, D.C., office for a meeting. He said to them, "Tom has a tough job ahead of him. He's going to have problems that are difficult to foresee, breakdowns, setbacks, but I urge you to support him, stick by him, don't bail out at the first sign of trouble. Stand behind him all the way." Those GM officials pledged that they would be there for TAW, and they did. They never let us down.

With GM's assistance and direction, our goal was to gradually make TAW a full-service vehicle leasing company. Those plans were excellerated when a transportation crisis crippled copper-rich Zambia's export business. The dispute involved Zambia and its neighbor, Northern Rhodesia (now Zimbabwe).

Here's what happened: Southern Rhodesia's Prime Minister, Ian Smith, a strong advocate of white rule, denounced Zambia as a haven for black freedom fighters, who conducted periodic raids into Rhodesia. Reports indicated that both countries had established training camps along the border and both supported cross-border raids. Smith decided to punish Zambia by closing the trade route Zambia used to ship its goods through Rhodesia to the port of Beira, Mozambique, but he exempted copper from the blockade because he wanted his financially troubled Rhodesia Railways to continue to transport Zambia's anual thirty thousand tons of copper to the Beira seaport. At the time, Zambia was the second largest producer of copper in the world. Kenneth Kaunda, Zambia's president, had no interest in doing any business with an enemy. He sought other options. The Chinese were building a railroad from Dar es Saalam, Tanzania's capital, to the copper belt in Zambia, which would have taken years to complete. Kaunda didn't wait. He announced that Zambia would reroute its copper by truck along the Tanzam Highway to a seaport in Dar es Salaam, a 1, 200-mile stretch over some unpaved roads and through rugged terrain.

I was home in Teaneck, New Jersey, when I learned of the Kaunda/Smith standoff. I quickly contacted GM and then left for Zambia, eager to set up a meeting with the Zambian government officals. We already had a leasing operation in Zambia, but this was an opportunity to expedite the full-service maintenance plan that John Rock and I already had discussed. I told the Zambian officals that TAW could provide Zambia with three hundred trucks with related services and an additional 80 trucks immediately.

I spent the next three weeks in discussion with various parts of the Zambian government. Almost without exception, each government agency, that I spoke to, expressed an interest, however, none were willing to commit. After three weeks, I decided that my offer of TAW's full service leasing program was "not to be "at this time in Zambia. I decided to return home to the U.S. On the way home, I stopped in Nairobi Kenya to spend a few days with Ernest Kalibala, the TAW manager for East Africa. After the second day in Nairobi, I received a phone call from Rupiah Banda, telling me he had set up a meeting with President Kaunda to dicuss TAW's leasing program. I immediately returned to Zambia and met with President Kaunda. I told President Kaunda that TAW could provide Zambia with 80 trucks immediately and 300 trucks with full service, at a date to be negotiated.

President Kaunda liked it, and the negotiations began. They ended with TAW acquiring its largest contract since operating in Africa, and our commitment to send an initial shipment of eighty trucks to Zambia in ninety days.

The deal, which would involve more than twenty-one million dollars in U.S. exports, loomed as a major game-changer for TAW. Little did I know that the day-to-day negotiations to finalize the deal also would lead to a significant change in my personal life.

CHAPTER 18

"There is no country in Africa where it is not essential to know to which tribe, or which subgroup of which tribe, the president belongs. From this single piece of information, you can trace the lines of patronage and allegiance that define the State."

CHRISTOPHER HITCHENS

For more than ten years, Kenneth Kaunda together with others fought to free Northern Rhodesia from British rule. When the nationalists' movement prevailed in 1964, Kaunda became the first president of his country of birth, which was renamed Zambia from Northern Rhodesia. Kaunda and Harry Nkumbula were among several nationalists' leaders who mobilized native Africans against the European-dominated federation of Rhodesia. Many thought Nkumbula would have emerged as the logical choice for president. Leaders of the country's three major tribes–Eastern Group, Bemba, and Tonga–couldn't agree on a president. They represent the country's controlling political forces. Though Kaunda was born in Zambia, he was not a member of a local tribe. His parents were missionaries from Malawi.

As head of the United National Independence Party, Kaunda pledged to unify the country; the people chose him. Kaunda understood that the power to govern resided in the leaders of the three major tribes, not the people. I believe he maintained his power by alternately pitting two tribes against the third. At three- or four-year intervals, he'd turn a former enemy tribe into an ally, or an ally into an enemy. Kaunda continued his my-enemy-my-friend switch among the three tribes throughout his twenty-seven-year reign. Many African leaders may not know the intricacies of science or nuances of the business world, but many of their leaders are savvy politicians.

TAW's goal was to relate to the African people not just as customers, but as business partners and investors. I believe many Zambians trusted that TAW, which employed many of their own, would seek to get the deal completed in a way that would benefit the Zambian people. As Alan Dynner said, our goal was unique to the times. "That's not how it was done before TAW arrived," Alan added "The reality was the former colonial countries, England, France, and Belgium, had a death grip on the economies of the former colonies. Their big national banks, the British banks, Standard and French banks, wouldn't lend money to a local African. Tom saw the potential in these people trying to start their own businesses, but they couldn't get funding....TAW gave it to them. Tom's idea was amazing and very progressive."

From my perspective, the most progressive development occurred when Kaunda closed the deal with a handshake, not a request for a bribe. Back then, the payment of bribes was–and might still be–an acceptable part of business transactions in Africa. I expected Kaunda to follow through with a where's-my-under-the-table-cut later. He never did.

Two other developments arose from the TAW/Zambia negotiations worth noting. The first involved the use of an IBM Magnetic Tape/Selectric Typewriter (MT/ST) machine, forerunner of the word processor, which expedited the negotiating process.

The second–and more personal matter–concerned the presence of Dorothy Walker, the IBM office products manager in Lusaka Zambia. She captured my heart.

The IBM MT/ST machine was a model of the IBM typewriter. TAW had an MT/ST machine in our New York office. IBM had a policy which allowed companies operating in any foreign country to use the MT/ST in an

IBM office wherever available. Luckily, IBM offices in Zambia were equipped with MT/ST machines.

I went to the closest IBM office and there was Dorothy. She wouldn't take my offer of money for helping TAW, so I took her to dinner several times which I would have done for a male in the same circumstance, that's how the relationship began. We shared some of our experiences and learned that we had a lot in common. Dorothy was an early member of the independence movement, which lifted Kaunda to the presidency. She knew, personally, all the political and economic players in Zambia, and was a Kaunda ally. In the late 1960s, Kaunda sent Dorothy, who's mother was a member of the Tonga tribe, to London as Zambia's "chief of protocol."

The top tier restaurants in Lusaka, Zambia, all had bands for the dancing pleasure of their patrons. To my surprise, Dorothy was one of the very few people who could follow me when I danced. I don't use the commonly taught dance steps. I kind of move in rhythm with the music. Everyone dances in Africa: grandmothers, old uncles, children, Nelson Mandela. I felt very much at home.

My sister tried to teach me to dance when I was a teenager; she failed. When my two daughters were teens, they tried to teach me. Same result. I was surprised that Dorothy was able to keep up with my random dance steps. As we danced, I thought about Ginger Rogers and Fred Astaire—she did the same thing he did only backwards and in high heels, as the saying goes.

Dorothy dressed smartly when she was on the job. She wore silk stockings and high heels and was looked upon by her fellow Zambians with a high level of respect.

Once while walking with me along the main street in Lusaka, an old woman from the village of Dorothy's mother approached her. When Dorothy recognized the woman, she fell on her knees, bowed her head, grasped the woman's hand, and then mumbled what sounded like a chant. She was following an African custom, showing respect for an elder from the village of her mother. It reminded me of the rituals that U.S. college fraternity pledgees perform publicly for frat brothers. The more time I spent with her, the easier it was for me to understand why her fellow Zambians respected her. Dorothy was one of only a few people in the sparsely populated colored community who supported the independence movement, another reason she was held in high esteem.

At another time, while Dorothy and I walked along the Kafue River, a different woman approached us. She spoke to Dorothy in Tonga, a language where you use the phrase "eh, eh" quite often. The woman might have been in her sixties; Dorothy was in her thirties. It turns out the woman was one of the nannies that helped raise Dorothy as a child. She remembered Dorothy's father, James Walker; they talked about him.

Dorothy was the product of a mixed-race relationship—a Zambian mother and a British father. Often when we were together in public, many people thought we were related or married. Sometimes, even Africans weren't sure of her heritage. For example, when I took her to an upscale Kenyan restaurant, the waitresses and waiters joked and exchanged personal comments about us in their native language, unaware that Dorothy understood every word they said. She spoke Tonga, Swahili, and French, as well as English, each fluently.

Her father was a descendant of one of England's prominent legal families. He grew up in Lancashire, which is in the western part of Britain. He had two older sisters; both became lawyers, but they didn't pursue law careers. One of them scaled Mount Everest.

Like his sisters, he had no interest in the family law business. While in his late teens, he visited Zambia, fell in love with the country, and, of course, Dorothy's mother, and decided to live there. His father bought him a twenty thousand-acre spread, and he became a farmer. Dorothy's mother lived with him. This was before Zambia gained its independence, so they couldn't marry legally. They had six children.

When his wife died at an early age, James Walker wanted to ensure that Dorothy received a first-class education. He wanted her to attend the

"Cathedral," a Catholic school that was considered the best in Southern Rhodesia (now Zimbabwe). He asked a friend, who was the Minister of Education in Southern Rhodesia, to enroll his daughter there. The Minister, who assumed Dorothy was white, agreed to take her. Though they weren't greeted warmly, school officials allowed her to take classes but wouldn't allow her to live with fellow students in the convent. The minister arranged for her to live with a colored family in Zimbabwe.

Dorothy learned to be equally comfortable in a European setting or African setting. Her father built two homes on the complex. Her father and mother, wanted to raise their children to appreciate the lifestyles and cultures of both parents. One half of each house in which they lived was "the English house," where they had linen, silver, and china. The family gathered at the table for meals and had conversations in English. The other half was the "African house," which was decorated more plainly. Family members sat on the floor and scooped food out of a pot with their hands, just the way they did in other African villages. Conversations in the African part of the home were in Tonga, the mother's language. Conversations in the English part of the home were in English.

It's rare, I believe, when you meet someone, especially from a different country, different culture halfway around the world and discover that their values are your values. She brought out the best in me.

To me it was remarkable that many people meeting Dorothy and I, for the first time commented "that we could be sister and brother", just as different people at a different time, made the same comment about Barbara and I.

Dorothy's expertise with the MT/ST machine made her an invaluable asset during the negotiations. Though Dorothy was the IBM office manager, she agreed to do the late-night typing because she could not pay staff members overtime. The TAW team members routinely pulled nearly all-nighters, but we were always at the negotiating table each morning at 9 sharp. Alan Dynner and Ernie Kalibala chose to do goofy stuff to stay awake. Sometimes, they fought off the sandman by playing catch, substituting big wads of paper or other tubular items for baseballs. Other team members took quick naps.

After each negotiation session, Dorothy collected the material and spent the rest of the night transposing all the comments, amendments, and other changes into the MT/ST machine. She'd then crank the tape out, so we'd have twenty "clean" copies of the edited document for the negotiating teams to review. Twenty clean copies! No erasures! No pen or pencil marks! Twenty clean copies!

The Zambians were amazed. They'd never spent a day negotiating and the next day reviewing clean copies of everything that had been discussed. They didn't understand how we accomplished it. Our work ethic at the time was impressive and unusual for businesses, even in America, and our heavy workload stretched us to the maximum.

Besides crossing our "t"s and dotting our "i"s with our pact with Zambia, we also worked on solidifying agreements with two other partners—Fruehauf Trailer Corporation and Ryder Corporation. GM would furnish TAW with three hundred trucks; Fruehauf would provide four hundred trailers and Ryder would build infrastructure along the 1, 200-mile route and manage and maintain the fleet of trucks that would take Zambia's copper to the Dar es Salaam seaport.

Hence, in 1973, GM agreed with TAW to develop full-service truck maintenance, training, and parts facilities in Africa, beginning in Zambia. Then it struck me that this Harlem-bred grandson of a slave was a principal negotiator in an eighty million-dollar deal that loomed as a promising stimulus of economic growth for the African people. If we successfully broke the blockade by delivering the copper to market via our trucks, TAW would become a major business player on a part of the global stage. What a satisfying thought.

Thanks to favorable coverage by black U.S. media and word-of-mouth-praise among fellow entrepreneurs, some U.S. business investors and bankers took note. I was humbled, too, by the expressions of pride by many working-class blacks who knew of my success. Black waiters often would whisper in my ear "God Bless you," when they served meals. Taxi drivers, maids and other hotel employees also greeted me with proud smiles. Even now, I get goose bumps just thinking about how good they felt about our success. In its December 1973 edition, Black Enterprise (BE) magazine touted TAW's accomplishments with a cover story and the headline: "Black Africa on the Road to Economic Takeoff." The photo tagline: "Thomas A. Wood, Pioneer of Afro-American Black Business." The inside story headline read: "TAW- The success story of the black American company that is the first in equipment leasing in Africa."

Excited as I was about having the GM deal finalized, I realized, too, that we'd need an experienced manager to head the Zambia project. That was my next order of business. Hughlyn Fierce, a Chase manager, guided me to Frank Savage, who was then president of Equitable Life Community Enterprises Corporation, which provided capital for small black companies. Frank earned his undergraduate degree (BA) from Howard University and a masters' degree from Johns Hopkins University. He made his first trip to Africa as a Howard student with Operations Crossroads Africa, a harbinger to JFK's Peace Corps, which was established in 1961. Frank was among a group of students that built tennis courts for a boys' club in Zambia (then Northern Rhodesia). That same group traveled to several other countries, including Nairobi, Kenya. Frank stayed long enough to develop a serious crush on the African continent.

Hughlyn Fierce and Ernie Kalibala knew Frank when he was a bank officer at Citibank; they all were among the first blacks to hold managerial positions at major U.S. financial institutions. They believed Frank would be a great hire, a major asset. Hugh gave Frank a brief sketch of TAW, its CEO, and the eighty million-dollar truck leasing deal. Frank had trouble believing that a black man was the chief architect behind the deal. In his autobiography, The Savage Way (John Wiley & Sons, 2013), Frank revealed his inner thoughts as he listened to the Hughlyn sketch. He wrote: "Listening intently,

I wondered if I would wake up soon. Africa? (Multimillion-dollar) contract? Am I dreaming?"

Later, when I asked Frank to consider returning to Africa to work for TAW, he was truly stunned and intrigued. As he pondered the offer, I urged him to fly to Nairobi to meet with Ernie and then visit Zambia. He agreed to do both. Frank and Ernie were way-back friends during their start-up days in banking in New York. Ernie was with Manufacturers Hanover and Frank was with Citibank when they first met. Ernie greeted Frank at the Nairobi airport, showed him the TAW operation in Nairobi, and then took him to Zambia, where Frank had worked years ago as a Howard student. The trip might have made the difference.

I was excited and delighted when Frank agreed to join TAW as head of the Zambia project. He was delighted when I gave him a hefty signing bonus, which was enough for him to purchase a Westchester, New York, home his wife wanted. The pieces were falling into place, and as they did, my confidence level spiked. Yet I sensed the possibility of sinister forces unleashing havoc at any moment. We were, after all, operating in a foreign country new to independence, accustomed to unrest and distrust. If the Kaunda administration was to be successful in its plans to move tons of copper 1, 200 miles from Zambia to a seaport in Dar es Salaam, our bond with the Zambian government had to be strong, steeped in truth and trust. There was still much work to be done.

CHAPTER 19

"We must accept finite disappointments, but never lose infinite hope"

MARTIN LUTHER KING JR.

—

Before the Zambia/TAW contract had been finalized, General Motors demonstrated its commitment to the project by sending engineers and mechanics to Zambia to personally inspect the hazardous terrain and roads along the 1,200-mile route to the seaport.

The roads in several stretches were quite steep as they passed through rocky terrain. Unless specially designed, most trucks crept up those hills going only 5 mph to 10 mph. The GM techs returned to the States and designed a transmission in the new model that would allow the trucks to move up those hills at 25 mph.

Ryder pushed GM to make the trucks easier to maintain; GM pushed Ryder to provide top-of-the-line servicing. We wanted to make these Zambia-bound trucks five times better than the standard made-in-America-type. We tried to address every possible need of the drivers, mechanics, and maintenance crews and to anticipate every problem that might arise along the Tanzam Highway.

The system that we had planned included positioning three recreational vehicles (RVs) with complete workshops at three hundred- to four hundred-mile intervals along the route. Each transport truck would have its license number on top, and an airplane would monitor the position and condition of each truck. If the truck became disabled, the pilot would call the nearest RV station to have a mechanic dispatched to the disabled vehicle.

Nothing like this had ever been done before in Africa. That's why our European rivals didn't want us to succeed. They knew we were on the road to putting them out of the truck sales business. We knew that several key members of Kaunda's administration desperately wanted the TAW/Zambia deal to fail, the sooner the better. The possibility of saboteurs disrupting Zambia's first convoy of copper-filled trucks bound for port raised our anxiety level considerably. In fact, during this period, several European saboteurs were caught and imprisoned for blowing up bridges along the proposed truck route, which confirmed our fears.

Our known adversaries were:

* Rhodesia's Prime Minister Ian Smith, who closed the trade route that Zambia had used to transport its exports to the Beira seaport. Smith, however, told Kaunda that he could continue shipping Zambia's copper using the same route, obviously because it would benefit Rhodesia's struggling railways. Smith fumed when Kaunda rejected his offer and chose to transport the copper via trucks provided by TAW.

* Some members of Kaunda's administration loyal to the European truck suppliers questioned the competence of TAW's leadership; leaders of other tribes also searched for viable reasons to overthrow Kaunda. Before TAW established its leasing business in Africa, European companies provided Africa with its trucks and buses. They showered Kaunda's mid-level and some top administrators with gifts and other benefits.

* We saw Roland "Tiny" Rowland, chief executive of the London and Rhodesian Mining and Land Company (LONRHO), as our most dangerous foe. He was placed alone in a separate category. There was nothing small about "Tiny," who was 6-5, nor in my opinion, there were very few things nice about Tiny's business practices. Tiny shaped public opinion in several African countries through the newspapers he owned, including the Times

of Zambia, whose publisher was Vernon Mwaanga. Tiny once called Vernon the most hedonistic person he'd ever met. I expected Tiny to do whatever was necessary to derail the Zambia/TAW deal. Indeed, a day after the contracts were finalized, a sign posted in LONRHO headquarters read, "Kill the TAW deal!"

In my opinion, Tiny bribed officials in several African countries. When a country gained independence, he treated some of the African leaders as equals and they fell all over him. He knew many of the Africans power brokers "achillies heel" better than I. If a minister's child was sick, he'd fly the child to a London hospital for treatment. He would walk into a prime minister's office without being announced. Tiny was a very clever guy.

Tiny's modus operandi was to establish economic roots in a country by buying its newspaper and its Mercedes dealership. Then he would provide Mercedes cars to government officials and and others and control public opinion through his newspapers. Tanzania was one of only a few countries that said "no." Most of the others, including Zambia, said "yes." Tiny became known as "the unacceptable face of capitalism." Much later, after the arbitration, several of my friends in Zimbabwe, remembered when Tiny "salted"his first mine to get started". Many suspected, (including me)that Tiny Rowland was one of the sources of U.S. and British Governments' Intelligence on information about African Leaders.

Tiny and I had similar objectives, but I believe mine were more honest and altruistic than his. Through my leasing company, I wanted to improve the lives of the African people throughout the continent but particularly in the fourteen countries in which TAW operated. Creating jobs and business opportunities would be a primary contribution. TAW's plan was to support— but not, in any way try to control, the development of the African economies in those countries. The early phase of our plan was completed quite successfully, but the road ahead was fraught with danger. I knew staying on course wouldn't be easy.

I didn't really socialize with the ex-patriots in the countries in which I established leasing businesses; I socialized with the African leaders, administrators, and businessmen. I'd learned long before then that intertwining business with pleasure isn't necessarily a harmful mixture.

I formed particular working/social relationships with two of Kaunda's top confidants—Rupiah Banda, Kaunda's minister of foreign affairs, and Aaron Milner, Zambia's minister of home affairs. On one occasion, Aaron invited Mwaanga, a Tiny Rowland loyalist, to play doubles with us on Milner's backyard tennis court. Mwaanga suggested that we determine partners by skin color. "Why don't we have the coloreds play against the Africans?" he said.

Milner and I were light brown; Banda and Mwaanga were darker. Rupiah Banda quickly vetoed Mwaanga's suggestion, picking me as his partner. "Tom is black; Aaron is colored," Banda said. His comment meant a great deal to me because it summed up the way I wanted to be viewed by the African people. Africans who knew me saw me as Rupiah Banda did: one of them, partners in a business venture that could lead to a better life for most Zambians. TAW had no secrets, no hidden agendas, no under-the-table payoffs.

Much later, Rupiah Banda became the 4'th President of Zambia.

Kaunda appointed Peter Siwo, Permanent Secretary in the Ministry of Works and Supply, as Zambia's point person on the TAW/Zambia project. I invited Peter to come to the United States and observe my discussions with GM regarding the changes we wanted in the specifications of the trucks that would transport the copper to the seaport. As an engineer, I knew that GM's standard trucks wouldn't last long on Africa's rugged terrain. If favorably impressed, I believed that Peter, one of a few college-educated members of Kaunda's administration, would reassure his superiors of TAW's commitment and desire to secure the best possible deal for Zambia.

Peter and I bonded on that trip. We shared stories about our lives as students and young men. Peter, a chemistry major, was among the first graduates of the University of Fort Hare, one of Africa's primary institution of higher education (1915 to 1959) for Africans. Located in South Africa, Fort Hare offered a Western-style education to students from throughout sub-Saharan Africa and created a black African technical elite. Sebastian Zulu, who was Zambia's solicitor general in the early 1970s, is also a Fort Hare alumnus. I also took Peter to California to meet Barbara's parents. Her father, Henry Sr., was then the retired head of Alabama State University's chemistry department. I knew they would have much to talk about, and they did. Peter was an honest, straightforward person. He was diligent and fair.

For a while, the operation to provide Zambia with a fleet of GM trucks rolled along trouble-free. The initial 80 trucks arrived on time. The three RVs that were to be used for servicing disabled trucks that broke down on the road, arrived ahead of time, as did the tires and a simulator to train the truck drivers. Then we hit a major snag. After the delivery of the 80 trucks within 90 days, as called for in the contract with the Zambian Government, (under which the Zambian Government was not charged for the cost of the vehicles, they were only charged for the operation of the vehicles) GM notified us that it couldn't meet the set deadline for the delivery of the three hundred trucks. GM representatives cited several transportation-related events worldwide that would cause them to miss the deadline. They included specifically, the U.S. requirement for emission controls, resulting in a change in scheduling for the GM truck model that was to be sent to Africa.

The new model would include emissions controls, which are used to limit the discharge of noxious gases from the internal combustion engine. Most Americans who bought trucks back then wanted trucks without emission controls, which caused greater gas consumption. Unlike automobiles, new truck models are not automatically produced every calendar year. A backload of orders, created by truck owners who didn't want emission controls, forced GM to extend the model for another year.Pushing the TAW trucks scheduled for the next model year back in time.

Immediately after I was informed of the delay by GM, I held an emergency meeting with our creditors in Washington, D.C. They wanted to be assured that Zambia would agree to an extension. I told them I would request a waiver. I had my secretary locate Peter Siwo, who was in London. I met Peter in London, informed him of the delay, and he agreed to OK an extension. He didn't want to sign it in London because he believed some might think our action and meeting were contrived. He asked me to return to Zambia with him, and he would sign it there. When we returned to Zambia, he decided to run it by Kaunda.

It took him several weeks to get back to me, but when he did, he said, "Everything is OK." I flew to New York to inform our bankers, suppliers, and OPIC of the waiver. They all were relieved and promised to continue providing support. However, they did want Zambia's waiver approval in writing. I promised to request the written approval, once the trucks were at the Baltimore dock ready to be shipped to Zambia. I did not want to request a written waiver, at that time, for the possibility of another delay in the production of the trucks. I asked Siwo to send someone to Detroit to watch the trucks come off the assembly line. He sent an assistant, Kafumakachi, who wrote his name on the chassis of one of the trucks. As he wrote his name, Kafumakachi said, "When the trucks arrive in Zambia, I can say, That's the truck I saw coming off the assembly line in Detroit!" Upon Kafumakachi return to Zambia, Siwo provided TAW with a written waiver.

We then focused on the next step, which was completing the funding for TAW's full service operation for the Zambian contract. Prudential, which had contributed seven million dollars of the 10.8 million-dollar package that launched TAW two years earlier, quickly agreed to provide additional funds, in addition to others. Then fate struck with a hammer-like blow. Two days before the deal was to be finalized, a phone call from a Prudential official burst our festive balloon. "We're not going to do the deal," the Prudential official said. "We learned that the Prudential person who's negotiating this deal and others, took a bribe from another Prudential customer.* We've decided not to touch any of the deals that he's involved in."

*It should be noted that the person negotiating this deal was not in the crew that negotiated the first 10.8 million dollar deal.

I hung up the phone, wondering how I possibly could block this potentially deadly blow. Sam Pierce, my lawyer friend, came to mind. Like Obi-Wan Kenobi was to the rebels in the first Star Wars movie, Sam became my only hope. He had come to my rescue earlier in my career when I was CEO of Decision Systems, my computer firm. Sam resolved TAW's dispute with RCA, simply by placing a phone call to NBC president Robert Sarnoff, his friend and Cornell University classmate. In the real world that's how some business disputes are settled.

Sam, a former member of Prudential's Board of Directors, worked his magic once more on my behalf. He told the Prudential board, "Tom and I have been friends since we were kids. I can vouch for him. He's an honest man and I know he would never have anything to do with this or any other dishonest or shady deal." Sam's passionate plea in my defense evoked favorable action: Prudential's board reversed its decision in the TAW case.

READER ALERT: Africa in not unique in this practice.

It also gave me and TAW managers, Frank, and Ernie along with our outside lawyer Alan something to celebrate later that night. We had dinner at a Greek restaurant in Manhattan close to the office. That night, Jimmy "the Greek" Snyder was among the diners. As a member of CBS' NFL pregame show, Snyder had become a celebrity of sorts. Working with cohosts Brent Musburger and Phyllis George, Snyder's job was to predict the final scores of each game. Acting silly, Snyder entertained the diners by dancing. Alan earned his fifteen seconds of fame by trying to coax Ernie into belting out a song. He introduced Ernie to the crowd as a "great African singer." With absolutely no talent as a singer, Ernie wisely refused to play along.

After our festive dinner, I sent Frank to Zambia to deliver the news that the trucks were on the way. A week after he arrived in Zambia, Frank called with alarming news: Zambia had canceled the TAW/Zambia contract. I told Frank to meet me in Nairobi, Kenya, in a few days to plan a response.

CHAPTER 20

"Real integrity is doing the right thing, knowing that nobody's going to know if you did or not."

OPRAH WINFREY

"For my friends, accomodation;
For my enemies, the law"

ANONYMOUS

We were obligated to inform the banks, OPIC, and suppliers that the Government of Zambia had canceled the contract. GM halted its shipment of vehicles from Detroit, took back the vehicles that were sitting on the dock in Baltimore Maryland ready to be shipped overseas. All the vehicles to be delivered under the contract had already been produced. The project that once had TAW moving steadily toward great success suddenly had veered into a death spiral.

Prior to the Zambian cancelation TAW was ranked by Black Enterprise magazine as the tenth largest black business in the U.S..

Zambia's willingness to return to the negotiating table slowed our descent, which was all I could ask for at the time. I wanted our restore-the-contract strategy to remind Kaunda that TAW's presence already had bolstered the country's economy. Our firm employed many Zambians at every level, including management. Other Zambians, with TAW's support and expertise, learned to start and operate their own businesses.

Zambia's representatives at the meeting included an attorney and someone from the Minister of Transportation. A family emergency kept Alan Dynner, TAW's attorney, at home in the USA. Joe Brigati, one of Alan's partners, and Frank Savage, director of the Zambian project, and Sabastian Zulu, joined me on the opposite side of the table.

I began the session expressing our disappointment and surprise in Zambia's decision to cancel the contract. The Zambian representatives sat stoically across the table, listening with their heads often bowed. They never asked any questions. As soon as I completed my presentation, Zambia's lawyer thanked me, then said, "The fact remains that TAW did not meet the obligations of the contract; therefore, the contract was canceled."

We realized that nothing we suggested would change their minds. Sensing the futility of the moment, Brigati said, "Before we conclude the meeting, it is my obligation to remind you of the provisions of the contract, which states that in the event of a dispute, if a dispute cannot be resolved amicably between the partners, the issue would be remanded to the International Court of Justice in London, where three judges will decide the outcome of the contract and whether any damages should be awarded. We don't want to go to arbitration. We want to continue to execute under the contract. That is our wish."

In response, the Zambian attorney said, "Mr. Brigati, we fully understand the contract provisions."

Rupiah Banda, a Kaunda's top advisor, later told me that our meeting was a meaningless formality. The decision to cancel the contract had been made earlier at a gathering of Zambia's leaders, including Rupiah and Kaunda, who had argued in favor of reinstating the contract. According to Rupiah, Kaunda told the group, "Why are we doing this? We have an obligation to honor the contract!" Kaunda's pleas fell on deaf ears; he was overruled.

I mentioned earlier that Zambia's three major tribes controlled the government and that Kaunda held onto the presidency for twenty-seven years with a tactic of alternately pitting two tribes against one. This time, Kaunda couldn't get the swing vote; he didn't think he would survive if he pushed too far to get it. Philosophically, I understood why Kaunda backed away. His decision was a variation of an anonymous adage some times credited to Julius Ceasar and used by many others in politics and business routinely: "For my friends, accommodations; for my enemies, the law."

In my opinion, it didn't matter how great of an impact the decision might have on his country; Kaunda did what he had to do to avoid a coup. From his perspective, he had no choice but to accept the tribal-influenced vote and allow an arbitration court in London to make the ultimate decision. Indeed, such political tribalism has lurked in the halls of the United States Congess, as demonstrated by the Republican Senate Majority leader Mitch McConnell's message to the Republican GOP to say "No" to anything Democratic president Barack Obama proposed, even at the expense of the country.

My thinking is that someone below the top level of Kaunda's government wanted to void our contract with Zambia.

With our backs to the wall, Mainza Chona, Kaunda's vice president, made one final stab at converting me to the bribery side of business in Africa. A few days before our failed meeting, Chona invited me to his office after business hours. I arrived still wearing a suit and tie. When I entered his office, Chona already had taken off his coat and tie and was stretched out on the floor. I sat in a chair and wondered if the room was bugged. We made small talk for a while, then in effect he said, "If you're willing to take care of us, we'll see about reinstating the contract." I told him I couldn't do that. The next day, Chona spread the word that I insulted him, By tribal standards, I had insulted him. I should have sat on the floor with him. But by my standards, he had insulted me.

I believe when other members of Kaunda's administration learned that I hadn't paid any bribes for the contract, they decided that I had to go.

My philosophy in Africa was that I was there as a businessman. I wasn't going to be involved in corruption or offer bribes to get business. Perhaps it was self preservation. I didn't want to have to look over my shoulder for the rest of my life. Since my first job with the Detroit Tank Arsenal, I adhered to my personal guideline which says, "You can accept or give anything that can be consumed or used in one day—dinner, theatre tickets, sporting event tickets, and so forth." That was my guiding directive in the United States, and in Africa.

The cancellation of the contract, which led to an arbitration hearing in a London court, eventually set us on a scramble for survival. Bankruptcy loomed as a real possibility.

We in the United States do not have under our laws a requirement that the plaintiff is required to pay the legal fees of the defendant, if the plantiff losses the lawsuit. For this reason the plaintiff is required to put up a bond to cover the defendents legal costs. Under English Law, which governed the contract, this is the case. This requirement does tend to prevent "frivolous law suits". I personally believe that requirement is a "good one". However the requirement caused TAW a great deal of financial hardship.

My financial problem was twofold:

To set aside as a bond payment of approximately 250, 000 U.S dollars every six months to pay Zambia's court fees if the arbitrators ruled against us in the contract dispute.

To negotiate a "composition or workout agreement" that would keep OPIC and other creditors at bay.

My primary goal was to avoid bankruptcy and maintaining sufficient funds to keep TAW operational in Zambia and several other African countries until the arbitrators rendered their decision. Arbitrations generally last at least a year, but with delays, they might last several years.

Just days after the Zambia contract was canceled, the strangest thing happened. Bill Sword, the Morgan Stanley executive who did not fulfill his commitment to finalize the fifty-two million-dollar deal that would have given TAW a rainy-day cushion, resurfaced. Without any discussion with me, Sword called the creditors and advised them that Morgan Stanley would serve as TAW's investment advisor during the workout agreement. His stature in the banking industry drew them to his office without protest. "We're not going to have a panic sale," Sword said. "We're going to have an orderly transition and work this thing out." Though appreciated, I believe Sword's action was another indication of a guilty conscience, born of his decision to walk away—without saying a word—from our fifty-two million-dollar deal.

Over the next few months, we negotiated an agreement with OPIC. OPIC was, the government agency that was created to assist Americans who invest in overseas businesses and provides insurance against being nationalized or expropriated. OPIC director Marshall Mays, who had replaced Brad Mills upon his retirement, eventually initiated bankruptcy proceedings and worked overtime to ensure that the negotiations weren't favorable to TAW. I believe his actions were driven by racial animus.

In 1973, under Brad Mills, OPIC's first director, TAW was viewed as a hero, an ally, and competent business partner. Brad saw me as a peer and he treated my staff and me fairly and with respect. In a statement before a U.S. Congressional Subcommittee on International Policy, Brad described the TAW project as "one of those pioneering ventures that opened new fields of activity." Brad stated that a financial project (like the TAW project) "must pass a detailed analysis against three basic tests: reasonable prospects of financial viability over the full term of the loan; likely to make a significant, preferably innovative contribution to the host country's development and likely to produce net economic benefits for the United States." Brad added, "To pass these tests a project must be soundly conceived, supported by realistic market and other analysis, be assured of competent management, and capitalized with enough cushion to survive the almost inevitable setback and surprises."

That's how TAW was viewed when Brad Mills was OPIC's director. Here's what happens when your government turns against you.

In 1974, under Marshall Mays, Brad's replacement, I became a villain and TAW was considered poorly managed and incapable of achieving its goals. Mays, I assumed, felt that I, Tom Wood, had committed the "unforgivable sin of being black." At the time Zambia cancelled the U.S.$ 80 million transportation contract with TAW, the dollar amount of the guarantees which OPIC had provided TAW was U.S.$7 million, less than 1/3 of the U.S.$ 25 million plus TAW owed to multiple creditors. The other major creditor was General Motors. GM and most of the other creditors were willing to work out the debt over time. Not so with OPIC, OPIC initiated the bankruptcy proceedings. After completing the "work out agreement", in November of 1974 and after we had repatriated 250, 000 dollars and drawn checks to pay that amount pro rata to all of TAW's creditors, then OPIC, suddenly and without warning accelerated and demanded immediate payment of all loans, seized all of TAW's bank accounts in the United States, and filed lawsuits against TAW. I believe Mays' plan was to put TAW in bankruptcy as quickly as possible. Moreover, terms of the agreement, set by Mays, required TAW to make illegal quarterly payments into a joint bank account with OPIC and TAW as the account holders, with only OPIC allowed to make withdrawals.

Having a resident (TAW) and a foreign national (OPIC) on the same bank account didn't make sense.Previously, I asked Mays, "If I pay money to you, why do you want my name on your account?" I told the creditors that I don't want the money in TAW's name because I don't want you to play games maneuvering the money out of the African countries. I wanted the creditors to set up bank accounts in OPIC's name only. I didn't want the names of any TAW employees on the bank account. Despite my protest, Mays, a South Carolinian, kept TAW's name on the account. We complied reluctantly for several months.

It soon became clear to me, and others, that I, not TAW, was the target of Mays' hostility. He seemed unable or unwilling to establish a cordial working relationship with a black CEO. Alan, my attorney, said, "I don't think Mays was a roaring bigot, but racism can take a whole bunch of forms. Marshall Mays couldn't believe he was dealing with Tom Wood because Tom was black. We never accused anybody of racism, but there's no question in my mind that (racism) was a factor."

Sam Pierce, my attorney/friend, arranged for me to discuss the Mays' matter with Marshall Mays' patron, Sen. Strom Thurmond (R-SC) in his Washington, D.C., office. Sen. Thurmond opposed the civil rights legislation of 1964 and 1965 to end segregation and enforce the constitutional rights of black citizens.

In 1925, Sen.Thurmond fathered a mixed race child by the family maid when she was 16 and he was 22, Sen Thurmond paid for her education. Her name has been added to his memorial at the state capital.

I explained to Sen. Thurmond that Mays, among other things, forced my company to become involved in a dubious banking arrangement in Africa. Thurmond listened but provided neither assistance nor guidance.

During this time, Sebastian Zulu, attorney, who was Zambia's solicitor general before becoming TAW's legal councel in Zambia, advised me that the OPIC/TAW joint bank account violated Zambia's foreign exchange control regulations. "It's illegal for the U.S. government to have a local currency account in Zambia" Zulu said.

Based on Zulu's advice, I stopped making payments to the OPIC/TAW accounts.Marshall Mays said, "You have to."

I said, "You're crazy. It's against the law."

Mays accused me of being self-serving and he was right. But if serving your own interest means conforming to the law, then basically, in my opnion, that's not self-serving. I didn't want to break the law. Mays refused to provide TAW with a legal opinion that the TAW/OPIC accounts were legal, and insisted that we continue to make the payments through the joint accounts. I sought congressional help.

In 1976, I testified in the U.S. Congressional hearings which led up to the 1977 Foreign Corrupt Practices. Act. Alan Dynner's firm contacted Stephen Solarz, a Democratic congressman from Brooklyn, New York, to sponsor a bill pursuant to the pending Foreign Corrupt Practices Act, which stated that the U.S. should not break the laws of foreign governments. I provided testimony during those May-June 1976 hearings before the Subcommittee on International Economic Policy. My testimony included this statement: "We recognize the creditors' right to that money. We never disputed that. We were objecting to being forced to break the law. Primarily because we had employees in Africa; they are subject to the laws of these countries, which include criminal penalties." I also submitted to the sub-committee letters of support written by judges from several different African countries. My creditors, led by Marshall Mays, persisted. Mays tried to bank-rupt TAW in Kenya. The Kenyan judge wouldn't let them. He said, "You're breaking our law!"

OPIC then sought to bankrupt TAW in Kenya, for non compliance with the "work out" agreement, by refusing to make the"illegal" payments. In Court, OPIC claimed, falsely, that the subject bank account was "in full control of TAW not OPIC". The Judge told OPIC that if the Court were to believe that statement then TAW should be able to withdraw funds from the account at TAW's discresion. The Judge then told Alan Dynner and I, to, at the lunch break, with draw funds from the account. (the bank was across the street from the courthouse). At the lunch break, Alan and I attempted to withdraw funds from the account. The Bank refused to comply with TAW's request to withdraw funds. We reported "what happened" to the Judge. After consideration, the Judge dimissed OPIC's legal action, with the statement that

"OPIC's actions have violated Kenyan Banking Laws".

It should be noted That:

As president, Trump asked his administration to kill the Foreign Corrupt Practices Act of 1977, as reported in the book "A Very Stable Genius" authored by Phillip Rucker and Carol Leonning. They wrote that "in the spring of 2017 Trump was at a briefing with Rex Tillerson, the then Secretary of State, and at the mention of a bribery law, Trump "perked up" and told Tillerson that he wanted Tillerson, to get rid of that law. Tillerson explained that he could not simply repeal the legislation, that Congress woud need to be involved in any effort to strike it down".

Solarz introduced a bill to forbid OPIC from violating laws of foreign countries, but it was never passed. I took my case to the media, purchasing a half page ad in The New York Times, charging OPIC with trying to coerce TAW into breaking the law. When a situation like this occurs, a government agency such as OPIC usually ceases its action, then investigates the charges rather than persist in its questionable action. OPIC never did that. I tried to get the Congressional Black Caucus to support us, but there was virtually no response. Andy Young, then U.S. Ambassador to the United Nations, and then Democratic Congressman Parren Mitchell from Maryland were the only politicians to support TAW. Still, I refused to make the payments. I told Marshall Mays, "You may put me in bankruptcy, but you'll have do it in Macy's window". You're not going to do it surreptitiously. You can't take that kind of stuff if you want to survive.

I believe that particularly if you are black, you must be "clean of corruption", if you are to win a fight like this one. I knew that freedom is the "freedom to succeed" and also the "freedom to fail", and I was determined "not to fail".

In my case, Marshall Mays/ OPIC scrutinized my business life looking for financial impropriety (dirt), and when they could not find any, OPIC turmed their scrunitiny to my private life. There, they found my relationship with Dorothy. Marshall Mays/ OPIC decided to raise her name in a creditors meeting, a meeting in which I was present, hoping to intimidate me. It did not work ! It only served to increase my resolve "to win this fight" and not fail in my business career.

My inability to stop Marshall Mays/ OPIC from demanding that TAW violate the Foreign Exchange Laws in several African countries caused me to place an Advertisement in the New York Times newspaper explaining "my view on the insistence of OPIC for TAW to make these illegal payments".I will include, at this point, the NY Times "ad" as it covers concisely the difficulties it placed TAW in. At the time I assumed the "ad" had some, if minor political repercussions, for Marshall Mays began to "run away" from what he had wrought.

The title of the New York Times advertisement was

"An Open Letter To President Ford From A Black Businessman"

The "ad "reads as follows:

Dear President Ford;

The advertisement sponsored by the President Ford Committee, which recently appeared in more than twenty Black newspapers with the caption "For Black Americans, President Ford is quietly getting the job done".

It has compelled me to call your attention to the testimony which I gave to the Sub-Committee on International Economic Policy of the Committee on International Relations of the U.S. House of Representatives, in which I stated that a federal agency, the Overseas Private Investment Corporation (OPIC), under your administration forced a Black U.S. company, TAW International Leasing, to break the law in eight African Countries under the threat of placing the company in bankruptcy. TAW is a multinational leasing company doing business in ten African countries. In forcing TAW to make these payments OPIC used the U.S. embassies in these countries as illegal conduits to remove over $440, 000 from these developing nations in violation of their exchange control laws.

In addition OPIC forced TAW to transfer illegally more than $238, 000 to bank accounts established and maintained in an East African nation friendly to the U.S., for the benefit of OPIC and others. OPIC is currently refusing to obey an order by the Central Bank *of that nation to return these funds. This action is also contrary to the statement that you made in your second debate with Jimmy Carter on October 4, 1976, "that our foreign policy must follow the highest standards of morality."*

OPIC has denied that it instructed TAW to violate African exchange control laws. However, I consider this denial a blatant misrepresentation of the facts, reminiscent of the stonewall tactics used in the Watergate Case. I presented to the Congressional sub-committee a letter from the treasurer of OPIC in response to my written request that OPIC provide TAW with written representation that the payments could be made legally. The letter responded that "OPIC is not in a position to render to TAW any opinion as to the local laws of the various African countries in which such transfers are to take place." Yet in the same letter OPIC wrote that OPIC "would expect you to immediately resume or instigate payments".

I also presented letters from some of the African countries where the transfers took place stating that the transfers were illegal. The fact that TAW owes over $20 million to OPIC and others is not any reason for OPIC to violate the exchange control laws of other nations to receive payment. TAW has not contested the amount owing to OPIC and others only the requirement to violate the laws of the countries in which it operates in order to make payments as directed by OPIC. These exchange control violations are punishable by up to five years' imprisonment and an unlimited fine, depending upon the country in which the violation occurred. All of TAW's African personnel who are nationals of the countries involved have been placed in jeopardy by these violations. Currently there are two Black Americans in a Zambian prison for exchange control violations. OPIC's conduct in this instance was the latest stage of a long history of misdirection and duplicity by OPIC.

In 1974 after the cancellation of TAW's largest lease agreement, OPIC began to bring increased pressure on TAW. In November 1974, OPIC and others suddenly demanded immediate repayment of all loans, seized all of TAW's U.S. bank accounts, and fileed lawsuits which would have the effect of placing TAW in bankruptcy. OPIC in this way seized the money TAW would have used to pay premiums on its' $27.6 million of leased equipment. Then OPIC cancelled the insurance on the grounds that TAW could not pay the premiums on time.

TAW negotiated with OPIC and other creditors for time to repay what it owed. Under threat of bankruptcy, TAW signed a Composition Agreement which is designed to destroy TAW rather than to protect the financial position of the creditors. For example, the agreement requires TAW to sell 95 percent of it's assets by January 31, 1977, regardless of the price it can get. This requirement contradicts good business judgement.

OPIC has attempted to stonewall any legal claims by TAW through through countersuits against TAW. TAW sued in New York State Supreme Court to order OPIC to reverse the illegal transactions by returning the OPIC-directed payments. TAW also asked the court to restrain OPIC and others from requiring additional payments and from placing TAW in bankruptcy for refusing to continue them. OPIC and the lenders had already deprived TAW of funds to continue a lengthy court case by seizing all TAW's bank accounts in the U.S.

When OPIC knew that TAW for lack of funds was unable to pursue it's legal case in New York, OPIC began a lawsuit in Africa to force TAW into bankruptcy. However, in Africa, TAW has funds to finance a legal battle. On learning that TAW would fight back, OPIC immediately withdrew it's legal action.

TAW's problems with OPIC and the actions of the U.S. embassies have caused a member of each of the Houses of Congress to ask for an explanation from Secretary of State Kissinger. In a letter to Mr. Kissinger they asked, why U.S. embassies accepted payments that they should have known were illegal. In addition they asked if the State Department intends to comply with the request by the Central Bank concern. To date, Mr Kissinger has given no reply. These actions by OPIC under your administration, have significantly harmed a Black Business which was listed among the ten largest Black Businesses by BLACK ENTERPRISE in 1974 and is currently the largest Black American business in Africa.

Sincerely,

T.A. Wood

October 27, 1976

Years later, in a Federal Times story, Mays denied breaking foreign currency laws in eleven African countries. In the article, he said, "I think that probably occurred after I left OPIC. I couldn't recall any specifics." I believe that any rational person, looking at the evidence of the date's would come to the conclusion that this is a blatant lie. The Times story also reported that Mays was OPIC's president from 1973-77, which coincides precisely with the 1973 cancellation of TAW's contract with Zambia and the years OPIC ignored African laws while pressing to put TAW in bankruptcy. In 1981, Mays was one of eight candidates competing to become comptroller general of the General Accounting Office (GAO). He didn't get the job.

While I was busy fending off OPIC's full-court assault in congressional hearings, I asked Frank Savage to develop a plan to restructure and streamline the company in a way that would convince OPIC and our creditors to allow us to stay operational at least for a year. Because Zambia had canceled the contract without notification, I was confident we would prevail at arbitration. At that point, we needed our creditors to provide more patience, not money.

Frank met with our creditors in New York at Chase Manhattan Bank. In Frank's book, The Savage Way, Chase manager Hughlyn Fierce, speaking for TAW's creditors, told Frank, "We reviewed your plan and would be prepared to change the terms of the servicing of your loans for a period of a year until the arbitration. We would even consider giving you a further extension if your plans don't work." In a phone conversation with me shortly after the meeting, Frank told me there was one condition: "They wanted me to replace you as the CEO of TAW International Leasing and run the company."

I wondered why Chase would consider such an implausible move. I owed Chase one million dollars; I owed the other creditors 24.6 million dollars. The creditors were lenders, not stockholders. I owned the majority of the shares in the company. Aware that I wouldn't accept bankruptcy without a fight, I considered the possibility that Mays might have suggested that a black representing the investors become the head of TAW. That way, he wouldn't be accused of being prejudiced.

David Rockefeller offered an interesting observation, comparing the government of Zambia's action in an earlier contract dispute with the Chase Bank with the Zambian cancellation of the TAW contract. Many months before David's comment, the government of Zambia borrowed one hundred million dollars from each of several U.S. banks, including Chase, to improve its copper mines. Instead, and in violation of the loan agreement with the banks, the money was used by the government of Zambia to pay for the nationalization of Zambia's copper mines. At the time Zambia was the second largest exporter of copper behind Russia. When the Zambia contract was discussed at a Chase meeting, as a favor to Rupiah Banda, I stood and defended Zambia's indefensible decision, by presenting to the Chase board the Zambian government's point of view. Later, when the Zambians canceled my leasing contract, David reminded me with a smile, "The Zambians did it to the Chase Bank, and then they did it to you."

Frank met with Ernie and me in Nairobi a few days later. In earlier conversations, Frank had made me aware of his desire to leave Africa and TAW once the Zambia contract dispute was settled. He said he had no interest in becoming TAW's CEO. He suggested that I send him back to New York and tell the creditors that their condition was unacceptable. I said, "That's fine."

Frank delivered my message and reported to the creditors. In response, Hughlyn said, "We don't like it, but we'll work with you, and we'll give you as much leeway as we think is prudent." That provided the breathing room we thought we needed. Turns out, we needed much more.

More than four years passed before the Zambia vs. TAW arbitration received a court date. Why so long? Kaunda's administration repeatedly stalled the process. During the first year the arbitrators held a couple of preliminary meetings with the TAW/Zambia legal teams to review the lawsuit and outline arbitration procedures. The Zambians slowed the process in subsequent years, requesting additional postponements for a variety of reasons.

Their main reason, however, was to force us to make sizable bond payments, which aren't required in U.S. courts. Zambia's pockets were much deeper than mine and they obviously hoped that I would cut my losses and give up. I never considered caving. Zambia had close to two dozen lawyers working the case, about a dozen of whom were working in the courtroom. I had to come up with roughly 250, 000 dollars semiannually to cover the Bond requirement covering Zambia's legal bills, or we would lose the lawsuit, that with our own attorney fees, was quite a financial strain.

Frustrating as the Zambians' delaying tactics were, they helped me identify two high-level persons that I had to fire: Mamadou Ba, manager of TAW's French-speaking African countries, and former U.S. Supreme Court Justice Arthur Goldberg, our pick to serve on the three-judge arbitration panel in the TAW vs. Zambia case.

In Mamadou's case, I no longer had to wonder why TAW began to lose money in the French-speaking countries. Mamadou had become very political and was leasing equipment to political allies, friends, and relatives without collecting payments. He had used TAW's funds for political purposes, trying to get elected to be the President of the country of his birth, Guinea. Though that kind of corruption and dishonesty may have been common practice in some African countries, Mamadou should have known it was something I wouldn't tolerate. He was dismissed immediately. He did run to be President of Guinea unsucessfully, more than once.

Sam Pierce, my well-connected attorney/friend, at my request, had asked Goldberg to serve as TAW's arbitrator and Goldberg agreed. Turns out Goldberg's skills–and perhaps his attention span–diminished considerably after he left the United States Supreme Court. During one of our early preliminary sessions, the arbitrators discussed an issue that was highly detrimental to TAW. Goldberg sat silently and didn't object. Alan Dynner and I were among those allowed to witness the proceedings, but we could not participate. Lord Patrick Devlin, the independent arbitrator, turned to Goldberg and said, "Shouldn't you be objecting to this on behalf of your client?" Goldberg didn't respond. That's when I said, "That's it, we've got to get someone else."

Our British solicitors suggested we replace Goldberg with Sir Henry Fisher, the son of the Archbishop of Canterbury, and we did. Sir Henry had an American connection; he was on the board of directors of the Equitable Insurance Company in Europe. He served us well, but he couldn't stop Zambia's request for delays. Our debts grew larger.

At one point, TAW owed more than twenty-six million dollars, half of which I personally had guaranteed. We managed to meet our cash bond deadlines to the court for the first 3 ½ years, but the financial strain kept getting worse, not better. Of the fourteen African countries in which TAW had leasing deals, Uganda was the only one in which I had sufficient funds from which to draw. I had no other choice but to visit the country ruled by Idi Amin, aka, the Butcher of Uganda.

CHAPTER 21

"In any country there must be people who have to die. They are the sacrifices any nation has to make to achieve law and order."

Idi Amin

As Ernie Kalibala and I walked through the Uganda airport, I said, "This country is run by Idi Amin, nicknamed, the Butcher of Uganda. Instead of allowing me to withdraw fifty thousand dollars, a portion of the money that TAW has in a Uganda bank, he might shoot me!"

We traveled to Uganda about a year after the Zambia contract was canceled. I asked Ernie to tag along mainly because of his family connections; Uganda is his birthplace and his grandfather was a tribal leader. The hotels in town were unavailable, but we found accommodations at the airport. We stayed in a building that didn't have a ceiling, and we could hear people moaning and screaming throughout the night. Later, we learned that the facility was one of Amin's torture facilities.

We made it through the night and set out in the morning for the bank. Since I wasn't withdrawing a six-figure sum, I hoped the transaction would be smooth and quick. I almost got my wish. We went to visit Uganda's Minister of Finance in his office several times, but he was never there. Ernie poked around, learned where the Minister lived, so we made a house call. The Minister was a bit upset when he saw us waiting in front of his house as he arrived in the early evening. I knew that the Minister was a General in Amin's

Army. So I decided to appeal to his Army responsibilities to those under his command. I told him, that I needed the funds to pay my employees, and that I had a responsibility to them, just as he had a responsibility to the soldiers under his command. Then I said, "I need fifty thousand dollars." He understood and let me have the money.

As we flew out of Uganda, it occurred to me that Ernie's presence in Uganda at some point might become problematic, especially for his family members living in Uganda. My understanding is that when Amin first seized power he had planned to appoint Ernie's father as president because he had a lot of respect for him. Instead, he appointed himself and warned Ernie's family to stay out of politics and out of Uganda's major cities. I decided it was too risky for him to return to Uganda.

When the arbitration dragged on for an additional two years, I made a second collection-of-funds visit to Uganda. This time, I needed seven hundred thousand dollars, desperately, to pay TAW's legal costs, and the security deposit required under the arbitration. If I was unable to make the security deposit by the due date, TAW would lose the arbitration. When that possibility passed through my mind, I had visions of myself shuffling around someone's kitchen washing dishes, pots, and pans forever.

Fiancially TAW was sinking. Its financial bank accounts held in other African countries were nearly bare, except in Uganda. TAW opened for business in Uganda in 1970, a year before Amin's coup d'état. I'd never met Amin and I certainly wasn't anxious to chat with him about withdrawing US seven hundred thousand dollars in foreign currency from one of his banks. I had no other options. Since I needed that much money, I knew, at some point, I'd probably have to face the 6'4," 300-pound leader, dubbed by historians as one of the more notorious despots in world history.

Amin's military expertise and exploits propelled his rise to power. He was appointed commander of post-colonial Uganda in 1966 after Prime Minister Milton Obote abolished the ceremonial presidency of King Kabaka Mutesa II and appointed himself executive president. Obote named Amin commander of all of Uganda's armed forces. Concern about Amin's growing military power compelled Obote to snatch control of the armed forces from Amin in October 1970, reducing him to commander of the army. Three months later, while Obote attended a summit meeting in Singapore, Amin and a small group of his loyal followers seized control of Uganda. The take-over was bloody and ruthless.

In his book, A State of Blood, author Henry Kyemba described Amin as a leader who might on one day shower a Ugandan village with affection, shaking hands, hugging everyone within reach, smiling all the time, and on another day, while armed with a handgun and a deadly gaze, strike fear into the hearts of the same villagers with threats of torture and death.

Amin's regime was accused of human rights abuses, political repression, ethnic persecutions, and economic mismanagement. Amin's forces slaughtered up to five hundred thousand people during his eight-year reign. In the prologue of his book, Kyemba wrote, "When (Amin) seized power, my friends were killed – even my brother. I saw corpses by the hundred. I heard of horrendous massacres. I experienced the death throes of a whole nation as it spiraled down toward mere subsistence, its population cowed by thugs who were bribed with luxury goods and easy money to kill on Amin's orders." Kyemba dedicated his book to one hundred of the hundreds of thousands "who have died at Amin's hands".

Despite the danger, I focused on doing whatever needed to be done to get TAW's money out of Uganda and have its bank transfer the funds into "hard" currency. There were no other options. Three months before the payment was due in Switzerland, I returned to Uganda, knowing that this would be a long and arduous process. There were no commercial flights to Uganda during that time, so I chartered a plane which dropped me off on Mondays and picked me up on Fridays for my return to Nairobi. I stayed in the "fanciest" hotel in Uganda, which seemed as comfy as a torture chamber. There were no working elevators, no hot water, no air-conditioning, no food, there were roaches and a lot of other creeping things on the floor, so I slept with the lights on all night to keep the bugs away. For those weeks, I subsisted on pineapple juice and oatmeal cookies that I brought with me when I returned each monday."Even in Africa cold showers are not pleasant."

Day-after-day, I went to Uganda's Minister of Finance to discuss withdrawing TAW's money and converting it from Uganda shillings to a hard currency, such as U.S. dollars or German marks. The funds had to be in a "hard" currency when I deposited it with the ICC in Switzerland. For three weeks, I met daily with different people on Uganda's finance committee to get this done, but nothing happened.

Week four of my stay in Uganda began with a visit from a stranger. He had the demeanor of a CIA agent and asked me only one question: "What do you want?" I told him I wanted to withdraw TAW's money and convert it to a hard currency, that is, U.S. dollars, German marks, and the like. He left. Two more weeks passed and, still, nothing happened. I had meetings with them one day, then wouldn't see a committee member again for two-to-three days. At that time, the phones usually did not work in Africa, but fortunately during my stay in Uganda, they were reliable internationally and domestically.

One day, Ernie called me from Kenya and said, "I know someone who might be able to solve our problem." The person's name was Dr. Carlos Russell, a Panamanian/U.S. citizen who was a poet and playwright at Brooklyn College. Carlos, a civil rights activist, who was inspired by the assassinations of the "3Ms"–Medgar Evers, Malcolm X, and Martin Luther King Jr.–founded Black Solidarity Day in 1969. Celebrated annually on the first Monday in November, it is a day that blacks supposedly gather to discuss for whom they should vote on Election Day, as well as take a holiday from school and work.

Previously, Carlos had made a number of favorable statements regarding Amin to a New York newspaper.

I called Carlos from Uganda and told him my story. I also told him that I would pay him US 25, 000 dollars, which was, at the time, almost equal to his annual teaching income, if he would assist me in what I needed to do, that is, withdraw seven hundred thousand dollars of TAW's money from Uganda's bank and convert it from Uganda shillings to a hard currency. Carlos said, "Well, I need more information."

I flew to New York and met Carlos at Kennedy airport. We talked intently for about an hour. After Carlos made a phone call, we flew back to Uganda, via London and Nairobi, then a charter to Uganda.

When Carlos and I arrived at the Kampala Airport in Uganda, Amin was there to greet us! I didn't expect that, but it convinced me that Carlos had called Amin before we left New York to let him know when we would arrive and why we were coming. Amin put us in an old Mercedes with a driver and made reservations for us at the hotel where his army officers were staying. We had a suite, a bedroom on either side of a large living room, and we had hot water, food! And, of course, the elevator was working.

Amin came by our suite later the same night. He was accompanied by Frank Terpil, a renegade former member of the CIA, and an African Ugandian female army sergeant with a machine gun. Terpil had been described in published reports as a significant player in several terrorist-type operations. He was suspected of supplying torture devices to the Amin regime. When Amin's rule ended Terpil was on Amin's plane, loading, gold before they flew out from Uganda.

Previously, Terpil had left the CIA due to misconduct in 1971. In 1980 a US court indicted him for illegal arms dealing. Terpil was born in Brooklyn New York. After a tour in the United States Army, he joined the CIA in 1965. In 1970 Terpil was in India living "the good life" and needed to supplement his U.S. government pay. He then began to deal in "quasi legal" currency exchange. After India Terpil arrived in Libya as an Arms Dealer. After Libya Terpil moved on to Uganda under Idi Amin. Idi called Terpil, "Waraki" or "white lightning". After Amin was deposed Terpil finally ended up in Cuba. Terpil posed as Robert Hunter, a Australian retiree. Terpil had a Brooklyn accent, which belied his cover. At the time Cuba attracted a number of fugitives including the American Robert Vesco trying to evade U.S. justice.

Reports indicate that Frank Terpil died in March 2016, however, some feel that he faked his own death.

I met Terpil as he came into my hotel suite with Idi Amin that night. Amin was huge, so big he really couldn't fit in the chair in our room. So, he sat on the floor. His English wasn't great, but I understood him, and he understood English. When he spoke English, he was like me trying to speak French. Amin spoke Swahili and his own tribal language fluently. He asked me what I wanted, and I told him that I was involved in arbitration with the Zambian Government and that I needed the seven hundred thousand dollars in a "hard currency" to make the next semiannual bond payment. Then I told him that the only African bank that I had sufficient funds to withdraw to make the bond payment was here in Uganda, and that if I didn't make the bond payment on time, I would lose the arbitration. Amin expressed his dislike for Kenneth Kaunda the president of Zambia for a few minutes, and then Amin says, "You can have the money".

Relief swept through me like a cool breeze after a long, muggy day. Instead of condemning me to one of his torture chambers, Amin had tossed me a lifeline. Carlos had earned his money, and it was time for me to get TAW's.

I could not go to the bank the next day, as Amin invited us to be his guests, as he entertained Mobutu Sese Seko, president of Zaire. He insisted that we travel with him to the airport to pick up Mobutu. Amin involved us in some of the head-of-state activities that he had planned in honor of Mobutu. He took me to the woman who gave him massages. I got a massage. I even shot hoops with him. He was a boxer as a young man and was still a reasonably good athlete. We played H-O-R-S-E, a basketball game in which you must duplicate your opponent's shots. Of course, I didn't dare try to win. We also were among a select few to accompany him on a boat ride in which he took Mobutu to visit a group of islands, one of which Amin named for Carlos Russell. Carlos had a PhD, so Amin referred to him as Dr. Russell and he started calling me Dr. Wood.

Right after the boat ride, I headed for the Minister of Finance office to withdraw and convert the funds. I didn't have written orders, the Minister knew that Amin had OK'd the release of the funds. Still, he gave me a reason why it couldn't be done before closing time, so I went back the next day, and the next day. The delays continued for several days. I didn't want to whine to Amin, saying "he won't let me get the money," but the deadline for paying the bond in Geneva was getting closer and closer.

Finally, we were down to the last day before our chartered flight to Nairobi Kenya was to depart in order to meet the arbitration deadline. We knew that Amin normally stayed up all night, and slept sparingly during the day light hours, because he was afraid of an overthrow of his reign, which quite often is attempted in the dead of night. For this reason, Carlos and I were concerned that we would not be able to contact Amin. We called Amin, and to our good fortune, we reached him. He said, "What, you don't have your money? Be in my office in forty-five minutes." When we arrived in Amin's office, the Minister of Finance was sitting in a chair, shaking. I mean literally trembling. And there might have been a few tears in his eyes. Amin had been known to pull out his pistol and shoot people dead on the spot. The minister said, "We can't give you a check in U.S. dollars, but we can give you one in Deutsche marks. "That's fine," I said.

Amin then pointed to a bank official and said, "I want you to take Dr. Russell and Dr. Wood to lunch and when they get back, have the cashier's check ready." We went to lunch, came back, and the check was there. The minister was still shaking, but he seemed a little calmer.

Amin looks at me and says, "I like you. The water supply in Kampala needs to be replaced. I want to give you the contract to do it."

I said, "But I'm not that kind of engineer."

He said, "You just get it done. I will give you a contract."

What am I to say, "No"? So, I say "Yes."

Amin turned to Carlos and handed him an envelope and said, "This is for bringing Dr. Wood to me."

The envelope contained ten thousand dollars. To make my connections to Geneva, Carlos and I flew to Nairobi, and left there that night for Paris, where we parted ways. I put him on the Concorde to New York. He had never ridden on the Concorde and he never forgot it. I then flew to Geneva, where the next bond payment was due.

My association with Amin didn't end when I left Uganda. Later, during one of my stays in New York, Frank Terpil, the ex-CIA agent, showed up in my office. He told me that long before Amin came to power, Uganda owned a vacant lot directly behind the U.S. Mission to the United Nations, which was across the street from the UN building in New York. Amin wanted to put Uganda's Embassy on that lot and he wanted it to be taller than the U.S. Mission building, so he could look down on it. That's figuratively, of course, because he knew he was never going to get into the U.S. Terpil told me that Amin wanted me to handle the contract for that building, but I didn't pursue that. According to media reports, Terpil died in March 2016 in Cuba. As I said many believe the former CIA agent might have faked his death.

Amin's strong support group dwindled significantly after he waged war against Tanzania, and despite support from Libya's Muammar Gaddafi, Amin sought refuge in exile after Kampala was captured in April 1979. Years later, I received a message from Carlos Russell, who had returned to his native country, Panama. The message read: "This is Carlos. Manuel Ortega, the president of Panama, wants to see you." I didn't respond to his message. I last saw Carlos on TV in Washington, D.C., when he testified before Congress on behalf of Ortega.

Years later, Alice Burnette, Alan Dynner, my attorney, and I were dining at a Chinese restaurant with Peter Johnson, who wrote a biography of David Rockefeller. Peter told us that he had shared my Uganda horror story experience with David. Peter said David Rockefeller sat listening intently, his mouth wide-open during his telling of the story.

CHAPTER 22

"It's a great life, if you do not weaken"

ANONYMOUS

(I use the phrase very frequently Tom Wood)

From the witness stand, I sighed in relief, as I watched the three arbitrators lean back in their chairs, set to begin the hearings in the TAW vs. Zambia arbitration. Lord Patrick Devlin, the chief independent arbitrator, shifted his eyes to Sir David Hirst, TAW's barrister, and said, "Mr. Hirst, would you like to make a brief statement?"

Sir David replied, "I'm obliged."

Calmly, and in that charming English accent that so many Americans love to hear, Sir David Hirst spent the next twenty minutes explaining why TAW should win its 26.5 million-dollar lawsuit against Zambia's government for canceling its contract with TAW. "Can I, first of all, take a bird's eye view of the case and particularly of TAW's position," said Sir David, moving about in his inimitable penguin-like style. "When one reads the pleadings, and I am thinking of the defendant's, Zambia's, pleadings, one has an overall picture of the TAW companies as bucket shops, on their knees financially, hounded by their creditors and wholly unable, and almost it seems sometimes suggested, un-anxious to deliver the goods they had contracted to supply. That picture perhaps is a very different one from that which you find in the documents . . . "

Before the arbitration began, each side submitted a summary of its case to the arbitrators. TAW contended that Zambia violated the terms of the contract by terminating it without giving notice; Zambia argued that I was dishonest and fraudulently had entered a leasing agreement knowing that my company wasn't financially able to deliver the three hundred trucks and other equipment as promised. Each side was to present witnesses for cross-examination by the opposing barristers.

I was the first to take the stand and was subjected to twelve consecutive days of sometimes withering cross-examination by Conrad Dehn, the Zambia's barrister. A Holt Scholar of Gray's Inn, Dehn was a member of one of Great Britain's preeminent law firms. His reputation as a "master" of the cross-examination had prompted Frank Presnell, my assistant solicitor, to bet Alan Dynner, my U.S. attorney, that Dehn would reduce me to a bowl of mush, and therefore TAW would loose the arbitration. Dehn's goal was to reveal me as a liar and a con artist; my goal was to make sure Alan won his bet.

Team TAW arrived in London three months before the hearings were to start. Our daily preparations for the arbitration hearings were often arduous and long. I am grateful to Lolita Valderrama, Frank's wife, for routinely finding excellent dining facilities where the TAW team could relax and spend part of their evenings enjoying a fine meal. Lolita, a fine arts painter, is an engaging personality. She is fluent in a half dozen languages, including Swedish, Spanish, Italian, and French. She is affable, and engaging personality. It was very difficult too for large groups to get reservations at the best London restaurants. Sometimes the wait was two weeks. At that time, London's top restaurants were like that; you had to wait unless you were a regular patron. Lolita, however, often managed to get us tables that same day. On several occasions, I'm sure her skills as a linguist helped.

We used our work days to familiarize ourselves with the summary disclosures that Zambia had submitted and to prep me for what I should expect during Dehn's verbal assaults. Before this, I never realized that lawyers routinely prepped their witnesses before they faced opposing attorneys in court. We held mock sessions in which Sir David Hirst, TAW's barrister, and Sebastian Zulu peppered me with tough questions. In addition to the questions they added comments, such as, "Don't say that! Don't look down! Don't smile! Don't roll your eyes!" More than once, Sir David said, "Don't be like a typical American, don't be abrasive."

I didn't do well in the mock sessions. I said to them, "The adrenaline is not flowing now. Wait until I get to the arbitration hearings". I'll be ready when the real competition starts. I'm not going to leave my game in the locker room." We had disclosed written documents about the case to the Zambian legal team. I remembered virtually everything that we had disclosed, because I lived it. I could just about turn the pages of the documents in my head and read from memory every word in all the documents. I had no problem recalling any of the information in the documents. I assured my team that I could handle the situation.

However, during my first few days on the stand, I was far too passive in my responses. Dehn launched what seemed a full-frontal attack that first day. He tried his best to rattle me with repetitive charges and accusations. He hammered and hammered and then hammered some more. I was far more passive than I should have been, but I was never overwhelmed by his tactics or angered by his side remarks. He, on the other hand, seemed unnerved whenever I responded to what I considered, his frivolous exchange with a bemused smile.

Dehn: What do you mean by the last financial statement?

Wood: The statement we had available when this document was published.

Dehn: Where is the statement?

Wood: I assume you have it.

Dehn: Show us where it is in the bundle.

Sir David, TAW's barrister, interrupts: "I think it is attached to this memorandum but to ask Mr. Wood to find something in twenty volumes is a bit steep. I am told it is on Page 28. If Mr. Dehn would refer that sort of question to us, we will try to help him. Obviously, Mr. Wood does not know the exact pages of everything."

Alan and I were not allowed to discuss the case once the hearing began, but Alan used a technically legal way to evaluate my performances as TAW's key witness. Frank Savage and Herb Cummings relayed the evaluation. During the morning session of Day 4 of my testimony, I remained locked in a passive demeanor while Dehn stayed on the attack. At lunch, Herb and Frank Savage discussed my testimony between themselves as I listened. Speaking to Herb, Frank said, "Tom has been too nice, too deferential. He's letting Dehn walk all over him. He should be more forceful, go on the attack."

That afternoon, I came out charging and challenging nearly everything Dehn said. I looked at Dehn and said, "I'm no longer going to sit here and listen to you suggest that I'm a liar, denigrate my character, and imply that all the things I achieved as TAW's CEO in the Zambia project were impossible, didn't happen." Dehn tried to silence me by protesting to the arbitrators, saying that I was out of order and that I wasn't answering his questions. The arbitrators said, "Let him talk, let him have his say."

I was as emotional as I could get. I demonstrated the flaws in Dehn's linear approach to arguing his case, saying, "You can pick two points and draw a straight line and assume that a point in between is on that straight line. But most high school students know that you can draw an infinite number of lines through two points."

Then I said, "Consider the stock market, whether it's in New York or London. Let's say the market closes at 2, 100 on one day and 2, 300 two days later. You can't say the market closes at 2, 200 on the day in between because you know the market isn't predictable. It could close at any number. Which means you can't always draw a straight line between two points and assume you know everything that's occured between those two points is on that straight line.

"You tell me I couldn't produce the trucks, but when the Zambians canceled the contract, the trucks were sitting on the docks ready to be delivered. If I couldn't do this, how did the trucks get there? You've seen photo evidence that the trucks were sitting on the docks ready to be delivered and still you tell me I couldn't do it. It's like watching someone sit in a chair and you tell me no one's there."

My transition from punching bag to counterpuncher was complete. It was my unplanned rope-a-dope tactic that turned the tide. I felt a spark inside.

After that exchange, in answer to many of the questions Dehn asked, I responded, "That's not correct." The English "lawyers" have a way of starting a question, saying, "I put it to you." That's their way of starting a question: "I put it to you." Each time he said that, I replied, "What's the question?" He'd say, "I put it to you." I'd say, "What does that mean?" That disconcerted him. Then I changed tactics completely. Rather than apologize for not understanding a question, I searched for ways to counter most claims regardless of how trivial they seemed. From time to time, I anticipated his line of questioning.

As an example, at one point, Dehn attempted to show that I was a liar by challenging my assertion, in responding to a question, that I always used Pan Am Airlines when traveling to Europe. I watched as one of Dehn's assistants hand him a TWA bill, but before Dehn could say "How can you say that you always fly Pan Am to Europe, when here's a TWA bill"? I said, "Your assistant is about to give you a piece of paper that would suggest I flew TWA, not Pan Am. If you look carefully, you will see that the bill came from TWA, but the flights were all on Pan Am." Dehn, without saying a word, gave back the TWA bill. Back then, some airlines provided charge cards instead of credit cards. TWA offered charge cards, with a four hundred-dollar deposit, but I also could use it when I flew Pan Am.

The early credit cards also required full payment when billed.

Another instance during which he tried to expose me as a liar occurred when he questioned my assertion that I had made a business phone call on Easter Monday. "How can you make a call on Easter Monday? Nobody works." I said, "I do." All the Americans and the three arbitrators laughed. "Americans don't observe those holidays like we do," one of the arbitrators said. "They work."

Dehn opened one session with this question: "I understand that you were a man of substance." My response: "I believe I am a man of substance, and I hope that I will always be a man of substance." The English use the word "substance" as a synonym for wealth, whereas we Americans tend to equate substance with character. The arbitrators smiled when I said that perhaps knowing that I meant it as a double entendre.

When Dehn couldn't paint me as prevaricator, he then attempted to show that I was too inexperienced to be an effective CEO and that I exaggerated TAW's value and financial stability. In other words, he tried to say that I had committed fraud. During the next seven days, he flitted back and forth, using lines of inquiries attempting to cast me as a liar or a fraud. My responses to Dehn's queries were delivered coolly, but at times with palpable defiance.

Dehn: You did not have the financial capability to provide something of the order of three hundred trucks and trailers on lease at that time?

Wood: We did.

Dehn: You were not in a position to acquire that number of trucks and trailers because you did not have the money, did you?

Wood: If you define "position" for me, I will be able to answer the question.

Dehn: You needed to borrow the money, did you not?

Wood: Which is a normal case for a leasing company, yes.

Dehn: You were not able to borrow the money at that time to acquire the trucks, were you?

Wood: It was not necessary to acquire the trucks and pay for them at that time.

Dehn: You were not in a position to borrow the money to get hold of those trucks. That is right?

Wood: It is not correct.

Dehn: I suggest to you, Mr. Wood, that the only chance you had of being able to borrow the money was by inducing some major credit-worthy customer such as the Government of Zambia to place a major order with you. That is right, is it not?

Wood: Is that a question?

Dehn: Yes.

Wood: I thought it was a statement.

Dehn: I was suggesting it to you.

Wood: It is not correct.

Dehn: I suggest to you, Mr. Wood, that you could do that only if you deceived that major customer as to your experience and financial capability and ability to deliver quickly. I put that to you. That is right?

Wood: It is not correct.

Dehn: I put it to you that even the lenders would refuse to lend because of the other difficulties in TAW's financial position?

Wood: That is absolutely not correct, and you know it. The money was borrowed and the conditions that were requirements at that time were waived in order to allow us to borrow the money.

Again and again, using variations of the same "How can you borrow money if you don't have money?" theme, Dehn persisted, but his persistence only underlined his lack of knowledge of how, in many situations, business is done in the USA. Sir Henry Fisher, TAW's arbitrator, offered Dehn this helpful information. "In America, the ratio of what you can borrow could be 5-1, or 10-1. Maybe that's why American businesses beat us. In England, you can't do that. Here, if you put up a dollar, they'll lend you fifty cents." The courtroom buzzed with laughter.

Dehn's frustration mounted, as I had answers for every question he put to me. After Day 12 of his cross-examinations, Dehn was done. "I have no more questions," said Dehn, his body language revealing the true depth of his fatigue. I had tried my best to refute every charge against me he had made. "I don't know how you endured," said Alan, my attorney.

Later, Alan took the stand and Dehn tried to denigrate him, too. In his unpublished memoirs Alan recalls his three-day cross-examination by Dehn. "I knew the facts backwards and forwards and saw exactly what Dehn was trying to get me to say. On my third day of testimony, independent arbitrator Lord Devlin finally interrupted. He said, "Mr. Dehn, don't you realize that you're not doing your client any good? You are simply giving Mr. Dynner the opportunity to plead TAW's case in detail!" After Devlin's observation, Dehn informed the arbitrators that the Zambian government had completed its cross-examination. He then sat down.

Near the end of my testimony, I overheard the arbitrators talking among themselves during a break. We had won, the arbitrators said, because Zambia had to show that we had committed fraud, and they concluded that there was no fraud. The arbitrators also said that Zambia never gave TAW any notice before canceling the contract. The law requires that one can not arbitrarily cancel a contract. One must give cause and notice.

When the Arbitrators announced their verdict "that TAW had won", Alan and Frank left their seats and were "dancing in the aisles", hugging each other. All I could do was to smile, for I was very close to tears. Alan said to Frank "This day is due to Tom's will, he persevered when many were wavering."

Upon reflection, I've occasionally wondered if the Zambians ever intended to honor the terms of the contract. When our negotiations with Kaunda's administration began, I was convinced that the initial 80 GM trucks that were delivered immediately would be used to transport tons of Zambia copper to seaport at Dar es Salaam, Tanzania. However, the arbitration testimony revealed that the trucks weren't used to transport copper. The eighty trucks that TAW delivered early to Zambia were sent all over the country for various reasons, but not to transport copper. As to why the trucks were never used for the purpose for which they were leased, well, as someone once said, "That's above my pay grade."

After serving TAW with the contract cancellation notice, the Zambian government did not return all of the trucks for more than 4 months.

During the initial negotiations, we noticed that the Zambians were in no hurry to get the deal done. Throughout the sessions, one of my team members would occasionally catch the eye of another team member and say with their eyes, "They say they need these vehicles, but they don't appear to be in a rush. They're taking their time!" There must have been some political reason for their nonchalance.

The Zambian government didn't testify. Instead, it offered TAW a proposal to settle. I told the Zambian representatives, "If my creditors accept the offer and relieve TAW and me from any and all financial liability, then I'll take it."

I then invited Sir David Hirst to speak on TAW's behalf when we met with TAW's creditors in New York to discuss Zambia's offer. I knew the creditors' attorneys held British lawyers in high esteem, probably because American law stems from British law.

CHAPTER 23

"Tom Wood does not get ulsers, He gives them to the opposing side"

ALAN DYNNER

The meeting was held in the New York office of General Motors' legal general counsel, who was a black man. I don't remember his name. I thought it ironic that GM would not consider hiring me after I graduated from Michigan in 1951 because I was black and there I was twenty-five years later, a black CEO of an international firm, negotiating terms of a settlement in the office of GM's top lawyer, a black man. Times indeed had changed. Sir Hirst David talked to the creditors and they respected what he said.

The message Sir David delivered reminded me of a business joke that involves a conversation between a high-powered businessman and a lady of the night in an exclusive hotel negotiating a short-term business arrangement. The businessman asks, "Would you go to bed with me for one thousand dollars?" She says, "No." Businessman: "Would you go to bed with me for one hundred thousand dollars?" She says, "No." Businessman: "Would you go to bed with me for one million dollars?" She says, "Yes." Then the businessman says, "Now that we've determined the principle, let's talk about the price."

Sir David's pitch to TAW's creditors was a variation of the businessman's tactic. He told them that the arbitrators had determined that the Zambians were at fault. "Now we need to determine how much the Zambians should pay," Sir David said. "We can accept the offer the Zambians made, or we can go through the process of assessing damages, which could take three to four months or three to four years."

TAW didn't have the resources to drag it out for six more months, much less one or two years. TAW wouldn't have survived if the creditors had opted to do that. After Sir David sat down, I told the creditors, "Either you accept this offer or I'm going to accept the Zambian offer and then put the money in a Swiss bank and fight you until the money runs out." I told them that by attempting to put TAW into bankruptcy soon after TAW's contract with Zambia was canceled, they gave the Zambians a reason to delay the arbitration nearly three years, hoping that we would use our resources until we were forced to declare bankruptcy. I told them that TAW would fight them on the basis that they had forced TAW to set up illegal accounts in nine African countries and that OPIC had established those accounts on behalf of all the creditors. The creditors knew that they had broken the law in many African countries.

The creditors accepted the Zambian settlement offer to TAW's 26.5 million-dollar breach of contract suit, awarding TAW four million dollars. In addition we received 80% of the two million dollars we had posted in legal expenses, and we kept the 1.8 million dollar deposit we received at the signing of the contract. TAW settled with all its creditors, including Morgan Guaranty, First National Bank of Chicago, Chase Manhattan Bank, OPIC, Ryder Overseas Services, and General Motors.

The Government of Kenya surprised OPIC when its Central Bank refused to transfer the illegal TAW/OPIC joint account funds into an OPIC only account. The Central Bank told OPIC that the original transfer into a joint TAW/OPIC account was illegal, and without TAW's written consent, and an admission by OPIC, that the initial transfer was illegal, the Bank would not release the funds to OPIC. This "back and forth" went on for more than a year, before OPIC agreed to admit that the requested transfer "did not conform" with the Kenyan Banking Regulations. When the funds were finally transferred to an OPIC only account, as a result of the negative change in Kenyan currency with respect to the U.S. dollar during the elapsed time between the settlement with TAW's creditors and OPIC's admission of "did not conform", OPIC finally received approximately 1/3 of the amount originally transferred by TAW into the Kenyan "illegal" bank accounts.

Another example that "Crime does not Pay" (smile).

Initially, the Zambians refused to pay despite the arbitrators' ruling. Zambia used "sovereign immunity" as a reason for not abiding by the arbitrators' decision. Nigeria had used the same reason a few years earlier, but when a Nigerian Airlines plane landed in London, the plane was impounded. We made it clear to Zambia that the next time one of its Zambian Airlines planes landed in London, it would be impounded. That's when Zambia paid.

Usually when work kept TAW's staff, or members of TAW's legal team up many nights, or away from their families for extended periods, I made it a practice to send flowers to their wives as a token of my appreciation for their understanding and sacrifices. I decided that the wives of TAW's seven-member legal staff at the arbitration deserved no less. I sent each of the wives two dozen roses. In the U.S., I'd always receive thank you notes from the wives. But in England, I received notes from the British barristers and solicitors (with one exception), I was told that in England, under no circumstances does a man send flowers to another man's wife. They forgave me because I was a crazy American.

CHAPTER 24

"We won the last battle, but lost the war."

ANONYMOUS

"Tom Wood has been able to do difficult things,
some things that
Have not been done before,
done while keeping his ethics, and always
With the ability to laugh at himself"

ANDREW YOUNG

My nearly five-year fight to keep TAW alive had taken its toll on me, physically, mentally, and emotionally. When the arbitrators rendered their decision, I watched Alan and Frank jump up and down, celebrating as if we'd won the World Series. I sat quietly for a while, relieved, but could only manage a smile.

For his expertise, hard work, loyalty, and friendship, I gave my attorney, Alan Dynner, his wife, and their three children a trip around the world.

In 1979, sometime after the arbitrators' decision was announced, I told a Wall Street Journal reporter, "Now we can breathe easier. With the litigation behind us we can devote our energy to new areas and other pursuits."

In my mind, the outcome was never in doubt. I just knew we were going to win. The same stars in my eyes that had glittered so brightly on my arrival in Africa ten years ago regained their glow. Time and again during the arbitration, I had said to myself, "They can't do this to this black man. Right has to win; we have to prevail." Blind faith kept me going those five years and that was a long time to keep the faith, given the forces against us, including my own Federal Government.

The arbitration victory allowed TAW to be solvent and operational. I went back to work, sans the zest and optimism that I carried within me while forming TAW. I wondered, too, if I would ever recapture the fire inside or relax the ethical values that shaped my business decisions. More than once, I asked myself, "Am I the right person to run TAW?" The ethical values that shaped my business decisions were counter to many of the business norms in most of Africa.

It should be noted that; President Trump tried to eliminate the "bribary" statute in the 1977 Foreign Corrupt Practices Act.

My thinking was that it would be wise to apoint some one with international recognition and esteem as my successor.

What happened on a trade mission helped me to decide who and when.

While I was engaged in these "on again off again" conversations with my self, I received an invation to accompany Ambassador Andrew Young on a trade mission to Africa. I accepted. The trade mission began as Andy Young was ending his tour as the U.S.Ambassador to the United Nations. The trade mission started in Liberia and had scheduled visits in the Ivory Coast, Nigeria, Cameroon, Kenya, Tanzania, and Senegal.

The trade mission was chronicled by Ebony magazine's Pulitzer prize winning photographer Moneta Sleet.

When the trade mission arrived in the Ivory Coast, President Felix Houphouet Boigny was out of the country due to illness. When he returned to the Ivory Coast, he was very disappointed that Ambassador Young was not welcomed by his government with a special ceremony. TAW however, had hosted a major event in Ambassador Young's honor. When Houphouet Boigny returned to the Ivory Coast, he showed his gratitude by depositing the equilivant of U.S. one million dollars in CFA franc in TAW's bank.

During the trade mission's stop in Nigeria, Ambassador Young included me and several other members of the delegation in one of his meetings with Nigerian President

Shagari. In the meeting as I remember, President Shagari said something to the effect "Ambassador Young is very well respected throught Africa and particularly here in Nigeria. As I understand the purpose of a trade mission is to promote business, and we here in Nigeria want the Young mission to be successful, Nigeria will award the American company Pullman-Kellogg a U.S. 340 million dollar contract to build a chemical fertilizer plant here in Nigeria".

Later, during the trade mission's stop in Kenya, Uganda's president Godfrey Binaisa sent a message to me, that he would like to see me during the trade mission's visit in Kenya. I invited Bruce Llewellyn (the then president of OPIC, and a cousin of Colin Powell)—my how the times have changed—and Ed Jones, a fellow member of the trade mission to accompany me in my meeting. During the meeting with President Binaisa he stressed the urgent need to get Uganda's coffee crop to "market", and the transtortation problems Uganda was experiencing in trying to accomplish this objective. President Binaisa then said that he would award a contract to TAW to provide trucks to transport Uganda's coffee crop to market. However, one of the conditions would be that Ambassador Young's trade mission include a stop in Kampala, Uganda and meet with President Binaisa, at the meeting Binaisa would sign a "letter of intent" for the leasing of trucks from TAW.

At my request, Andy Young, included a stop in Uganda, and the "letterof intent"was signed.

My thinking at that time, Binasia wanted the validation that a visit from the U.S. Ambasaor to the United Nations would bring—sound familiar—

These events suggested to me that Ambassador Andy Young would be a great replacement for me. Andy had the ability to be a "Rain Maker" on behalf of TAW. The fact that Andy was a "man of the cloth", a man of faith, and the esteem which African leaders accorded him, and because of his international stature, as he demonstrated more than once during the trade mission, would tend to deflect or eliminate the "bribery pressure" on TAW.

As the trade mission was on its way home, I asked Andy to consider replacing me. He promised to think about it. Months later Andy called to let me know that he preferred to stay in U.S. politics. In 1981 Andy began a campaign to become Atlanta's mayor, a position he held for eight years (1982-90).

When the Trade Mission returned to the U.S. President Carter hosted the group at the White House. During the White House meeting President Carter asked "since the trade mission had been such a success, when did Ambassador Young plan to return on another trip to Africa".

Six months after the arbitration, I held a meeting in New York with Ernie Kalibala, director of TAW's English-speaking African countries, and Seth Dei, who replaced Mamadou Ba as director of the French-speaking countries. I wanted to hear their thoughts on how we should move forward. I wanted them to have a say in what we were going to do.

Frank Savage had previously announced that he was moving on. I didn't try to stop him. Unloading his hefty salary eased our financial burden. Ernie had considered forming a partnership with Randy Daniels, then a CBS foreign correspondent, to establish a television station in Nigeria, but I convinced him to stay with TAW. I told Seth and Ernie that I was tired, needed a break, and that I wanted them to continue as CEOs of their respective operations. Seth would control the French-speaking countries and Ernie would continue to control the English-speaking countries. They agreed and understood that it was only a temporary solution.

After the arbitration, my life in Africa and in the United States seemed less complicated, more tranquil, but rarely dull. I had a couple of remarkable experiences during this time of my life. The first was a rare historical admission in the United States by a major university. A friend, a significant Georgetown financial supporter and graduate of Georgetown suggested I meet the President of Georgetown primarily because he was a fellow New Yorker in my age group. I met President Timothy S. Healy in his office in Healy Hall. After chatting a bit about Fordham, CUNY, and Columbia University, I joked, "As a fellow New Yorker, how is it that you just became President of Georgetown, and your name is on the building"? He told me, that the building was named after President Patrick Francis Healy -no relation- and that Patrick Healy was of African descent. I had not heard that before. It is now my understanding, that this knowledge was suppressed, for obvious reasons. However, this information about his African descent became some what public in the 1950's. More than another decade passed before Georgetown admitted "known" black students. Elmer Ripley my first basketball coach at Columbia in 1944 came to Columbia from Georgetown. He was very supportive as my coach and a friend after he left Columbia for Notre Dame.

President Patrick Francis Healy, S.J. the 26th President of Georgetown, is considered by many "the second founder" who transformed the college into a major university. To me this is truly a remarkable American story. President Healy was born in 1834 as a slave in Macon Georgia to an Irish plantation owner and his African slave. The then existing law—children had the legal status of the mother. President Healy was legally a slave when he was born. His father, Michael sent all of his children by his African slave Mary Eliza Smith north and on to Europe to be educated and to have opportunities not available in the slaveholding American south. In 1873, Patrick Healy was named President of the largest Catholic college in the United States, he modernized the curriculum, expanded the law and medical schools, and built a significant number of new buildings.

Contrast Patrick Healy's story with comparable stories about Alexandre Dumas (French)and Alexander Puskin(Russian) with similar African descent. With known African heritage, Puskin is considered by many to be the greatest Russian poet and the founder of modern Russian literature. Alexandre Dumas, with known African heritage is one of the most widely read French authors, works such as, The Count Of Monte Cristo, and The Three Musketeers, of motion picture fame.

I believe the difference in Europe as compared to America in the treatment of these historical figures results from the impossibility of America to reconcile the Declaration of Independence with slavery. To make the point, the 3/5 ' ths clause in the original US constitution was a compromise reached during the 1787 United States Constitutional Convention. The compromise solution was to count a slave as three/ fifths of a person. Because "We hold these truths to be self-evident, that all men are created equal, that they are endowed by their Creator with certain unalienable rights", America had to dehumanize slaves, which most of Europe and ancient Greece did not, to justify American slavery.It should be noted that at the time of Americas independence, most of the world had not accepted "that all men are created equal"

Another one of my more memorable experiences occurred when Dr. Alfred Cannon, a psychiatrist friend and Columbia classmate, asked me to come to California to advise actor/comedian Richard Pryor on a business matter. Pryor was Al's patient. Al and I met Pryor at his Northbridge, California home.

Pryor showed me several dubious accounting transactions that concerned him. I referred him to Alan, my attorney. Then we climbed into Pryor's Rolls Royce, and he drove us to dinner at a Chinese restaurant. He loved Chinese food. Pryor used a lot of profanity when we were with him, but he was also very polite, very subdued. He called me "sir" and called Al "Doctor." I spent three days with him, so I don't think it was an act. He seemed to turn on a switch when he went on stage.

Pryor rose to stardom as a comedian in the 1970s by examining the racial and contemporary issues of that time in a groundbreaking style, laced with profanity and racial epithets. His best-selling albums included That Nigger's Crazy (1974) and . . . Is It Something I Said? (1975). Jerry Seinfeld called him "the Picasso of our profession." Bob Newhart referred to him as "the seminal comedian of the last fifty years." During that same decade, Pryor won an Emmy Award (1973), three of his five Grammy Awards (1974-76), and appeared in several popular comedy films, including Uptown Saturday Night with Sidney Poitier and Bill Cosby and Silver Streak with Gene Wilder. His enormous success brought him international stardom and a bundle of problems caused mainly by drug abuse.

Remember when Pryor shot his car? One of the conditions of his release, without jail time, was for him to seek treatment. None of Hollywood's top psychiatrists wanted to deal with him. Finally, someone asked Al, who was then an assistant professor at UCLA, to treat Pryor, and he did. Al was Pryor's psychiatrist when he set himself afire while freebasing cocaine. During that fiasco, Pryor ran down the street of his California home and suffered second- and third-degree burns. He was making a movie at the time and the producers wanted him back on the set as soon as possible. They paid Al to stay with him twenty-four hours a day for more than a month. Al told me that Jim Brown and Marlon Brando were the only people who came to see Pryor during that time.

Al and Pryor became buddies. In the early 1980s, Al purchased an eighty-acre farm in Zimbabwe and moved there to help develop a better health care system. He invited Richard Pryor to visit him and the trip proved to be a life-altering experience for Pryor. In one of his made-for-movies concerts, Pryor talks about seeing millions and millions of Africans, and the realization that he had lost the urge to call anyone "nigger." That experience, he said, convinced him to stop calling anyone "nigger". My Columbia classmate, Al Cannon had influenced his decision to drop the word "nigger" from his vocabulary.

Surprisingly, I had become somewhat of a celebrity in the African countries where TAW had leasing agreements as well as here in the U.S.. Before the London arbitration was resolved, Houphouet-Boigny, president of the Ivory Coast, decorated me with his country's highest honor. The ceremony was held in Washington, D.C., during an Houphouet-Boigny visit. My award was for leadership in service to his country. During the presentation he said, "You, Thomas Wood, were able to put more Ivorians in business than my own state companies were able to do."

This comment, from the President of an African nation, made me feel that TAW had made some progress in accomplishing one of its goals. President Houphouet-Boigny's comment caused me to recall a episode that occurred when Mamadou Ba (TAW's manager in the French speaking countries)and I visited the Central Bank of the Ivory Coast. Walking down the hall to our meeting, we passed by an office in which two men were having a very heated argument (in French). I learned later that the arguement was centered around TAW. The argument was between an Central Bank African manager and his white French boss. The African manager was argueing to his boss, that he, his boss woud not allow him to have any "real authority"i.e.to sign off loans above what he characterized in French as "petty cash". The African manager used TAW as an example. He said that TAW's African managers had the authority to sign off on transactions significantly larger than "pettycash"(I do not recall the specific amount).

As in the case, when David Rockfeller appointed me to the Chase Manhattan Bank board, due to David Rockefeller's statue, it started a movement. TAW started a movement in both the English and French speaking countries to move Africans into more senior positions in their respective financial institutions. As in the Chase Manhattan Bank case, this movement did not occur because of me personally, it occurred because it was an American company that had African managers who were makng these significant financial decisions. Thus making African managers with significant financial authority no longer an outlier or anomaly.

It shoud be noted that the "titular" head of these financial institutions had been in African hands since independence.

At a later date, president Houphouet-Boigny built, a Catholic Basilica in the town of his birth, Yamoussoukro. The Basilica of Our Lady of Peace has personal air-conditioning for each seat, and is larger than its counterpart, St Peters in the Vatican City in Rome.

I also occasionally addressed gatherings of Africans from various countries who were interested in becoming entrepreneurs or starting their own businesses. The then CBS foreign correspondent Randy Daniels shared his personal observations and impressions of my mentoring sessions in Nairobi during my final few years as TAW's CEO. Said Daniels:

"Occasionally, I'd join a large group of black ex-patriots and Africans when they met with Tom. He was treated like a well-respected elder, though he didn't live in Nairobi.. He knew how to compete for contracts with foreign governments against international competitors and did so boldly and successfully for years. When you sit on Fortune 500 boards of directors, you're exposed to different legal issues and complex accounting principles. He gave you something extra to think about. Clearly, Tom emerged from that process as a very sophisticated businessperson. He was way ahead of his time, and he opened my eyes to a world I didn't know at that stage of my life."

As described earlier, after the arbitration was history and on a trade mission with Ambassador Andy Young, I met the president of Uganda, Godfrey Binaisa in Kampala, where I made a proposal to the Ugandian Government, to lease trucks to be used to move the Ugandian coffee crop to market.

As a result of the experience General Motors had under the Zambian contract with TAW, it would be a gross understatement to say it took a little persuasion by me to convince General Motors to send a technical team to Uganda to drive the proposed routes and produce the "numbers" needed to execute a contract for the trucks between the Ugandian Government and TAW.

All that TAW and GM had done was for naught. President Binaisa was overthrown, and I was told that the new Ugandian Government did not intend to proceed to contract from the letter of intent.

TAW's reputation, having won the arbitration suit against the Government of Zambia, as I was told, caused the new Uganda government to have concerns that TAW might again sue and win. Little did they know that I did not have the resource, or the will, that I had in the Zambian case.

Once again, I wondered, "am I the right person to run TAW".

The effort to sign a final agreement to provide trucks to the Uganda government, produced another "African Adventure" for Alan Dynner. While in Kampala Uganda, putting the finishing touches on the agreement "which was not to be", unannounced, Uganda closed its borders under a program to replace or exchange their paper currency. This was considered to be necessary, to prevent individuals, or any one who held Uganda currency outside Uganda (which was illegal) from participating in the replacement program. Since the border closing was "indefinite", the TAW people felt that Alan and I should leave Uganda. They arranged for us to be driven "after midnight" the 60 miles from Kampala to Jinja, a town from which the Nile river leaves Lake Victoria bound for the Mediterranean Sea. There were many road blocks along the way, and much to Alan's concern, very young, heavily armed soldiers with AK-47's, pointed through the car window at us, , stopped us to ask what were we doing this late at night. It was still dark when we arrived at the border and "just like in the movies", Alan and I walked the hundred or so yards between the Uganda border post and the Kenya border post alone. On the Kenyan side, one of Ernie's people was waiting, he drove us to a small airstrip where a plane was waiting to fly Alan and I to Nairobi Kenya.

After the arbitration, and on another trip to Africa, the finance minister of the Ivory Coast invited Dorothy and I to dinner at his house. After dinner, he pulled me aside and said, "You've got to do something about Seth Dei and your people, they're running amok. Your airplane is being used for wild parties, they're just having a good time, not caring about the business. You've got to do something."

The finance minister was in effect warning me that TAW's status as a credit baille might be jeopardized if corrective action wasn't taken. The solution to that problem was easy. Seth, who, had asked me on several occasions to let him buy me out, give him complete control of the French-speaking countries. When he asked again, I said, "Yes." Ernie chose to pursue other interests.

I have good memories. I'm especially grateful to Cornelius Shields & Company, which provided the funds I needed to become the first black CEO to sell his company shares over the counter on Wall Street, as well as Herb Cummings' 1.2 million-dollar investment that made it possible for me to launch an international leasing company in Africa.

Businessmen, far wealthier and powerful than I, experienced rocky times, as well. Sam Walton, founder of Walmart, survived a financial crisis earlier in his career and someone came to his rescue, as Herb came to mine. Walmart's net worth rose to 8.6 billion dollars in 2018. Years before Rupert Murdoch built his media empire, financial woes in his newspaper business nearly drove him into bankruptcy. European banks refused to loan him money, but he finally convinced a female banker in the United States to vouch for him, and the rest is history. Murdoch's News Corporation's net worth in 2018 was 15.9 billion dollars. Wealthy entrepreneurs, I'm sure, have had their share of cliffhangers. I'm just as sure, however, that I dealt with many more because of my race.

In the early 1990s, Robert "Bob" Adams, head of the Smithsonian, asked me what could whites do to improve race relations. My answer to him was in general that blacks do not have credibility/ beleivablity in mainstream America. In general, we are deemed untrustworthy or not believable and are not treated with respect. Treat everyone with respect. In the early years of the National Basketball Association (NBA), emerging black superstars such as Bill Russell, Wilt Chamberlain, Oscar Robinson and Elgin Baylor had to be paired with a white player in media advertising spots to appeal to the NBA's fan base. Barack Obama didn't receive the respect he deserved when he was president of the United States.

An excellent example of this, is the incident which occurred during President Obama's address to a joint session of congress in September of 2009. This incident is particulary remembered by American blacks. President Obama, in his address to the joint session, was making the case for the passage of the Affordable Care Act. In making the case, President Obama made the statement that "There are those who claim that our reform effort will insure illegal immigrants". This too, is false." Congressman Joe Wilson, a South Carolina Republican, in the congressional audience, shouted out, loud enough for all to hear, "YOU LIE". Obama was not lying, however that is not my point. The point is that an estimated 30% of the American public believed Joe Wilson, not the President of the United States, a black man who has a well earned reputation for being accurate in his public statements. It should be noted that being accurate is not the case for the current occupant of the White House.

The acceptance (30%) by the American public of Trump's unsubstanciated claim that Obama is a "Kenyan born Muslim" is another facet of this phenomen. Trump has yet to fully admit to the fact that his claim was false. McCain's encounter, during his run for the President of the U.S., with a woman who said that she could not vote for Obama because Obama is a "Kenyan born Muslim" and McCain's forceful rejection of her reason, is yet another example.

For many people, the default position in the believe/trust, not to believe/not to trust, is to default to the believe/trust position. This is described in detail by Malcolm Gladwell in his book "Talking to Strangers".The dicotamy between who we believe/trust and who we do not believe/do not trust, most people tend to believe/to trust "members of their tribe". Membership of the "tribe" can be based upon, nationality, race, sport teams, education, religion politics, , school, university, or any number of factors. However this believe/trust, not to believe/not to trust, across racial lines the default position, for far too many Americans is not to believe/not to trust. Recent studies events indicate that this not to believe/not to trust is not as prevalent in the under 30 age group.

In many cases, Malcolm Gladwell believes that we default to the believe/trust position even when that decision carries terrible risks —- because we have no other choice. Society cannot function otherwise. In those hopefully rare instances where belief/trust ends in betrayal, those victimized by default to believe/trust deserve our sympathy, not our censure.

Black Americans–during my generation and this generation–have endured similar experiences almost daily. However, times are changing and will continue to change because all of the grandchildren of this generation won't think that way. They'll see the black superstars in business, politics, government, education, science, and, as well as sports and entertainment, and will accept this as the norm. Hopefully, more people will adopt as their own one of my favorite sayings, "It's better to do something than to be someone."

CHAPTER 25

"REFLECTIONS"

*"Any fool can KNOW, the point is
To UNDERSTAND"*

ALBERT EINSTEIN

*"America is not the product of any one person, because the
single most powerful word in our democracy is the word
"we".
"We the people"
"We shall overcome"
"Yes we can".
That word is owned by no one.
It belongs to everyone, Oh what a glorious task we are given, to
continually try to improve this
Great Nation of ours"*

BARACK OBAMA

As TAW turned into a bittersweet memory, Dorothy became the most comforting and stabilizing force in my day-to-day life. I cherished her and put her above everything else. I thought of her desires, her needs, her comfort before I thought about my own. It was not one way; I knew she felt the same. In a poignant moment, I felt her watching me as I shaved. When I lifted my arm to put on after shave lotion, she stopped me and said, "Don't put it on, I want to smell you as you are, naturally."

I tried twice to treat just the two of us to an around-the-world trip as a gift, but each time the trip was cut short because of business-related matters. In the early years of our relationship, my life with Dorothy had always been an especially sensitive issue, because she was single, and I was married. In the years between the contract cancellation and arbitration, our love grew stronger. Each day overflowed with the warmth and joy of a honeymoon, even when bad news from the business world beset us.

Despite the fact that all my four children were all over twenty one years of age, my divorce from Barbara was the most emotional and difficult decision that I have made in my entire life. Barbara is a good person, and a good mother to our four children. Barbara is a lady and should not have had to endure such a troubling period in her life. My obsession "not to fail in business"required at times, almost all of my energy, and attention. All Barbara wanted was for me to "be there" for her and the children. At the time Barbara and I married, neither one of us suspected that I would become "obsessed with succeeding in business"(if you call what I have done—success).

As each door in the business world opened to me, it required more of my attention and energy.Initially, with the computer programming company, I was able to be home on a regular basis. When the events described in previous chapters caused me to look outside the United States for business opportunities, I was away from home for long stretches of time. I operated in 14 African countries.The average air travel time from New York to Africa is more than 20 hours.

The burden on Barbara to be both mother and father to our four children became a very heavy one. My long absences' strained the marriage to the "breaking point ". I believed that what I was attempting to do was a"Noble Cause", and as such required sacrifice by myself and my family. Little did I know then, the magnitude and extent of the sacrifice that my family would have to endure. There was no pain-free option. The divorce, as stressful as it was, opened the door to my happiness with Dorothy.

Shortly after the arbitration, Dorothy and I were married. My wedding gift to her was a spacious house on a 55-acre plot of land on a hilltop in Zimbabwe, formerly southern Rhodesia. Dorothy had attended a Catholic school there as a girl. We bounced back and forth between our homes in Zimbabwe and on Roosevelt Island in New York City during our first year of marriage. Some separations due to business matters kept us apart.

At times, we wondered how content our lives would be if we found a career that we could explore together through our retirement years. In a reflective moment, an idea occurred to me. While attending my first computer programming course in the early 1950s, my classmates included a couple who worked for a government computer facility in San Diego. The couple also owned a 10-acre avocado farm in the San Diego area. They told me that they earned five thousand dollars each a year through their jobs and about twice as much owning an avocado farm. I said to myself, "That's what I want to do when I retire!"

Because the cost of land in Africa was far less expensive than land in the United States, our Zimbabwe home seemed an ideal place to establish an avocado farm. The acreage was sufficient; the climate was comparable to southern California's, and my wife was a farmer's daughter, who knew how to grow crops. I, on the other hand, grew up on the streets of Harlem and knew nothing about farming. As a way of familiarizing us with our new career, we decided to spend a year in California, learning how to grow and market avocados.

The University of California at Riverside is in the epicenter of the U.S. avocado industry. We took a six-month course at the university, talked to many avocado farmers and visited various segments of the industry in that area, absorbing all we could about planting, growing, marketing, and shipping avocados. We agreed that a right-hand drive car would be needed for this venture since Zimbabwe is a right-hand drive country. We flew to England to buy a car and arranged for it to be shipped to the port of Durban, South Africa. When the car arrived in Durban South Africa, we went to pick it up. On the drive back to Zimbabwe, we stopped and spent the night in Santon, South Africa, a suburb of Johannesburg.

Shortly after midnight, Dorothy bolted upright in the bed with a look of fear in her eyes and said, "I can't see you, something snapped in my head!" She fell back in the bed and, just like that, my 43-year-old wife was gone. Doctors determined the cause of death was a cerebral aneurysm, which is an abnormal bulge or ballooning in the wall of a blood vessel in the brain. Aneurysms can develop slowly over many years and strike without warning.

When I returned to Zimbabwe, I informed Joe and Bettye Pegues, Aaron and Phyliss Milner, Al and Hazel Cannon, the Craster's, and the Spencer's, my Zimbabwe neighbors, of Dorothy's death. The Spencer's told their children, who then were attending the Cathedral, the same school that Dorothy had attended. The Spencers later informed me that the Mother Superior at the school said she remembered Dorothy when she attended classes there.

The years I spent with Dorothy were some of the happiest of my life. We were compatible in every way. With her at my side, the frustrations, disappointments, and setbacks that I encountered as TAW's CEO—and in life in general—became easier to endure. It was more than just the physical attraction. She had become the most important person in my life. At fifty-six, I felt rudderless without her, undecided about what to do with the rest of my life.

I turned to Lester Florant, my life-long friend, who lived in Palo Alto, California. I spent the next six months with Lester and his family and thought about what to do. I remembered the discussions I had with D. Parke Gibson, a pioneer in multicultural public relations and founder of the first black-owned public relations firm. D. Parke published his first book, The $30 Billion Negro (1969), an examination of the consumer strength of the black community in the U.S. He advised large corporations to alter their communications strategies to appeal to this increasingly affluent community. In 1978, $70 Billion in the Black: America's Black Consumers, a revised edition of Gibson's first book, was published by Macmillan. D Parke was a member of the Public Relations Society of America (PRSA) from 1966 until his death in 1979.

Unfortunately, the research and marketing strategies that D. Parke presented regarding the consumer strength of the growing black population was ignored by corporate America back then, but I saw his work as fertile ground to develop a philanthropic institution which would benefit the black community. I decided to organize a foundation to raise money, primarily from the black community, to benefit blacks on a scale that, as we enginers say, could reach a critical mass where significant change can be made. I believed then, and I believe now, that what I was proposing would improve on the old proverb "it is better to teach someone to fish, than to give someone a fish". What I wanted to do was to show that someone "how to run a fish farm".

I believe, that if I started my foundation any time after the year 2000, instead of the 1980's, I would have had a significantly higher chance of success, than in the 1980's. When I created a charitable organization to accomplish these aims, the internet was a research project of the United States Government. The internet and world wide web was in its infancy and not widely used as it is today. World Wide users in 2017 were one half the world's population. The U.S.has a penetration rate of 80%.(Wikipedia)

The spread of low-cost internet access opened new possibilities for charities. Now, websites, such as Donors Choose, and Global Giving allow small-scale donors to direct funds to individual projects of their choice.(Wikipedia)

I was siginificantly helped in my efforts to establish a charitable foundation by Roy Cobb.Roy a long time friend from my high school days, was the first black salesperson hired by New York Life Insurance. When I and my partners started COMPUTRONICS, I selected Roy to handle our insurance needs.I also chose Roy when I founded TAW International Leasing.As a result of my relationship with Roy, I met Donald Trump, who knew then, in the 1980's, that Trump was destined to become a president of the United States.

Roy's cousin, who was a sports writer for the New York Post newspaper, invited Roy and I to a party at his home in Manhattan, near Riverside drive. There were many sports elites at the gathering, however the only few that I remember in addition to Trump are, "Whitey" Ford, the star NY Yankee pitcher, perhaps because I had met him before with another Yankee pitcher, Al Downing, at my friend, and Teaneck NJ neighbors' home, Elston Howard the New York Yankee catcher. In 1955 Elston was the first black player on the Yankee baseball team, eight years after Jackie Robinson had broken the major league baseball color barrier in 1947. Howard was named the American League's Most Valuable Player in 1963. The first black player in AL history to win the honor.(WIKIPEDIA)

Edward Charles "Whitey" Ford is a ten-time Major League All-Star and six-time World Series champion.In 1961 Ford won both the CY Young Award and Most Valuable Player Award.George Vecsey of the NY Times suggested that Ford was "The greatest living Yankee". Among pitchers with at least 300 career decisions, Ford ranks first with a winning percentage of.690, the all-time highest percentage in modern baseball history.(WIKIPEDIA).

I also remember meeting Allie Sherman the former head coach of the New York Football Giants, and Lou Carnesecca, the coach of the St.John University Basketball team.

When Roy and I arrived, there was Trump standing at the edge of the larger group. Roy and I shook his hand and exchanged a few words, then Roy and I joined the larger group around his cousin.

This may be an appropriate place to comment on the current "Trump phenomenon". As Trump's actions are effecting many, many around the globe. I at ninety plus and Trump at seventy plus, we both may be considered by some as "well past our sell by date", (the phrase made famous by John Le Carre of spy novel fame). I believe that I have become wiser with my advancing years, while knowing that I have lost some of my athletic and mental skills. I do not have an opinon on Trump's athletic and mental abilities, capacity, or wisdom, however, you, the reader will now be exposed to my opinon of Trump's political, and business activities. I do believe that "If it looks like a duck, walks like a duck, quacks like a duck, and it has no contradicting attributes, it is highly probable that it is a duck". I believe, along with many other New Yorkers, that all New Yorkers can not be fooled all of the time, even though one is successful in fooling some New Yorkers all of the time I would add one can not fool many New Yorkers any of the time, and this is applicable world wide (courtesy of Abrahm Lincoln).

Billionaire, former Republican and Mayor of New York, Michael Bloomberg said "Thoughout his career, Trump has left behind a well documented record of bankruptcies, thousands of lawsuits, angry shareholders, and contractors who feel cheated, and disillusioned customers who feel ripped off. Trump says he wants to run the nation like he's run his business. God help us. I am a New Yorker and New Yorker's know a con when we see one"!.

New York Mayor Bill de Blasio called Trump "Con Don".

New York City produced Bernard Madoff of the $50 Billion Ponzi con fame. Although the Madoff's con scheme was given the Ponzi name, its originator was a New York grifter William Miller who masterminded a $25 million(todays dollars) similar con in 1899.

Many Republican conservative intellectuals have run away from Trump.

I believe Donald J. Trump is like a virus, a virus that many, if not most New Yorkers have developed an immunity to. Previously the Trump virus spread beyond the New York boundaries, and is now spreading world wide.

(Webster's Dictionary in one of its definitions, defines virus as "anything that corrupts or poisons the mind or character, evil, or harmful influence).

The vaccine for Trumpism is TRUTH, FACTS, and REALITY, wherever and whenever Trumpism attempts to raise its head.

Speaking of a virus being spread, Bill Gates in 2018, lobbied president Trump, to fix U.S. virus preparation before a possible outbreak. Bill Gates said "if we start now we can be ready for the next epidemic". In my opinion, Bill Gates did not forsee that "a virus" would infect the white house before the corona 19 virus spread from China to Europe and the United States.—- smile

Understanding the fact that most Americans, did not vote for Trump, Fintan O'Toole, the international author of "The politics of Pain" has commented, "Trump has destroyed the country he promised "to make great again", O'Toole also commented that "The world has loved, hated, and envied the United States, now for the first time, we pity it. O'Toole added "Trump has actively spread a deadly virus".

Many in the American community of color believe that if Trump is not a racist, as he and his supporters claim, Trump makes a excellent, convincing impersonation of a racist.

In my opinon and that of many others, virtually every endeavor, business that Trump created failed.Even Trump's election to the presidency of the U.S.I believe was only accomplished with Russian assistance.

I grew up in Harlem, in the 1930's -1940's, a black community with legitimate grievances and concerns. A community that felt its legitimate grievances were not being addressed by its government. I saw, as a youth, the attraction to and the demise of such con artists as Father Divine, primarily because the community had lost hope for a change in their circumstances in their lifetime.

Today I can quickly recognize the attraction to Trump that many Trump base supporters have. These Trump's base supporters have similar concerns and feelings about their elective reprentatives not addressing their perceived concerns, which in a number of cases "is not based in reality".

The loss of personally unearned status can be very bewildering, frustrating, and can lead to actions that have unintended consequences. The importance of not being "of color" is deeply rooted in far too many peoples psyche. I remember, in several African countries in the early days after independence, witnessing on a number of occasions, a white person automatically going to the front of any line that was composed of black Africans, as was the custom before independence. This kind of thinking was on display during "Indian Removal" in the early 1800's in Georgia, as well as other sections of the U.S. At the time Georgia was the largest State in terms of land area. The thinking went along these lines, "because "Indian title" was "permissive"and was derived from "mere custom", the State of Georgia could legitimately seize land from Creek Indians whenever it wished, and that the white citizens of Geogia had a "God" given "right" to the Indian lands. This morphed from Indian removal to Indian extermination. Remember the often quoted expression of the 1800's, "The only good Indian is a dead Indian".

As of this writing, one should look across the pond to find another example of what the perceived loss of status can do to a group of people. As many contempory British observers have commented, "it is not right for England to be a normal European country" as it is under the European Union. Most of us remember that Britain, the U.S. and its allies won World War Two. However it was Britain that shortly thereafter "lost" its vast world wide empire. This British feeling of oppression is imaginary, loss of status is imaginary, and many feel, it is the primary driving force in Brexit. Fintan O'Toole in his book "politics of Pain", comments, "the bedrock assumption was that England was humiliated by being in the E.U., ...that England had become a colony of the E.U.". O'Toole concludes "the route to such irrational outcomes cannot be entirely rational. It must run through a strange and dark terrain that, on the mental maps of a very particular reactionary discourse, is called England".

Unfortunately, this dark terrain is also present today in many areas of the world, including the United States. Many professionals in this field call it "TRANSFERENCE". A definition of TRANSFERENCE—a defense mechanism in which an individual or group projects qualities that are unacceptable to the projecting group on to another different group or individual, or on to itself. Too many of us in the United States need TRANSFERENCE to square present reality with our self-image "as the defender of liberty, equality, and law and order", one hand and the domination by the white population over other racial groups, that is the result of systemic racism existing in America since the "settlers" arrived. This phenomenon is in our founding documents (the 3/5 clause).

For some Americans this TRANSFERENCE took the form of conquest of the "wilderness" as an epic struggle of sacrifice and suffering. Not for the victims, but for the victors. The pain of the oppressed transferred to the oppressors. The often quoted "WHITE MANS BURDEN" is an example. Another current example is the claim by some American whites that "now the unspoken real problem is that American whites are discriminated against more than American Blacks. Another relatively recent example of TRANSFERENCE is the experience of Nelson Mandella as a prisoner at Robin Island in South Africa.

Father Divine did some good, but ten times the harm to his followers. Father Divine had followers of all races in the U.S., France, Switerland, Canada, and Australia.Father Devine attracted crowds of ten thousand or more. In the 1940's Father Divine became such a national figure that songwriter Johnny Mercer wrote a song on the basis of a Father Divine sermon. The song is "You got to accentuate the positive and eliminate the negative", which Mercer wrote with Harold Arlen of "Over the Rainbow" fame.

A much more serious concern that I have about the "Trump Phenomenon" is Trump's apparent advancement of Russian interests and points of view, that are in direct opposition to long held U.S. interests and points of view. My concern heightened when in Helsinki Finland in July 2018, Trump took the Russian position and not the U.S. Intelligence Agencies' position. This strange advocatcy caused me and many others to question, WHY ! WHY!.

This strange advocacy reminded me of the thoughts that went through my head shortly after Trump was elected in 2016. I will model, Trump's kind of language to describe my thoughts. I heard, people said, it has been reported, I read, that shortly before election night, Trump confided to his close associates that he, Trump, did not expect to win the Presidential election. Then as president, among Trump's first initiatives he sought to remove the U.S. sanctions on Russia. These thoughts as well as my belief that Trump does not do any thing that requires a cash outlay, unless that expenditure will benefit Trump and or his family personally. These thoughts reminded me of the 1968 movie "The Producers" directed by Mel Brooks. The movie is centered around a Broadway producer, and his accountant who discover that they can make more money on a Broadway "flop", than they can on a Broadway "hit". On basis that if the show is a "flop", their investors do not expect to be paid. Thus they sell 100% of the shares in a Broadway show, over and over to each of multiple, multiple investors.

The Broadway Producer and his accountant develop what they consider to be "the worst broadway show ever" However when their "sure to lose" show is a hit, the pair end up in jail. It is remarkable to me, how much Trump physicaly resembles the balding, comb forward, corpulent, overweight Zero Mostel as the low rent broadway producer.

A hypothetical comparision of the movie and Trump's Presidential run can be made by anyone who would care to do so. In my hypothetical, Trump, in his own mind, thinks he is smarter than everyone else, and he is, in his own mind, is the master of the con, as demonstrated by his past success at this "art form". Trump makes a "business" deal with Putin/Russia that will net Trump/family hundreds of millions of U.S. dollars in return for a change in U.S. policy toward Russia, when he, Trump becomes President of the U.S.. Trump does not really think his presidency will occur, and therefore he will not have to deliver on his part of the deal. Putin outsmarts Trump by using "information technology" including the internet, to trash Trump's opponent and Trump wins the U.S. Presidental election of 2016, and now Trump has to deliver his side of the business deal.

Again, to use a Trump fallback when Trump is cornered concerning his veracity, and responds "that is what the word is"....many roads through Trump lead directly to Putin, "that is what the word is".

As the saying goes; the past is prologue. With this in mind, I feel I can go out on a limb and predict that after Trump is defeated in the 2020 Presidental election, Trump will go the way of Father Divine.

I will go futher out on the proverbial limb and say, that there is a 50/50 chance that when Trump is not re-elected and the relative U.S. authorities prevail in prosecuting Trump, he will seek asylum in Russia claiming political persecution, joining his fellow American, Edward Snowden.

In the 1980's, I met Alice Burnette, then an Assistant Secretary and principal fund-raiser for the Smithsonian Institution in Washington, D.C. She previously had been the principal fundraiser at Howard University. Before that, she, as one of three, raised the funds that built Morehouse College's School of Medicine in Atlanta, Georgia. Alice is a co-author of "Achieving Excellence in Fund Raising", a staple in the fund raising field. Her father, Dr. Hugh Gloster, a past president of Morehouse, was also a notable fund-raiser.Dr. Gloster was Morehouse's seventh president and its first graduate to become president. Under Dr. Gloster, the campus doubled in size, and the endowment quadrupled.

Alice played a significant role in helping me shape my ideas about how to accomplish my fund raising goals, and in the process, she became my life-time partner. She was seventeen years younger than I and we were together for nearly twenty years. She died of cancer just before my eightieth birthday.

Alice designed and managed the two hundred million-dollar campaign to build the Smithsonian's National Museum of the American Indian. The Museum has become one of the Smithsonian's most popular tourist attractions since its September 21, 2004, opening. Her boss, Smithsonian Secretary Robert Adams, considered the establishment of the American Indian museum his most significant accomplishment. Bob earned three degrees, including a PhD, from the University of Chicago. His specialty was archaeology and most of his research and study in the Middle East, but he had never been to Africa. In 2002, he received the Gold Medal Award for Distinguished Archaeological Achievement from the Archaeological Institute of America.

When Bob announced his plans to retire, as one of his retirement gifts, the Smithsonian gave Bob and Ruth, his wife, a trip to Zimbabwe to visit our home, Victoria Falls, and Great Zimbabwe, the largest collection of ruins in Africa south of the Sahara. Alice learned that there were more than one hundred members of the Smithsonian in the Southern Africa area, and invited them to attend a party for Bob and Ruth at our home in Zimbabwe. Thirty of the group had never been to the United States. Many traveled more than two hundred miles to attend.

Alice and I began to spend the Christmas Holidays in Zimbabwe. Primarily because the fund raising "season" was then over, and would not really start until the beginning of the next year, as many potential donor had already made their decisions before the end of the calendar year. And it is summer there at this time of year. On one of these holidays in Zimbabwe, we received an invitation to the President of Zimbabwe's annual Christmas Party. Upon being introduced to the President, Alice said to him "I bring you greetings from my father". To which the President said, "who is your father". Alice replied "Hugh Gloster". The President immediately responded, "Ah, beautiful Atlanta, your father was my friend when I had very few friends, please give him my regards". I learned later that Dr. Gloster had arranged for the then freedom fighter Robert Mugabe to travel to Atlanta and receive an Honorary Degree from Morehouse College. It must have made an indelible impression.

After Alice left the Smithsonian, she became the Principal of Advancement Solutions, Inc., her own fund-raising consulting firm.

By then, the aging process and the usual forces beyond my control prevented me from continuing my D. Parke Gibson-inspired plans. I would have had to write another book to explain why my plans were set aside. Family matters took precedent.

NOTE:

Today, about forty million blacks, or approximately 13 percent of the U.S. population, reside in America. Though the average income of black households in the United States is 50% of white households, it is equal to households in Australia and Russia. However, blacks have only 10% the savings of U.S. whites, which is a huge disparity. It exists because we blacks don't save. Many of us don't save because we don't own homes.

During this period, I was given an "ad" by Dr. Robert Lowery, Alice's physician.

The "ad" read:

White Water Rafting!, on the Zambezi River, in Africa, with names like, Stairway To Heaven, Devils Toilet Bowl, The Washing Machine, and The Terminator. I had travelled Africa for almost two decades before I heard these words. Alice's physician Dr. Robert Lowery. an open heart surgeon, and his wife, because of Dr. Lowery's love of adventure, decided to visit our home in Zimbabwe to be able to go White Water Rafting at Victoria Falls on the Zambezi River. Robert said to me "the Victoria Falls White Water Rafting was the wildest one day white water rafting trip in the world". At 1,700 miles the Zambezi River (which means Great River in the language of the Tonga people) is Africa' fourth longest river. I initially felt that I had enough adventure in my career, and was only mildly interested. I was wrong. The rafting trip was for me a really great adventure and I later made many more white water trips on the Zambezi. The most memorable of these trips occurred when I visited my home in Zimbabwe with my daughter Vicki and my two grandsons, Daniel, and Eric. and their cousin, Nichlos. The Zambezi white water rafting is classified as a grade 5 by the British Canoe Union, with difficult, long, and violent rapids, steep gradients, and big drops.

We chose to raft on a Oar Raft, with an Oarperson (yes women can do this as well) controlling the raft, all we had to do was "to hang on to the raft", and to "high side" into the big waves as the raft hit them. Our first oarperson was a woman. The Oarperson felt that Eric was too young, Daniel and Nichlos was big for their ages, about six feet, and were allowed to raft. Vicki and Eric, as compensation would go, with a guide, in a canoe above Victoria Falls, in relatively calm water. Well, Daniel, Nichlos and and I capsized twice, and Daniel could not wait to tell his younger brother about his adventure, when we returned to the hotel. On arrival at the hotel, Eric was just as excited to tell his older brother what an adventure he had. My daughter Vicki did not share Eric's enthusiasm, because Vicki and Eric's canoe was capsized by a hippo above the falls, on what was supposed to be an uneventful calm canoe trip. Hippo's are grass eating animals, not carnivores, Despite their appearance hippo's are very territorial, aggressive, and responsible for more deaths in Africa than any other wild animal.

Many, many, years ago, on our drive back from taking Alice's younger son, Michael, to Morehouse, I noticed a road sign on I-95, announcing the exit for Milford, Virginia. I told Alice, "That's my mother's hometown. Let's stop. I haven't been there since I was six years old. Maybe some of my relatives are still there."

We stopped at the post office and I told a couple standing outside that I was looking for members of the Mont family. "They're relatives on my mother's side," I said. "Do you know where I can find them?"

The man looked at his watch and said, "It's four o'clock, Giles Mont will be picking lima beans in his field right now." He then gave us directions to the Mont farm. Sure enough, Giles Mont was in his field picking lima beans. His farmhouse was unpainted and rickety. His wife was blind. After chatting for a while, he told me that some other relatives lived nearby, Alice and I went to see them. There were several farmhouses in the area. We arrived at a suburban house on two acres.

We knocked on the front door, but there was no response. We walked around back, and as we approached the house from the rear, a woman appeared at the screen door. She stared at me as I moved closer then said with a wide smile, "You are ANNA'S BOY!" She opened the door and welcomed us in. I thought of my mother and felt her presence, as I sat with my relative in my mother's hometown, who had not seen me since I was about six or seven years old, sharing memories of my mother and a few laughs.

I'm sure my mother had been with me during my cliffhanger-filled journey through life, cheering me along the way and reminding me of the life-lessons that she instilled within me. My mother didn't play cards or any other board games. Neither did I. She was a serious, disciplined person, more of an introvert, like me, or more accurately, as I grew older, I became like her. Personality-wise, we were quite similar.

Having lived on this 3rd Rock from our Sun for more than four score and ten years, I have concluded that any bleak assessment of this Rock's long-term future is incorrect.

The Good News is — We in the United States can VOTE!

I believe that; on the world stage, all known forms of government are tyrannical, for by definition, the function of government is to govern. Governments expect their citizens to obey its laws, and if not, they punish them in one form or another.In a democracy the citizens collectively chose their own form of tyranny. When a citizen does not vote, that citizen is allowing others to make that choice for them.

In the recent presidential election, approximately 56% of those eliegible to vote, voted.The winner received less than 50% of those that voted, . Trump was elected by a hair more than a quarter of the eligible American voters. This has occurred before in U.S.history, where a U.S. President was elected by the Electoral College, without receiving the majority of the popular vote.

In my opinion, the apathy of the American voting public, cause our elected officals to listen more to lobbyist(s) than to their constituents. Reliable estimates indicate that there are between 15 to 30 congressional lobbyists for each member of congress.

Not too long ago, as the story goes, a reputable Public Relations firm confidentially told its clients, "You tell us what you want the American public to "think", and we will tell you, how long it will take, and how much it will cost, to make the American public "think" what you want them to "think".

Donald J. Trump in my mind, has created a new variety of this; accuse your rivals of what you yourself are guilty of, and the uninformed public will not think that you are guilty or at worse, the informed public will not know what to think, and thus Trump has neutralized the accusation of him.

"I alone can fix this", these words were uttered by Trump during the run up to his election. After his election, in too many situations to list here, these words have been followed up by excuse after excuse, as to why Trump has not been able square these words with his actions. It is almost always some one else at fault, or some thing preventing I, Donald J. Trump from fixing this or that. One can fill in the blanks . . . (the Chinese, the Iranians, the democrats, the liberals, and people of color from anywhere)

Trump supporters should really be aware of what Howard Stern, Trump's friend from the "old days" said recently. Stern opined "the oddity in all of this is the people Trump despises most, love him the most". "Trump prefers to rub elbows with the rich and famous", Stern added.

In my opinion, the normal apathy on the part of the American voting public, and the financial resources at the disposal of organizations or of some people with particular objectives, have made a very significant contribution to the "current state of affairs". An informed, voting American public can go a long way in improving on the "current state of affairs".

I believe what Martin Luther King Jr. said, in Selma, Alabama: "The arch of the moral universe is long, but it bends toward justice."

I believe what Jewish-Dutch philosopher Baruch Spinoza said: "Those who are governed by reason desire nothing for themselves which they do not also desire for the rest of humankind."

I believe what comedian Louis C.K. said in a standup offering that was published in Steven Pinker's book, Enlightenment Now, the case for reason, science, humanism, and progress. It reads: "When I read things like, 'The foundations of capitalism are shattering,' I'm like, maybe we need some time

where we're walking around with a donkey with pots clanging on the sides....
Cause now we live in an amazing world, and it's wasted on the crappiest generation of spoiled idiots....Flying is the worst one, because people come back
from flights and they tell you their story....They're like, 'It was the worst day
of my life....We get on the plane and they made us sit there on the runway for
40 minutes.'....Oh, really, then what happened next? Did you fly through the
air, incredibly, like a bird? Did you soar into the clouds, impossibly? Did you
partake in the miracle of human flight then land softly on giant tires that you
couldn't even conceive how they . . . put air in them? You're sitting in a chair
in the sky. You're like a Greek myth right now! People say there's delays . . .
air travel's too slow? New York to California in five hours. That used to take
30 years! And a bunch of you would die on the way there, and you'd get shot
in the neck with an arrow, and the other passengers would just bury you and
put a stick there with your hat on it and keep walking....The Wright brothers
would kick us all in (the crotch) if they knew."

Pinker also states the fact that "Racial and ethnic prejudice is declining
not just in the west but worldwide" He continues with "In 1950, almost
half the world's countries had laws that discriminated against ethic or racial
minorities (including the United States). By 2003 fewer than a fifth did, and
they were outnumbered by countries with affirmative action policies.

I believe, that the world is not going to hell. Nor as in Candide,
Voltaire's novella, "All is for the best in the best of all possible worlds." Nor
is the world, as Cervantes describes it, when Don Quixote experiences it in
rose-colored glasses.

I believe what President Barack Obama has opined. "The world, for all
of its challenges has never been healthier, better educated, wealthier, more
tolerant, less violent, more attentive to the rights of all people than today."

We may not be able to make the world "perfect." However, each of us
can make the world a "little better" by the way we live our lives and raise our
children. A "little better" is the civilized choice!

I believe that the United States of America, in spite of its current flaws, is the best country to live in for almost everyone(I am reasonably sure, that the Queen of England would not trade her British citizenship, and being the Queen of England to live in the US-smile). However we Americans can not rest on our hard fought, hard won equality, freedoms, and prosperity, for other envious nations and forces are presently attempting to bring an end to America's prosperity, leadership, and influence. We, as a people, must resist the forces that attempt to divide we Americans and prevent us from continuing to eliminate our flaws, and extending our prosperity to all of our citizens, and to "make good" on our premise "that we are all equal in the eyes of the law"

I also believe, (as someone recently remarked) that everyone should realize that, before anyone makes a withdrawal from "the Bank of Trust", a deposit must be made in "the Bank of Trust", by that person or entity.

I believe, as President Obama has commented;

"Change will not come

If we wait for some other person

Or some other time."

We are the change that we seek.

We are the ones we've been waiting for."

I believe that the world has become consistently better, more humane, more lawful over the last century. Dissatisfaction with humankind's condition has led to most of the improvements in our lives.

George Santayana said that "Those who do not remember the past, are condemmed to repeat it" However, one should always remember accurately, "how the past was".

In her book "CASTE" Isabel Wilkerson states a well known truth that is easy for me to understand. "When we go to the doctor, he or she will not begin to treat us without taking our history—and not just our history, but that of our parents and grandparents before us. The doctor will not hazard a diagnosis until he or she knows the history going back generations. Looking beneath the history of one's country is like learning that alcoholism, or depression runs in one's family—discovering that one has inherited the markers of a BRCA mutation for breast cancer. You don't ball up in a corner with guilt or shame—you don't—forbid any mention of them—you may pray over it and meditate over it. Then you take precautions to protect yourself and succeeding generations and work to ensure that these things, what ever they are, don't happen again.

Ezra Klein's brutaly frank and accurate remarks in his book "Why we're Polarized" are as follows "in America's early years, new arrivals from Europe drove out and murdered the indigenous peoples, brought over millions of enslaved Africans, and wrote laws making women second class citizens".(my comment—and we in the United States were "the GOOD GUYS"— smile)

These actions were not what made America great. What makes America great is the movement (unfortunately ever so slow) towards the ideas our founding fathers expressed in the Declaration Of Independence, not nessarily, the then actions of our founding fathers. These ideas and aspirations themselves were revolutionary at the time.

As an example of this duplicity; in one of his letters, Thomas Jefferson stated that "he desired to separate native people from their lands for their own good".

Jefferson also wrote in 1821 that "deportation of African slaves— would free up land for white laborers"

(Claudio Saunt)

From my perspective, the contest to decide the "way forward", beginning with our founding fathers until today, is the contest between our collective Brains and our collective Prejudices and Emotions. Fortunately, our Brains have won most of the contests.

We Americans, are better than we have been, despite hiccups and purtabations along the way, and I expect in the future, we Americans, in the long run, will be better than we are at the present time.

Among these ideas in the Declaration of Independence are:

"We hold these truths to be self-evident that all men are created equal". That they are endowed by their creator with certain unalienable rights that among these are, life, liberty, and the pursuit of happiness—

"Governments are instituted among men, deriving their just powers from the consent of the governed"

Both Martin Luther King and Barack Obama have more recently provided the following reasons for America's "exceptionalism".

Martin Luther King in his "I have a Dream speech" where he states "I have a dream that one day this nation will rise up and live out the true meaning of its creed: "We hold these truths to be self-evident: that all men are created equal". Barack Obama in his second Inaugual Address where Obama states "What makes us exceptional—what makes us American—is our allegiance to an idea articulated in a declaration made more than two centuries ago: "We hold these truths to be self-evident, that all men are created equal, that they are endowed by their creator with certain unalienable rights; that among these are life, liberty, and the pursuit of happiness:" Today, we continue a never-ending journey to bridge the meaning of those words with the realities of our time"

Since 1776 there have been over 120 declarations of independence, by different countries and different peoples.

"I constantly remember the words of Dr. Martin Luther King that he said to me during those long ago,

Never to be forgotten few days I spent with him in Montgomery Alabama in 1954.

"Every Mountain Top is within Humankind's reach, if we humans, just keep climbing".

I believe that no one alone causes any significant thing to occur. I have had many, many helping hands in my walk through the winds, rain, and sunshine of my life. I've leaned on and learned from too many of you to count, but you know who you are.

I hope that I have lived my life in such a manner that would make all those who came before me proud, especially black Americans. I hope that I have honored all the sacrifices they made. For those of you who believed that I possess abilities far greater than I have, I want you to know that I tried . . . I tried . . . and continue to try.

*"E pluribus unum
Out of many, one".*

TRADITIONAL MOTTO OF THE UNITED STATES,
APPEARING ON THE GREAT SEAL OF THE
UNITED STATES

APPENDIX

Early science in early Africa:

It is now acknowleged that the ancient peoples in Africa were the first to extract iron from the ore that is abundant in the interior of Africa, and to work the metal into tools.According to many scholars, early Africans were responsible for developing stringed instruments, domesticating cows, sheep, and goats. African people were the first to have an understanding of the planetary system. This curiosity and inventive habits did not disappear on the slaves ships that carried Africans to the "New World". Ivan Van Sertima in his seminal work, "They came before Columbus"— the African presence in the New World —reveals the presence and legacy of Africans in Pre-Columbian America, and the inventive skills necessary to accomplish this presence.

For those who are interested in the accomplishments of blacks in science, I would recommend ; Black Pioneers of Science and Invention by Louis Haber.

The book covers;

INVENTORS

Benjamin Banneker

Norbert Rillieux

Jan Earnest Matzeliger

Elijah McCoy

Granville T. Woods

Lewis Howard Latimer

Garrett A Morgan

SCIENTISTS

George Washington Carver

Percy Lavon Julian

Lloyd A Hall

Ernest Everett Just

Daniel Hale Williams

Louis Tompkins Wright

Charles Richard Drew

SELECTED BIBLIOGRAPHY

Anderson, Jervis. This Was Harlem (New York: Farrar Straus Giroux, 1982).

Banda, Rupiah - Wikipedia.com

Beach, E. Merrill, From Valley Forge to Freedom, 1975, Pequot Press

Black, Eli. Wikipedia.com

Black, Timuel. Wikipedia.com

Bower, Tom. Tiny Rowland: A Rebel Tycoon (London: Mandarin Paperbacks, 1994).

Boyd, Bob. Wikipedia.com

Cairns, Sir David. Wikipedia.com.

Call Them Heroes (New York: Silver Burdett Company, 1965).

Cornfeld, Bernard. Brittanica.com

Cummings, Herb. Nathancummings.org.

Daniels, Randy – Journal of American history.com

Decisions Systems, Inc. Prospectus, April 1964.

Dehn, Conrad. Checkcompany.com.

"Detroit Arsenal Army Base in Warren, MI," Militarybases.com

"Dred Scott Decision." History.com

DuMont, Allen B. Brittanica.com

Geneen, Harold. Wikipedia.com.

"Godfrey Binaisa" obit, The Guardian, Oct. 3, 2010.

Gonzalez, David, "In Sugar Hill, a Street Nurtured Black Talent When the World Wouldn't," The New York Times, Jan. 22, 2010.

Goodman, Roy M. Wikipedia.com.

Gourdine, Meredith - Blacks in Science, Transaction Books 1983.

Gravely, Vice Admiral Samuel. Wikipedia.com.

Hemenway, Robert E. Zora Neale Hurston: A Literary Biography (Champaign, IL: University of Illinois Press, 1977).

Hesburgh, Father Theodore. NotreDame.edu.

Hickock, Raymond. NYTimes.com

Hirst, Sir David. TheTimes.co.uk.

History of University of Columbia. Wikipedia.com.

History of University of Michigan. Wikipedia.com.

Howard, Samuel H. The Flight of the Phoenix: Thoughts on Work and Life (Franklin, TN: Providence House Publishers, 2007).

Jaffin, Charles. NYTimes.com

Johnson, Herschel. "TAW: The success story of the black American company that is first in equipment leasing in Africa," Black Enterprise, December 1973.

Johnson, Jack. Biography.com, Wikipedia.com

Johnson, James Weldon. Black Manhattan (New York: Knopf, 1930).

Jones, Fletcher. Wikipedia.com.

Kaunda, Kenneth. Brittanica.com

Kyemba, Henry. A State of Blood (New York: Ace Books, 1977).

Lewis, Reginald "Reggie." NYTimes.com.

Lincoln's letter to Albert Hodges on slavery, April 4, 1864.

"Martin H. Dubilier; Inventor and Investor" obit, Los Angeles Times, Sept. 7, 1991.

Masefield, John. Wikipedia.com.

Mays, Marshall, president OPIC - Federal Times, April 1981

Morton, James. "Obituary: Lord Devlin," The Independent, Aug. 11, 1992.

Murdoch, Rupert. Wikipedia.com.

New York's Stuyvesant High School. Wikipedia.com.

North American Aviation Corp. Wikipedia.com.

Paley, Bill. Biography.com.

Parks Jr., Henry G. BlackPast.org.

Pierce, Samuel. Wikipedia.com.

Pritzker, Penny. Wikipedia.com.

Pryor, Richard. Biography.com.

Pullman, George. Brittanica.com.

Ramos, George. "Had Apparent Heart Attack in Zimbabwe: Dr. J. Alfred Cannon; Health Crusader" obit, Los Angeles Times, March 11, 1988.

Ramos, George. "Robert Sarnoff: Former NBC Chief" obit, Los Angeles Times, Feb. 23, 1997.

Randolph, A. Philip. Biography.com.

"Reconstruction Era (1865-1877)." History.com.

Robinson, Jackie. Wikipedia.com.

Rock, John. Autoweek.com.

Rockefeller, John D. Biography.com.

Rockefeller, Laura. Brittanica.com.

Ross, Steve. Wikipedia.com.

Russell, Carlos. BlackCommentator.com.

Sattinger, Irving J. Applying Computers (Cleveland: Howard Allen, 1963).

Savage, Frank. - The Savage Way: Successfully Navigating the Waves of Business and Life (Hoboken, NJ: John Wiley & Sons, 2013).

Seaton, Earle. Biography.com, Wikipedia.com.

Shields, Cornelius. NYTimes.com

"Sir Henry Fisher: Brilliant lawyer and energetic public servant" obit, The Independent, April 14, 2005.

Siwo, Peter. Wikipedia.com, The Times of Zambia.

Solarz, Stephen J. - Congressional Hearings on International Economic Policy May – June 1976

Sosthenes & Hernand Behn. Brittanica.com.

Strategic Air Command (SAC). Wikipedia.com.

Stubblefield, Beauregard. Diaspora.com.

Sword, William. Towntopics.com.

Taylor, Kate. "Elite Schools Make Few Offers to Black and Latino Students," The New York Times, March 7, 2018.

Terpil, Frank. Wikipedia.com.

V-12 Navy College Program. Wikipedia.com.

Walton, Sam. Wikipedia.com.

Washington, Booker T. Up from Slavery: An Autobiography (New York: Doubleday, 1901).

Wilkins, J. Ernest, Wikipedia.com

William J. Damroth Jr., The Record/Herald News of New Jersey, March 28, 2010.